AFGHANISTAN: TRAVELS WITH THE MUJAHIDEEN

One day I had my beard trimmed by a refugee barber from Rokha, the main town of the Panjsher before it became a Russian base. He and his large family lived in a cave on the far side of the mountain facing Najmuddin's house. To do his rounds must have meant a daily walk of ten or fifteen miles. After clipping the straggliest bits of my beard he shaved my throat with a blade so blunt I cried out in pain. Looking hurt at what he took to be criticism of his professional skill, he asked Khalili what was wrong.

'Hasn't he got a sharper blade? That one is sheer agony.'

With a look that meant no Afghan would dream of complaining about such a trivial affair, he changed the old blade for one that was marginally newer. I gritted my teeth and endured the torture in silence. His charge was 50 Afghanis (25 pence). Khalili explained that he had a wider repertoire.

'He can do more than just cut beards, you know. He is dentist too. He is vairy good at pulling teeth, this old man. And he is surgeon, too. He can amputate legs and arms and do many operations.'

Praise for Sandy Gall

Also by the same author:
and available from NEL:

Don't Worry About the Money Now

About the Author

Sandy Gall was born in Penang, Malaya, went to school at Glenalmond in Scotland, and studied French and German at Aberdeen University.

He worked for Reuters, covering the Congo war in 1960–63 and in 1972. Now with ITN, he was thrown into jail by Idi Amin's soldiers and forced to run across the jail compound with a sub-machine gun at his back.

1975 found him in Saigon when the city fell to the Communists, and in 1980 he visited Vietnam and Kampuchea. His interest in Afghanistan began in 1982 when he and a TV crew spent two months with the guerillas in the Panjsher Valley. He has made three TV documentaries recording the events in Afghanistan, all of which have been widely acclaimed in Britain.

Sandy Gall lives in Penshurst, Kent, with his wife Eleanor and their four children.

Afghanistan: Travels with the Mujahideen

Foreword by the Right Honourable Margaret Thatcher, M.P.

Sandy Gall

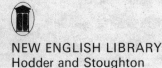

NEW ENGLISH LIBRARY
Hodder and Stoughton

British Library C.I.P.

Gall, Sandy, *1927–*
    Afghanistan: travels with the Mujahideen
    1. Afghanistan. Guerrilla wars
    I. Title
    958'.1044

    ISBN 0-450-50682-9

Printed and bound in Great Britain for Hodder and Stoughton paperbacks, a division of Hodder and Stoughton Ltd., Mill Road, Dunton Green, Sevenoaks, Kent TN13 2YA (Editorial Office: 47 Bedford Square, London WC18 3DP) by Richard Clay Ltd., Bungay, Suffolk.

To Jan Mohammed, whose unfailing good humour made the miles seem shorter and whose chips kept us going; to Masud Khalili, whose wit and knowledge illuminated the journey; to Andy and Noel who took the pictures and bore with me; and to my daughter Carlotta, who processed the words.

Andy Skrzypkowiak was killed in Afghanistan in October 1987 on his way in to Masud. His death is a heavy loss to the cause of a free Afghanistan – Sandy Gall.

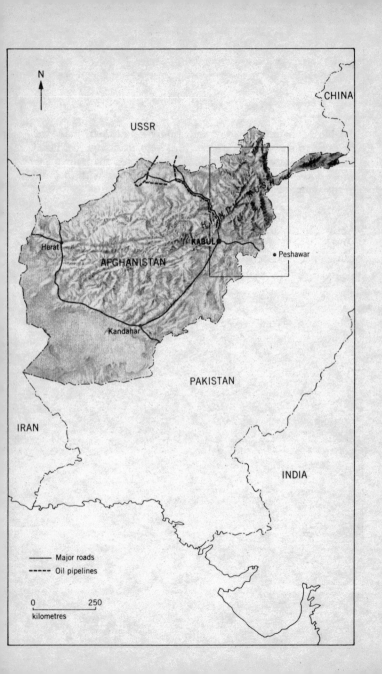

A Pathan Warrior's Farewell

Beloved, on a parchment white
With my heart's blood to thee I write;
My pen a dagger, sharp and clean,
Inlaid with golden damascene,
Which I have used, and not in vain,
To keep my honour free from stain.

Now, when our house its mourning wears,
Do not thyself give way to tears:
Instruct our eldest son that I
Was ever anxious thus to die,
For when Death comes the brave are free –
So in thy dreams remember me.

Anonymous, quoted by J. Bowen in
The Golden Pomegranate, John Baker,
London 1966.

ILLUSTRATIONS

FOREWORD

Since December 1979, one of the most heroic resistance struggles known to history has been taking place on the borders of the Soviet Union, in the mountains and plains of Afghanistan. This struggle, far too little reported, is at the time of writing nearly eight years old, which means it has been going on longer than either the First or Second World Wars.

Let us be clear about what is happening in Afghanistan. Virtually the whole Afghan nation is engaged in a war of national liberation against a Soviet occupation army of some 110,000 men, backed by large numbers of tanks, artillery, helicopter gunships and the latest jet fighters. If ever there was a battle between David and Goliath in contemporary terms, it is here.

When the Russians rolled into Afghanistan on Christmas Eve, 1979, few people would have given the Afghan resistance or *mujahideen*, with few arms and less organisation, any hope of lasting out against the Red Army for more than a few months. And yet, eight years later, the Afghans are still fighting for their liberty, with greater determination, and greater success, than ever before.

But the cost to the Afghan nation has been horrifying. Out of a pre-war population of about fifteen million, five million Afghans, or one third, are now refugees in Pakistan and Iran; and there are perhaps another million, if not more, 'internal refugees'. But even those facts. terrible as they are, do not illuminate the full extent of the tragedy. No one knows how many Afghan civilians have been killed in the war. Probably well over 100,000 and possibly half a million or even more.

Sandy Gall has made three trips to Afghanistan to report on what he rightly believes is a forgotten war. This is an account of his last journey, an arduous trek across the Hindu Kush to meet the guerrilla leader Ahmed Shah Masud less than a hundred miles from the Soviet border. On the way he came across many harrowing tales, but he also witnessed, undimmed, the Afghans' remarkable spirit of resistance.

Foreword

There has to be a political settlement in Afghanistan, based on a Soviet withdrawal. To understand how this can best be achieved, we must first understand the nature of the war and of the Afghan resistance. This book makes a valuable contribution to that understanding.

Margaret Thatcher

CHAPTER ONE

A small Afghan boy of about eight sat on the floor in an orphanage in Peshawar, in the North-West Frontier Province of Pakistan, and told me in his own language, Farsi, the story of how Russian soldiers had come to his village at night and burst into his house. As he told the story, jerkily and looking down, he kept fingering a little black scar above his right eyebrow.

First of all, he explained, there had been a battle and the *mujahideen*, the guerrillas who are fighting the Russians and their Afghan allies, had withdrawn.

> 'The *mujahideen* went back to the mountains. They [the Russians] came in our direction. We were all in bed. They broke down the door and came in. The door was smashed. We were all frightened and jumped up. My brother didn't get up but they forced him to stand up. They shot my father and my brother. They lifted me up and wounded me with their bayonets.' He touched the scar on his forehead. 'I lay down and cried. I was sad because my father had been killed. My father was dead and was lying on the ground. They took us outside. I saw lots of people had been taken out of their houses into the alleyways and killed. We went to the bazaar. The shops, the shops had been burnt. People had been killed. Everywhere women had been killed, men had been killed, even boys that high' – he gestured with his hand – 'had been killed. They didn't leave a single one alive.'

There are many stories like that in and around the refugee camps, countless reports of atrocities committed by Russian troops in Afghanistan over the years. These reports began to circulate soon after the Russians invaded their small neighbour on Christmas Eve, 1979. It is one of the mysteries of the Afghan War that so little has been reported, either in the papers or on television, of these atrocities, though some experts have recorded them. As long ago as 1982, Michael Barry, an American scholar who lives in France and speaks Farsi and Pashto, crossed the border from Pakistan to record the facts of what became known as the Logar Massacre. Before dawn on 13 September 1982, the Russians surrounded the village of Padkhwab-e-Shana in Logar Province. Fearing reprisals the menfolk of the village, more than a hundred of them, took refuge in the underground irrigation system known as *q'anat*. The story as told by one of the few survivors was that the Russians, having discovered where the men were hiding, brought up a couple of lorries and pumped some sort of chemical into the tunnel. They then added another substance which ignited the first and set off a big underground explosion, which from the eyewitness's description had the effect of napalm. Everyone who was underground, 105 men and boys, was burnt to death.

The eyewitness, whom I later interviewed on 'News at Ten', said that when the Russians had gone he and a few other men went down into the tunnel and found the victims so badly burnt that they were unrecognisable. Pointing to a cheap metal watch on his wrist, he said, 'The only way I recognised my brother was by his watch.' Somehow the watch had survived the holocaust and was still going.

As incidents like the Logar Massacre became commonplace, it is hardly surprising that in the years that have followed the Russian invasion, about one-third of the Afghan nation has fled abroad. Of the total pre-war population of about fifteen million, at least five million are now in the refugee camps of Pakistan and Iran, with a few more scattered across the world. Pakistan has borne the brunt of the Afghan exodus and given asylum to between three and three and a half million refugees, while Iran accounts for another two million. One more statistic: according to the United Nations, of the approximately ten million refugees in the world today, exactly one half are Afghans.

Statistics are not very moving, but it requires only a bit of imagination to put flesh on these bare bones and to grasp that in the Soviet Union's continued occupation of Afghanistan we are witnessing one of the great human tragedies of this and indeed any other century: another holocaust: an invasion and occupation as ruthless as anything that Genghis Khan or Tamerlane inflicted on the Afghans' ancestors. Even Alexander the Great seems to have been more merciful than Messrs Brezhnev,

Andropov, Chernenko and Gorbachev. In February 1986, the United Nations' Special Rapporteur on Afghanistan, Mr Felix Ermacora, wrote in his report to the Commission on Human Rights, 'Continuation of the military situation (i.e. the war) will, in the opinion of the Special Rapporteur, lead inevitably to a situation approaching genocide, which the traditions and culture of this noble people cannot permit.'

He estimated that 35,000 civilians were killed in the fighting in 1985. In an interview in *Newsweek*, 22 December 1986, he gave a revised figure of 37,000. For every person killed, three or four were probably wounded. In 1986, Mr Ermacora estimated that the number of civilians killed up until the end of August had dropped to around 12,000 to 15,000. A British diplomat in Islamabad remarked to me, 'That's because there are fewer Afghans left to kill.' The overall picture drawn by Mr Ermacora was one of a steadily escalating conflict, becoming more brutal and costly in human lives as heavier weapons were introduced on both sides and as the Russians made more determined attempts to block the guerrillas' infiltration routes and to destroy any sign of resistance, whether civilian or *mujahideen*. Seen against this apocalyptic background, Mr Gorbachev's protestations of wanting to withdraw the 115,000 Soviet troops in Afghanistan seem to many Afghans totally cynical. They say it is hard to escape the conclusion that, while cultivating a conciliatory tone and appearing anxious to negotiate, the Kremlin is still dedicated to its original goal of wiping out all opposition to the Communist government in Kabul and of making sure that Afghanistan becomes as solidly tied to the Soviet system as any other satellite.

Mr Gorbachev has described Afghanistan as a 'bleeding wound' and has assured the world that the Soviet Union *does* want to withdraw its troops. Yet recent visitors to Kabul report that the building of Soviet barracks and other permanent structures indicates that the Russians intend to stay for a long time.

At this point, the question presents itself: why did the Soviet Union invade Afghanistan in the first place? Some people, and not a few Afghans, believe that it was all part of the historic Russian drive for a warm-water port in the Indian Ocean. Other Afghanistan watchers, myself included, believe rather that although the strategic interest may be always at the back of the Russian mind, much more important were two other reasons. The first was to shore up a Communist government in Kabul which was on the point of collapse. The second follows from the first: to prevent the replacement of a Communist regime by an Islamic government which, although not necessarily as extreme as the Khomeini regime in Iran, would have been militant enough in Russian eyes to have inflamed to the point of rebellion the sixty million Muslims who live across the Amu Darya (the classical Oxus), in the Soviet Union. These Central Asian states of Tajikistan, Turkmenistan and Uzbekistan are the soft underbelly of the Soviet Empire. Until the middle and end of the last century, they were made up of a number of independent little Muslim khanates such as Bokhara, Samarkand and Khiva, when each in turn was overthrown and colonised in the insatiable southern march of the Tsarist Empire.

Let us for a moment look at the first reason for the Soviet intervention: the bolstering-up of a precarious protégé. The Communists came to power in Afghanistan on 27 April 1978 through a coup staged by a number of army and air force officers. The Communists did not carry out the coup but were quick to exploit it. They overthrew a republican regime, led by President Daoud, who had come to power himself by deposing the King, his cousin, in 1973.

While King Zaher Shah, whose critics said he was only interested in shooting and fishing, disappeared into exile in Italy, President Daoud, who had been Prime Minister from 1953 to 1963, entered upon an Afghan version of the *apertura a sinistra*, the opening to the left. He cultivated closer relations with the Soviet Union and brought a number of left-wingers into his government. In the process he alienated a number of traditional leaders like Pir Gailani and Professors Rabbani and Sayaf, who fled the country to neighbouring Pakistan. Gailani's passport was confiscated by Daoud until 1977, when after the intervention of King Khaled of Saudi Arabia he was allowed to leave the country for the Haj (the pilgrimage to Mecca). He did not return to Kabul. However, not long after he came to power, Daoud began to get cold feet about the extent of his dependence on Moscow and started to reverse the policy. He eliminated Communists from his government and purged leftists from the army. Moscow became increasingly angry, and by 1977 Brezhnev and Daoud were reported to be at logger-heads. In April 1978, the political murder of a leading Communist, Mir Akbar Khyber, for which Daoud was blamed, led to a big Communist-inspired demonstration in Kabul. Daoud retaliated by arresting Communist leaders, including Nur Mohammed Taraki, the founder of the party, who was detained on 26 April. Next day the coup took place, with or without the connivance of the Russians: the Soviet Ambassador was out of Kabul on a fishing trip, but that proves nothing. What is certain is that the coup was a last-minute affair, hurriedly set in motion by a handful of army officers, although the official version gives the credit to a close aide of Taraki's, a Russian-trained former air force officer called Hafizullah Amin. Daoud and his family were surrounded and trapped in the presidential palace and then systematically killed, down to the last child. It was a massacre worthy of the bloodiest excesses of Afghan political history.

The new government may have had the backing of key elements of the armed forces, but it soon became obvious that there was little support in the country at large, even among the small peasant farmers, in whose name the revolution had partly been made. Taraki was the President, Prime Minister and party leader, but the driving force came from Hafizullah Amin and before long he and Taraki fell out. Suspecting that Taraki and the Russians were plotting to get rid of him, Amin moved first and, in another chilling display of bloodthirstiness, seized Taraki after a gun battle in the palace and later had him killed: according to one report, he was suffocated on Amin's orders. This did not please the Russians, who saw the newly launched and leaky ship of revolution, which was already in dire straits, heading for the rocks under Amin's erratic and brutal command. Throughout the twenty months of the Taraki–Amin regime, opposition continued to grow in the countryside, and Afghanistan is predominantly an agricultural country.

This opposition came from the mosques and the village elders who considered the new Marxist government by definition atheistic and anti-Muslim. So much so that a *Jihad*

(Holy War) was declared against the Communists long before the Russians arrived on the scene. Fighting spread across the country: by 1979 it was clear that the Islamic guerrillas, the *mujahideen*, were gaining the upper hand and that it was only a matter of time before they reversed the Saur (April) Revolution and installed their own Islamic government in Kabul. This the Russians were determined to prevent – not least because it would torpedo the Brezhnev doctrine, which laid down that a Communist takeover was irreversible.

By the autumn of 1979, thanks to Amin's brutal and reckless rule, the country was on its knees economically and in flames politically. The growing strength of the *mujahideen* had led to a state of civil war which the Communists looked certain to lose. The Russians had seen this coming for months, and by December the die was cast for intervention. They waited only for the most propitious time: Christmas Eve, 1979.

The irony is that the Soviet Union, so paranoically sensitive about its security, has sent shock waves through its own empire by its invasion of Afghanistan. It has also internationalised the war, forcing the Americans and the West to come to the aid of the Afghans, and made it impossible to withdraw on what are, for Mr Gorbachev, acceptable conditions. The same sort of dilemma confronted the United States in Vietnam: that any admission of defeat would weaken it and its allies throughout the world. As he searches for a way out of what Dr Andrei Sakharov has called the 'tragic blind alley of Afghanistan', Mr Gorbachev must be highly conscious of the American disarray that followed Vietnam and be determined to prevent it happening in the Soviet Union. He has appointed Dr Najib, the former head of KHAD, the Afghan secret police, as the Communist boss of Afghanistan, with orders to broaden the base of his government and effect a policy of 'national reconciliation'. This, however, is seen by the Afghan *mujahideen* as being simply a ploy to keep control and achieve by diplomacy what he has failed to achieve by military force.

While he searches for a solution that will satisfy both the Politburo and the generals, Mr Gorbachev is prosecuting the war as vigorously as ever, and in some ways more determinedly than the Americans were able to in Vietnam. Many Americans used to complain that the United States was unable to unleash its full power in Vietnam, for example by bombing the North more extensively. These considerations do not deter the Russians in Afghanistan, where they bomb civilians in their villages as a matter of course and after the bombing send in ground troops to wipe out any survivors who still resist. There was one My Lai that we knew about in Vietnam, and there may have been half a dozen we did not know about: in Afghanistan there have been many hundreds of My Lais, if not thousands. But they are not reported because the Russians have strict control of their own media and the foreign journalists who enter the country with the Resistance are few and far between. Journalists who enter Afghanistan with the permission of the Communist authorities are naturally not taken to the scene of the latest atrocity.

This has worked to the political advantage of the Russians but in the end may not avail them much. Opinion throughout the world, including the Third World, is at last becoming aware of Russian atrocities in Afghanistan. Also on the minus side for Mr Gorbachev, there is the effect of the Afghan War inside the Soviet Union; and there are plenty of indications that it is every bit as unpopular among young Russians as Vietnam was among young Americans. Draft-dodging must be just as appealing an idea, if less easy to accomplish. Drug-taking, mainly hashish, is said to be a way of life for young Russian soldiers in Afghanistan, rather as it was for GIs in Vietnam; morale and discipline are equally suspect and conditions for ordinary Russian soldiers are said to be abject, without the medical and material advantages the Americans enjoyed.

There is, we know, a large number of incapacitated and disturbed American veterans of Vietnam. Little is known about that sort of problem in the Soviet Union, but it must exist and be as bad as anything the Americans faced. The Americans lost 58,000 men killed in Vietnam. The Russians do not publish casualty figures, as one would expect in their still secretive society, but Western intelligence estimates put Soviet casualties at the end of 1986 at around 30,000: 10,000 dead and 20,000 wounded. These figures may well be on the low side, but they are still a long way behind the American ones. However, they are almost certainly rising faster as the war progresses and the Russians have to do more and more of the real fighting, so there is little comfort there for the Soviet authorities.

Mr Gorbachev is clearly looking for a politico–military solution, as were the Americans in Vietnam. He has told Najib to keep pushing his 'national reconciliation' policy while the tanks and bombers keep the pressure up on the *mujahideen* and – equally importantly – on the hapless civilians caught in the middle. While 'national reconciliation' does not seem to have any real chance of success, the second strand of his policy, aimed at Pakistan, may have. The Russian and Afghan air forces bombed the Pakistani border many times in 1986 and 1987, killing hundreds of civilians, and Communist agents set off scores of bombs in and around Peshawar, the capital of Pakistan's North-West Frontier Province and also of the Afghan *mujahideen* in exile. Pakistani resentment of the war is growing and the *mujahideen* get the blame, however unfairly. The Kremlin obviously hopes that the combination of the big stick of bombing and the political carrot of offering ultimately to withdraw its forces will persuade the Pakistanis to accept a settlement which leaves the Russians masters of Afghanistan.

My own conclusion is that the Russians will genuinely withdraw when they see it as the *only* option, when all the signs point in one direction: world opprobrium, dissent at home, increasing drug-taking, growing casualties and the steady financial drain of the war, said to be costing the Kremlin about fifteen million dollars a day (against forty million dollars a day for the Americans in Vietnam). When that moment comes, Mr Gorbachev will have to tell his Afghan allies that they are on their own now, a step no Russian leader can possibly contemplate with any degree of equanimity. So I believe Mr Gorbachev will withdraw from Afghanistan and allow the Afghans to decide their own future only when he concludes that he has no alternative.

CHAPTER TWO

In the summer of 1986 I made my third journey into Afghanistan. I had gone for the first time to make a documentary film in 1982, when very little was known about the conflict, although it was already three years old. I remember being told that if I wanted to bring myself really up to date I would have to go to Paris to talk to a number of experts there. This I did with pleasure, not solely connected with matters Afghan. I went with my friend Charles Morgan, then a cameraman but now a maker of sports cars, and after completing our talks we toasted our anticipated success with a bottle of champagne in Brasserie Lipp on the Boulevard St Germain, at eleven in the morning. Charles and I, along with Tom Murphy, our young sound recordist, and Nigel Ryan, an old friend, a former editor of ITN and the producer of the documentary, eventually made a remarkable journey to visit the *mujahideen* leader Ahmed Shah Masud in the Panjsher Valley north-east of Kabul.

The trip took ten weeks, we were heavily bombed and at one point separated from all our camera equipment for a highly frustrating three weeks. The fact that we finally achieved what we originally set out to do, namely make a one-hour film about the war, seemed to me then little short of a miracle: it still does today.

I went back again in 1984, this time to travel with the Pathans, the main ethnic unit in the south of Afghanistan, near the Pakistani border. Our group, led by Din Mohammed, the second-in-command of Yunis Khalis's Hisbe-i-Islami Party, would have with it, I was told, a number of SAM 7B missiles, with which the *mujahideen* hoped to shoot down a Russian helicopter or two. As it turned out, the SAMs, which are Russian-made, proved completely ineffectual, either because it is a bad weapon or because these ones were in bad condition. That would not have been surprising as they had to be transported over the mountains on horseback and inevitably came in for some rough treatment. In the event, all attempts to shoot down a Russian helicopter failed.

During the last and most likely try, four helicopters flew past on their way to supply a government fort a few miles away. We were sitting in a village when we heard the familiar beat of the rotors and scrambled to put our boots on. I had an ITN crew with me (Paul Carleton and Jon Hunt), who snatched up the camera and sound gear and hurried outside just in time to see two Mi8s landing in a cloud of dust about a mile away. The other two, Mi24 gunships, flew in protective circles overhead, just in case the *mujahideen* tried to interfere. Ten minutes later the Mi8s took off and came back towards us on exactly the same route, following the old road which runs from Kabul to Jalalabad.

The guerrillas had one SAM ready for action as the helicopters came past, only a few hundred feet up and presenting what should have been the easiest of targets. The *mujahid* with the SAM took aim, got the necessary 'lock-on', which meant the heat-seeking missile was ready for firing, and pressed the trigger. Filming from about fifty yards away, we saw the puff of smoke as he fired and then watched with professional disappointment as the wretched missile, instead of streaking heavenwards, sped fifty or sixty yards and flopped like a wet pancake on the ground. The helicopters flew on without giving the slightest sign that they had seen us, although the SAM operator was standing right out in the open on top of a little hill in the middle of the plain.

We were told by the *mujahideen* afterwards that a kill ratio of one in ten was all they could expect with the SAM 7B, which they found not very encouraging.

A few days later, back in Peshawar, I bumped into an acquaintance, Andy Skrzypkowiak, known to his friends as Andy the Pole, a former paratrooper who after leaving the army had become a freelance cameraman and made several trips to Afghanistan. He was with his wife Chris, a still photographer, and they were about to set off for the Panjsher. Andy said to me, 'Sandy, why don't we make a trip together next year?' Knowing his reputation for fearless combat photography, I happily said, 'Yes, what a very good idea.' In fact, there were a number of problems to be overcome, and it proved impossible to make our proposed expedition in 1985. However, by early 1986 these had been resolved, and detailed plans were made for Andy and me to be accompanied by Noel Smart, a documentary cameraman at Central Television, who were commissioning the film. Noel turned out to be a wonderfully resilient and agreeable companion as well as a first-class cameraman and he and Andy made a brilliantly successful pair. We decided to revisit the elusive and now legendary Ahmed Shah Masud. It was to be the longest, in terms of miles, and the most arduous of my three expeditions, but in many ways the most successful.

We left London on Saturday, 14 June. It was a beautiful day, almost the first of the summer, and I experienced a small pang of regret at leaving the green, Palmeresque landscape of Kent, just as it was coming into full leaf. Nigel Ryan came to see us off at Heathrow, presenting me with a gift for the coming journey through Afghanistan: a box of lifeboat survival biscuits. He half wanted to come with me again, although for him the adventure of Afghanistan called less strongly.

My wife Eléanor had protested when I told her I was going back: 'You must be crazy. You're far too old for that sort of thing.' I was in fact a few months short of my fifty-ninth birthday, but I felt fit and, having made the journey into Afghanistan twice before, I was sure I could do it again. I knew that important as physical fitness was, mental fitness was even more crucial. If you are determined enough, you can force your complaining body up those terrible slopes, make light of the unappetising food and spartan conditions and put up with the vagaries of Afghan companions who have a very different concept of time and distance. To an Afghan '*nim sat*' (half an hour) can mean anything up to two or three hours. One day, after walking for a very long time and longing desperately to reach our destination we asked three passers-by in quick succession how far it was to the next village. The answers were variously: thirty minutes, one hour and an hour and a half. It turned out to be two.

But there were other considerations. Alarming stories had been coming out of Afghanistan of increased Russian activity on the infiltration routes: more bombing of arms convoys and more frequent use of Spetsnaz special forces, especially in night-time ambushes. Their method was to helicopter in and then walk to the ambush point where they lay in wait for the

11

unsuspecting convoy. Much disruption was said to have been caused and many men and animals killed.

The southern routes were known to be the riskiest and our friends in Jamiat-i-Islami (Society of Islam), the organisation to which Masud belongs, said firmly that we must go by the northern route, because it was safer. I knew, too, it was much higher, more difficult for men and horses, and longer. It led from the Pakistani hill town of Chitral, best known in the annals of the Raj for its famous siege in 1895, across the border into Nuristan, the highest and probably the most beautiful of Afghanistan's twenty-eight provinces. I had come out by this route in 1982 and remembered with a twinge of apprehension the five 15,000-foot passes that we would have to negotiate between the border and the Panjsher Valley. That had been our destination in 1982, because it was Masud's stronghold. But he had moved out of the valley and was now organising and fighting much farther afield, right up to the Russian border. The problem confronting us was not only where would we find him, but how long it would take us. We had been told secretly that he would probably be somewhere near Khost-i-Fereng, a town in the northern foothills of the Hindu Kush, about a week's march beyond the Panjsher Valley, but this was all very approximate we realised, because Masud moved about a great deal, keeping well ahead of the assassination squads and snatch teams the Russians had several times sent after him. He must by now rank as Public Enemy Number One, or at least be on the short list.

Apart from the chilling stories about the Spetsnaz, I was conscious that Andy and I must be on the KGB blacklist of journalists who made a habit of going to Afghanistan with the *mujahideen* to report what was really happening in the war. If the KGB were half as efficient as one expected them to be on intelligence matters, we had to assume that they would have fed into their computers the fact that the three of us were heading for Afghanistan in June 1986. But I have often found that in risky situations, rehearsing the dangers in advance is much more frightening than the actual experience. So it proved this time. I had a number of briefings and discussions before going in, and I emerged from them feeling that this would be my most dangerous assignment yet. After floundering about for years, the Russians were finally learning how to fight a guerrilla war under Afghan conditions. Others thought so too. My brother-in-law, Julian Smyth, the head doctor for the NAAFI, presented me with a Miraculous Medal to keep me safe. But I also knew that Noel and I could not have a better survival expert as a companion than Andy.

It was therefore with almost complete confidence, flawed by only a few scintillas of doubt, that I embarked on what I had already promised myself would be my last assignment to Afghanistan: not so much because of the danger but because I felt I was running the risk of becoming stereotyped. I was the only television journalist in Britain who took a deep enough interest in Afghanistan to have visited the country three times in four years and to have made three full-length documentaries on the war. It was time, I told myself, for a fresh eye.

At the same time, I was determined my swan song should be as powerful as I could make it because I felt very strongly that Afghanistan had been and still was neglected by the Western media in a way that contrasts strangely with our concentration on, say, South Africa, or Lebanon. I spent three years working for Reuters in South Africa, and I quite understand why, as a classic conflict of white versus black, it should have so captured the interest and compassion of the world. Again, the Lebanon, its civil war more bloody and convoluted than even Shakespeare could have conceived, is strategically important because it lies at the heart of the Middle East, with its oil, inflammatory politics and the Israeli dimension.

Afghanistan on the other hand, it can be argued, is so remote and so little known that it lies outside the immediate scope of British and Western concern. Now that we no longer have an Indian Empire, now that the North-West Frontier is no longer a place where young British officers win their spurs protecting the outposts of the Raj, it is only realistic, the argument runs, for us to concede Afghanistan to the Russians and their sphere of influence.

In any case, the argument continues, Afghanistan is a lost cause: there is nothing we can do about it. And then there are so many other problems, so many other issues with which one can feel a greater sense of identity.

To that I would simply say: freedom is indivisible. The

Afghans' struggle for independence against a foreign aggressor whose only justification is that might is right is in the heroic tradition of all wars of national liberation. I believe the Afghan struggle against the Soviet Union is on the same noble level as the American War of Independence against the British in the eighteenth century; Greece's war of liberation against the Turks in the nineteenth century; and the colonial world's struggle for independence in the twentieth; whether in Egypt, Algeria, Indochina, Cyprus or Zimbabwe. One also thinks of a different but no less heroic struggle: our own defence of freedom in the Second World War, virtually alone at the beginning against Hitler's Nazi Germany; and also, from 1941 onwards, the resistance of the Russians in their 'Great Patriotic War' against the same enemy.

It seems tragic that the Soviet Union, which fought so splendidly for its own freedom in the Second World War, should so brutally try to subjugate a small, underdeveloped but infinitely brave nation only forty years later. Leonid Brezhnev and his heirs have much to answer for.

CHAPTER THREE

We arrived in Islamabad, a modern artificial capital, at 5 a.m. on Sunday, 15 June. Unlike any other time I have been there, the airport was almost completely deserted, and despite our small mountain of luggage we had no trouble with the Customs. But once outside the terminal building we were besieged by a small group of persistent taxi drivers, all of them proud possessors of ancient Morris Minors, almost the last vestige of British imperial power left in Pakistan; a thin black and yellow line that cannot be expected to hold out much longer against the encroaching hordes of Japanese Toyotas, Datsuns and Suzukis. Surprisingly, the Japanese invasion has still not captured the low ground of the airport taxi.

We would need two Morris Minors, plus roof racks. Having selected his victims Andy bargained cruelly hard, beating the drivers down to what seemed to me an almost indecently low price. At one point I weakly protested: 'Andy, 150 rupees (about £6) is quite all right.' But he either did not hear or disdained my advice. '125 rupees. *Bus* (finish). OK?' He fixed the unfortunate drivers with such an imperious blue eye that after merely token argument they succumbed. 'OK, *sahib*, 125 rupees to Islamabad, no extra charge.'

Islamabad is built on the grid system, like New York, although there all similarity ends: in theory, however, any address is readily findable. But of course, being the Orient, things do not work like that. For example, the street you are looking for, let us say Street 11 in F2, a residential quarter which houses a lot of foreign families, should be between Streets 10 and 12, but someone has moved it and hidden it away round a corner next to Street 15. The deviation may be due to a small stream, or some other quirk which has bent the mathematical precision of the grid. Luckily our drivers knew their Islamabad, and despite the erratic numbering deposited us with great efficiency at the house where we had been invited to stay for a few days. Not surprisingly, our friends were still in bed, but although we unloaded our baggage as quietly as

15

possible, Francesca Black heard us and appeared in her dressing gown.

'Oh, hallo, I thought I heard a car.' Andy was an old friend, and I had met her once briefly in London. 'Leave your bags. Lal Khan will see to them. Come in and have a cup of tea.' Nothing could have sounded more invitingly British as we trooped into the cool of the house. I apologised for the earliness of our arrival. 'Oh, don't worry, Juliet Crawley forgot her key and I had to get up at three thirty to let her in.' Juliet, who appeared later, was a young and attractive English girl who worked for Afghanaid in Peshawar and clearly enjoyed her trips to the big city. Soon afterwards Christopher Black appeared, friendly and already dressed for the office, and we breakfasted together. He was both charming and intelligent, a businessman who worked for a well-known multinational and who had offered to help us make our arrangements, keeping in touch with our principal Afghan contact, Masud (it means 'lucky') Khalili. Khalili was the political officer for Jamiat and was going to act as our escort and interpreter for the journey.

Christopher had some not particularly good news to impart over the cornflakes. 'I spoke to Khalili the other day and he says that the passes are still blocked with snow. He thinks it will take ten days before you can get the horses over the first pass.' My jaw dropped. This was a complete surprise, although Afghanistan is always full of surprises. 'To be absolutely fair he told me this a couple of days ago and I decided not to pass it on, so if anyone is to blame it's me. But I knew you were all ready to leave and I thought to stop you at the last moment would have been pointless.'

Andy spoke between mouthfuls. 'I know he tried to ring me before we left but I was away. Maybe that's what it was about.'

A little later this was confirmed in a telephone call from Khalili. Andy came back into the room to announce, 'Khalili says there was a late snowfall two or three weeks ago. People are getting through on foot, but he says it's impossible for horses.'

That evening Khalili came to see us, small with very dark, darting eyes and a ready smile. His father, Professor Khalili, was probably the best-known Afghan alive after the King, and the greatest poet writing in Persian. He had become a symbol of the struggle against the Russians, was revered by Afghans of

16

all kinds and sought out by many of the Resistance leaders. His was the authentic voice of the Afghan people in all its tribulation and in all its heroism. He died, alas, in May 1987.

All Khalili could really tell us was that we were the victims of a freak storm which had deposited several feet of snow on the high passes and that he was trying to get an up-to-date report from the Jamiat people in Chitral, our jumping-off point. We also discussed our movements over the next few days and he was adamant that I, at least, should not be seen in Peshawar. 'You know, Peshawar is full of KHAD and KGB spies and someone as well known as yourself will be spotted immediately and your presence reported. It is just not worth the risk. It is far better if you stay in Islamabad until we are ready to leave.'

I am always nervous about being relegated to the rear, taking the view that I can exert more pressure if I am as near the point of departure as possible. I also knew from experience that the Afghans were far less preoccupied with time than we Westerners. One week here or there makes very little difference to them.

'How about Chitral? Is it a good idea to spend a couple of days there before we depart?'

Khalili shook his head. 'No, Chitral is just as bad. It's full of spies too. What you should do is stay in Islamabad until we can move, say in ten days' time, and then we will go straight to Peshawar and either fly or drive to Chitral. Spend one night with Atik, one of our people there, and then head for the border next day. That way, there will be less chance of you being seen. You know, there are always people around watching what's going on, and when they suddenly see three foreigners, with lots of television equipment, either in Peshawar or in Chitral, they don't have to be very clever to guess that they're going into Afghanistan to make a film.' He laughed loudly at his own perspicacity.

I knew perfectly well that this was good advice and we would have to take it. 'All right,' I said, 'we'd better move into the Holiday Inn. Is that the best place?' I addressed the question to the room at large. Francesca chipped in.

'You can stay here. If you go to the Holiday Inn, you're just as liable to be spotted by the KGB. The Russians use it all the time.'

'Well, is there some other hotel less frequented by the KGB?'

'Yes, but you wouldn't want to stay there.' Francesca laughed. 'You'd be much more comfortable here, and if you don't mind the children you're very welcome and we'd love to have you.' It was a generous offer which I felt it would be both ungracious and silly to refuse. I accepted with I hope not too much alacrity.

'Well, there are three of us, which is an awful lot, but it would be extremely nice for us, rather than living in some ghastly hotel ...' I looked round at the others. Andy had stayed with them before and was a special friend, so he had no trouble in accepting. Noel, who is very easy-going, said he would be very happy to stay in the house and he turned out to be a big hit with their three small boys. What none of us could foresee was that we would spend three weeks with our generous and long-suffering hosts, as Khalili commuted between Islam-abad and his office in Peshawar and monitored the state of the passes by telephone to Chitral, not always the simplest of operations.

For a change of scene and to buy some equipment, Noel, who had not been in Pakistan before, went to Peshawar with Andy, and had his first glimpse of the capital of the North-West Frontier. Peshawar was once the jewel in the Afghan crown, the old winter capital. Now, by historical chance, it has become at least partly an Afghan city again and the headquarters of the Afghan Resistance. Round it, scattered over the bare brown plain in mud-walled houses and tents, were something like three million Afghan refugees.

I stayed quite happily in Islamabad, trying to see my old friend President Zia, and gathering as much information as I could about the state of the war. The picture that emerged in Islamabad was not a very optimistic one. With the exception of the north-east, where Ahmed Shah Masud was said to be busy expanding his military and political base, reports from the rest of the country suggested that the war was going badly for the *mujahideen*. This was partly because the new Afghan government was trying harder and the Russians were using more effective tactics. But also, so my informants said, the trouble lay with the way the Pakistanis were running the war. Quite understandably, since both their commitment and vulnerability were so great, the Pakistanis wished to control operations as much as they could. They had definite ideas and undoubted preferences. If, as was the case for the Soviet Union and China in Vietnam, the Pakistanis were able to deal with a unified resistance, a single entity like the Vietcong (although it was in practice simply an extension of the North Vietnamese Communist Party), things would be much easier for them. But, through no fault of their own, they had to deal with a hydra-headed Afghan resistance, consisting of seven main political parties as well as a lot of minor groups.

Although the seven major parties form an alliance, with a rotating spokesman, not chairman it is worth noting, it exists only on paper. Each party goes its own way and is in competition with all the others for money, arms and influence. This has had the result of obliging the Pakistanis, as well as their principal backers, the Americans, the Saudis and the other Gulf states, to make choices as to whom they should support, and they have not always done so wisely. The Pakistanis, and through them the Americans and the Arabs, favour two parties, both called Hisbe-i-Islami, one run by an elderly man of God with no military pretensions, Maulawi Yunis Khalis, and the other by a ruthlessly ambitious politician who seems more interested in fighting other Afghans than the Russians, Engineer Gulbuddin Hekmatyar – Afghans use Engineer as a title as we do Doctor. Both are Pashtuns, or Pathans as the British called the border tribesmen in Kipling's day, the largest ethnic grouping in Afghanistan representing about forty per cent of the population. The Pashtuns have traditionally supplied the leaders and kings of Afghanistan, but, paradoxically, they have thrown up no outstanding guerrilla leader in the present conflict able to unite all the Pathans, let alone all the Afghans. They have not even produced a leader with the imagination and bold strategic mind of a Masud. The closest they get to it, in my view, is in the person of Abdul Haq, the Khalis commander for the Kabul area, who had talks with Mrs Thatcher when he came to Britain in 1986. On present evidence he is a brave and able tactical commander, but no strategist. Masud, on the other hand, is a potential Tito. But he is also a Tajik, and because of tribal jealousies is unlikely ever to be accepted as a leader by the Pathans, which is unfortunate for the Afghans.

The pro-Pathan bias of the Pakistanis is understandable for several reasons, mainly tribal and geographical. First, the Pathan tribes straddle the North-West Frontier between Pakistan and Afghanistan; they speak the same language; and have the same tribal system, based on the famous *Pashtunwali*, the Tribal Code of the Pathans. This sets great store on the honour and independence of the tribe and its individual members and is in some ways reminiscent of the customs and loyalties of the old Scottish clans. In the Tribal Areas today, as in the days of the British, it is the *Pashtunwali* which regulates the affairs of the local inhabitants, not Pakistani law. *Pashtunwali* is rather like Old Testament law: an eye for an eye and a tooth for a tooth. Revenge is not only sweet but obligatory.

Reinforcing this strong blood tie is the geographical argument. The Pakistanis see the Afghan Pathans, very naturally, as a buffer between themselves and the Russians. There is nothing the Pakistanis want less than a strong Russian presence on their border, however mountainous and inaccessible it may be for three-quarters of its length. So the main thrust of their policy is to encourage the *mujahideen* to build up a strong presence all along the border, strong enough to make it impossible for the Russians and their Afghan levies to establish military posts which command the crossing points. It is unfortunate to say the least that the Pakistanis' implementation of this perfectly sensible policy has been so maladroit, based on a sort of Maginot Line mentality, and has encouraged the Afghans to build bases along the border which are vulnerable to the hammer blows of Russian air power. This is exactly what happened at Zhawar, not far from the Pakistani border.

The colourful commander of Zhawar was a splendid-looking Pathan warrior called Jalaludin Haqqani, a Khalis man. Over the years he built a large, well-publicised base in the sheer rock face, tunnelling out ammunition dumps and living quarters, a hospital and a mosque. Several hundred *mujahideen* were based on Zhawar, and photographs appeared in French magazines of its extensive facilities and fortifications, including some captured tanks. In March 1986 the blow fell.

The Russians bombed the base heavily and repeatedly, then

landed special forces and overran it, despite spirited resistance, capturing or destroying a large amount of carefully hoarded equipment. It was a classic demonstration of how a guerrilla army should not conduct its affairs.

Gulbuddin seems to have forfeited some Pakistani support because of his arrogance and cussedness: Yunis Khalis, on the other hand, irreproachable from a religio-political point of view, now seems to be the Pakistanis' favourite son and the proud recipient of the first American Stinger ground-to-air missiles.* In a report in the *Sunday Telegraph* in November 1986, a young freelance journalist, Radek Sikorski, said he had visited a Yunis Khalis base camp in Nangarhar Province, between the border and the city of Jalalabad, and seen five Stingers which the *mujahideen* had just acquired; they claimed that they had already scored several successes with the hand-held missiles, the first of an initial shipment of about three hundred. The report went on to say that the Americans were training the *mujahideen* in the use of Stinger at a secret base near Islamabad.

My informants, however, complained that it was not just incompetence and favouritism that was playing havoc with the performance of the Afghan Resistance. Corruption was an all-pervading and sapping influence which had not only in some cases castrated the *mujahideen*'s zest for the *Jihad*, but was threatening the very stability of Pakistan itself. I was reminded of the case in 1984 of a Pakistani colonel and two of his majors who were selling arms to the *mujahideen* – arms that had been bought with American money and should have been handed over free. The colonel and his two subordinates were jailed, but I was told that the same sort of thing was still prevalent. What happens is this: a middleman acting for Pakistani officers who are entrusted with supplying free arms to the *mujahideen* is approached by a *mujahideen* commander. He says he needs weapons to send to his people in Afghanistan.

---

* The arrival of the Stinger at the end of 1986 has transformed the war. It has significantly raised *mujahideen* morale: for the first time, they feel they have an answer to Soviet air power. Conversely, it has made life more dangerous and more costly for the Russians. In 1987, Soviet and Afghan Government losses were estimated at about 40 aircraft (fixed wing and helicopters) a month: more than one a day.

The middleman says he can let him have, say, fifty Kalashnikov rifles, at a price. The commander, who wants, let us say, a thousand Kalashnikovs, accepts because he knows that he can sell them in the local bazaar for US$500 apiece. With the money from the sale, the commander returns to the middleman and this time buys perhaps five hundred Kalashnikovs. Again a bargain is struck, and the commander sells the five hundred new weapons in the bazaar at the same price of US$500. His wallet full, the commander goes back again to the middleman and this time says he wants a thousand Kalashnikovs. He has the money to pay for them, the deal is done, and the Kalashnikovs, finally, are on their way to the *mujahideen* who have been waiting all this time for modern weapons with which to fight the Russians. Corruption on this scale is enormously damaging, not just to the *mujahideen*, although the effect on them is the most obvious.

I was quoted the case of an able commander in the Kandahar area called Asmatullah (Muslim) Achakzai. Like all the best Pathan commanders, he is a larger-than-life character, wild and a law unto himself, but brave, resourceful and a born leader. Asmatullah, I was told, became increasingly disenchanted with the corruption surrounding the supply of weapons to the *mujahideen* and finally, when there was an attempt to frame him on a charge of either belonging to or supporting the Al Zulfikar terrorist organisation, founded by one of Bhutto's sons, he defected to the government side, taking his men with him.

> O, young Lochinvar is come out of the west,
> Through all the wide Border his steed was the best.

So Asmatullah. He was now said to be as useful to the Russians and their Kabul allies as he previously was to the *mujahideen* cause. Since his defection, it was said, the government forces had virtually sealed off the infiltration routes to Kandahar, forcing the *mujahideen* to make a much longer and more difficult journey right round the city. According to this view, the Afghans had become the rather inefficient sepoys of the Pakistani army and had been transformed from wild tribal fighters into rather tame levies, subservient to the conventional military thinking of the Pakistanis. Although I found it hard to believe that the natural guerrilla genius of the Afghans, which had slaughtered one British army in 1842, and inflicted serious casualties in two other Afghan wars (1878 and 1919), had been extinguished so readily, I was told that this was indeed happening. My informant described how he had talked to a group of middle-ranking *mujahideen* commanders near Quetta who had all complained bitterly of the way they were being obliged to fight.

'They say that the Pakistanis force them to fight in large groups, to build conventional posts opposite government posts, where there is no cover. They say, "We know this is not the way for us to fight. We have always fought in the traditional tribal manner. That is the way we have always fought. Unless we return to what we know best we will be destroyed."'

'How can the Pakistanis force them to fight in a way they don't want to?' I asked.

'They withhold the arms and ammunition. Unless the *mujahideen* obey instructions, they don't get the supplies. The Afghans are desperate but there's nothing they can do.'

It is exactly because he does not intend to be forced into this kind of position that Masud refuses to place himself under Pakistani control. This, of course, has made him *persona non grata* with the Pakistanis. They say they only want to help him. He says they want to control him. He insists on fighting the war in his own way. 'How,' he was to say to me, 'can a Pakistani who is not in Afghanistan and doesn't even know the country tell me how to fight the Russians, which I have been doing for seven years in any case?' It seems an unanswerable argument. Nevertheless, the whole squabble is highly unfortunate for both Afghans and Pakistanis. Only the Russians benefit.

As someone who admires the immensely courageous struggle of the Afghans for their independence, as well as the generous support they have been given by the Pakistanis, at no mean cost to themselves, I believe that it is indisputably in the world's interest that a more effective and finally successful Afghan Resistance should force the Russians to withdraw from Afghanistan. The Afghans have, God knows, spilled a huge amount of blood and suffered untold agony in fighting for their liberty. The Pakistanis, largely because of the solid and unflappable support of their President, General Zia, have been resolute and indispensable allies. But I think they need to take a lesson from the way Britain backed Josip Broz Tito against the Germans in Yugoslavia in 1940. They gave him arms and money but, although they did not approve of his Marxist ideas, left him to fight the war in his own way.

I believe the Pakistanis need to support the best Afghan commanders in the field, people like Ahmed Shah Masud in the north, Ismail Khan in Herat and Abdul Haq in the Kabul area, irrespective of whether they are Pathans or Tajiks, regardless of their political and religious leanings, and purely on the basis of their military skill and leadership qualities. They also need to encourage Afghan unity, both inside Afghanistan and outside, by penalising anyone like Gulbuddin who acts out of personal self-aggrandisement, and supporting people like Masud who is trying to build a united resistance under the noses of the Russians. In this way only, I believe, will the Pakistanis achieve the goal which they and their friends, the Americans and the Arabs, the Afghans themselves, and indeed the whole of the civilised world so rightly desire: the withdrawal of Russian troops from Afghanistan and self-determination for the Afghans.

CHAPTER FOUR

I talked one day in Islamabad to an Australian diplomat who had recently been in Kabul: the Australians have a house there, although no mission, so they are given visas to visit their property periodically. He said that in Kabul you get the impression very strongly of a city under siege. 'The war seems to be always just over the horizon. The choppers are always in the sky and every so often at night you hear the thump of an incoming rocket.

'There are three concentric rings of defence round the city designed, unsuccessfully, to keep the *mujahideen* out. The outer one is manned by the Russians, the inner two by the DRA (Democratic Republic of Afghanistan) who're less reliable.'

But what struck him most about Kabul was the hatred of the Russians among all the Afghans he met, even people in the army. 'In one shop I went into, there was an Afghan soldier on leave. When he discovered I was friendly and not a Russian, he said, "I hate the Russians for what they are doing to our country."'

Khalili rang to say that Ashem, a *mujahid* from the Panjsher Valley, had just arrived in Chitral and reported that the snow was one and a half metres deep on the passes, with a danger of avalanches. He thought it would be another twenty days before horses could make the journey. This caused a slump in morale and it was decided that Andy and Noel should make another visit to Peshawar to exert pressure on Khalili. I also suggested that Andy should make contact with Agha Gul, Masud's chief of convoys, and ask him to start arranging horses for us and to be sure to get word to us as soon as the route was open. I wanted to be the first over.

Ashem was one of Masud's couriers and had a disconcerting story to tell. He had started out from the Panjsher, planning to take the easier, southern route. Somewhere near Bagram, a big Soviet airbase north-east of Kabul and not very far from the Panjsher, they were either ambushed or more probably waylaid

25

by villagers belonging to Gulbuddin's Hisbe-i-Islami Party. Ashem and his four companions were stopped, their weapons taken from them and they were tied up. The villagers sent word to a nearby Afghan army post, which despatched troops and tanks or armoured personnel carriers to arrest the Panjsheris. When Ashem heard the noise of the armour approaching he realised what was happening and managed in desperation to free himself and escape. His companions were not so fortunate: all four were shot. Ashem had then retraced his steps and taken the northern route. The story convinced us, if we needed any convincing, that the southern route was indeed too dangerous. It also suggested once again that the Hisbe were not to be trusted, and could on occasion be more dangerous than the Russians or the Afghan government forces.

Ten days after our arrival, I finally saw President Zia in his grand office in the new presidential palace in Islamabad. In the old days I would have expected to have seen him almost immediately, but bureaucracy flourishes like a weed in Pakistan as well as everywhere else. We spoke for about an hour and he seemed remarkably relaxed. I asked him first about Benazir Bhutto, who had made her spectacular return after a long period of exile a couple of months before. Some of the more apocalyptic commentators had pictured her overthrowing Zia in much the same way as Cory Aquino had recently forced out Marcos in the Philippines. I had thought that unlikely – although the Pakistanis are as volatile as anyone else – largely because Pakistan has become a relatively prosperous place as a result of the Soviet occupation of Afghanistan and the resultant flow of American and Arab aid.

President Zia said that Benazir had spent twenty million dollars on her campaign against him at that point, the money coming mainly from the Libyans 'and possibly the Russians'. He claimed that people were paid one hundred rupees (£4) to attend her meetings, many taking the day off work to do so. Organisers were paid so much a busful, Zia said.

'She also received moral support from Democratic Senators and Congressmen in the States. But I don't think the general population will come out on the streets in support of her call for early elections.'

Zia's position is that the present government of his Prime

Minister, Mr Muhammad Khan Junejo, is legally in power until 1990 and that there is no question of elections before that date.

'How long do you see yourself remaining in power?'

'Oh, until 1990, and then I think I'll have had enough.' He gave his famous chuckle.

We then talked about Afghanistan. I was looking for any sign that his resolve might be weakening. After all, his support for the *mujahideen* in their struggle against the Russian occupation, while making him a valued ally of the West, had created all sorts of problems for Pakistan and for Zia as head of state: he had been leant on heavily by Brezhnev, Andropov, Chernenko and Gorbachev in turn. In 1984 he had even told me that he thought a limited Soviet invasion of Pakistan, to teach him a lesson as it were, was a distinct possibility. The Russians are only one hour fifteen minutes' flying time by helicopter from their nearest base to the Karakoram Highway, across the Wakhan Corridor, the parrot's beak of Afghan territory that protrudes into China and has been in effect annexed by the Russians. 'We have no troops up there. It would be very embarrassing. We have a treaty of mutual assistance with the United States, but I can't see the Americans sending troops to defend Pakistan, can you? No, we'd be very much on our own.'

But his views on the rightness of the Afghan cause and what he sees as his duty to support it seemed as positive as ever.

'Unless the Russians agree to withdraw their troops from Afghanistan within months if not weeks, there can be no agreement and no return of the refugees.'

I had heard rumours of a possible sell-out of the *mujahideen* in order to get a quick solution to the war, so I pressed the point.

'Given the unpopularity of the war in Pakistan, would you consider sending back the refugees ahead of an agreement?'

'No.' It was categoric.

He leaned forward. 'The whole thing is the time frame of the Soviet withdrawal. We want to know the date when they are going to start withdrawing their troops and the date they'll finish.'

I suggested things might not be going too well for the *mujahideen*. He did not agree. 'Their morale is unshaken. They are as strong as ever.' He raised his fist to drive the point home.

His military secretary, Brigadier Durrani, put his head round the door. It was time to go. I got up and thanked him. 'We'll be praying for you,' he said, gripping my hand.

I had known Zia for a long time, since he was a brigadier in Jordan in 1970, at the time of Black September. He was then a member of the Pakistani military mission to the Jordanian army, and the adviser on tank warfare. He got me an interview with King Hussein, the first since the bloody battle with the Palestinians which led to the expulsion of the PLO from Jordan. I next met him in 1971 when India and Pakistan went to war over East Pakistan, now Bangladesh. Incongruously, we met in the coffee shop of the Intercontinental in Rawalpindi. He had been recalled from Jordan and looked a very depressed man: small wonder, Pakistan was on the verge of a terrible defeat in which they would lose East Pakistan, and have 90,000 soldiers taken prisoner. Curiously, that defeat led to the ousting of General Yahya Khan and his replacement by the former Foreign Minister, the ambitious Bhutto, and it was Bhutto who chose Zia, over the heads of more senior but, he thought, less pliable generals, to be his new Chief of Army Staff.

My next meeting with Zia came about in a fairly dramatic manner, shortly after he had led the coup which unseated Bhutto in July 1977: indeed I was presenting 'News at Ten' that night and when the story came over the wire from Reuters I said to David Nicholas, now Editor of ITN, who was producing the programme, 'Hey, I know this bloke. My old friend Zia. Do you want me to give him a call?'

But it was already close to our deadline and the call did not materialise.

A week or ten days later, however, the telephone rang in my cottage in Kent. I happened to be in the kitchen, where I took it. A strongly accented Pakistani voice inquired if I was Mr Sandy Gall, and when I replied in the affirmative, rattled off, 'Stand by please for the Chief Martial Law Administrator, Pakistan.'

Seconds later, a familiar voice came on the line. 'Hallo, Sandy, Zia here. How are you keeping? How's the family?'

Then he asked me to fly out to see for myself what was happening in Pakistan. 'I want you to hear at first hand why the army was forced to intervene and arrest Mr Bhutto. I will tell you the whole story when you come out.'

'I'd like to bring a camera crew with me and interview you. It would make a fascinating story.'

'I'll give you an interview with pleasure later. But I ask you this time to come without the cameras, see what's happening in the country – everything is peaceful – and hear the full story. You can go anywhere you like and talk to anyone you like. We have nothing to hide.'

I said I would have to talk to my editor. He made no objection so I flew out the following weekend and spent a couple of days listening to Zia's account of the coup. I also saw and had a brief talk with a frightened and bitter Bhutto, who had been released after being arrested at the start of the coup and was back in his house in Islamabad. When he discovered I was accompanied by a man from the Ministry of Information, one of his former officials, he became furious.

'How dare you come in here?' he shouted. 'Get out.' I felt very embarrassed and wanted to intervene, but did not know quite what to say. While I hesitated, the man, a nice, polite, middle-grade official, got up and left the room. I asked Bhutto what was happening to him. He looked at me angrily.

'What do you think's happening to me? I'm followed everywhere by the secret police. All the time.'

When I expressed surprise, not so much at the fact that he was followed as that he should be so upset at what must have been standard practice in his own heyday, he rounded on me: 'Where have you come from, the moon?'

After that I felt there was not much point in pursuing the conversation and took my leave. It was the last time I was to see Bhutto, although I reported the final stages of his trial for ordering the murder of a young opposition politician. The politician, a former Bhutto supporter, survived an assassination attempt but his father was killed. After Bhutto's appeal had been turned down and the death sentence confirmed, I asked if I could see Bhutto in the Rawalpindi jail, but Zia, after initially saying yes, finally said no. It would undoubtedly have been powerful propaganda in favour of a pardon and against his subsequent execution, and simple soldier though he was in those days, Zia recognised that.

The Soviet invasion of Afghanistan in 1979 brought us into contact again, although I did not tell Zia in advance of my first trip to report the war in 1982. I thought that he might just conceivably say he did not want me to cross the Pakistani border – the only practical route in – so I did not risk it. But I saw him when I came out and discovered that my fears were groundless. Far from being against my going in, he was very much in favour and applauded the documentary and my subsequent book, *Behind Russian Lines: an Afghan Journal.*

Since then, on two subsequent trips, I have been at pains to let him know my movements and he has always given me every possible help. His attitude has consistently been that the war needs to be reported as widely as possible and kept in the forefront of world attention. As he said to me once, explaining that he had no choice but to support the *mujahideen*, 'We have to. It is Afghanistan today, but it could be Pakistan tomorrow, you know. Even if it's in fifty years' time.'

We left Islamabad before dawn on Friday 4 July, American Independence Day, which I took to be a good omen. Francesca had left weighing scales in a prominent position beside the front door, with a notebook in which to record our weights. We did.

> Andy: 11st. 7lbs.
> Noel: 11st. 7lbs.
> Sandy: 13st. 0lbs.

My excuse was that I had my boots on, which must have weighed at least five pounds, but I was certainly a little heavier than my normal weight of twelve and a half stone.

Our plan was to drive in our borrowed jeep direct to Chitral, about four hundred miles to the north-east, bypassing Peshawar and, we hoped, its plethora of KGB and KHAD informers. It was, they said, a fourteen- or fifteen-hour drive, the road for the last two hundred miles or so being mountainous and in bad repair: the late snow melt had caused floods and landslides. We started off towards Peshawar on the Great Trunk Road, which runs the length of India right up to the

North-West Frontier, another relic of the British Empire. We crossed the Indus at Attock, famous for the great pink fort, built by Shah Jehan in 1581, its crenellated walls descending in a mighty swoop to the river below. As we crossed the bridge, I told Noel to look to his right.

'You see the line where the Kabul River joins the Indus? Brown on the right, that's the Kabul, blue on the left, that's the Indus.'

Today the Indus was a pale creamy blue, the Kabul brown and silty: the one an aristocrat, the other a proletarian.

We turned off before reaching Peshawar, began to climb and before long came to the Malakand Pass. From the top we had a sweeping view of scores of brown mountains, many of them crowned with small stone forts, called piquets by the British who strove, not always very successfully, to keep the unruly natives of the North-West Frontier in check for a hundred years and more until Partition in 1947. Beyond the Malakand we came to the most famous piquet of all, an eagle's eyrie overlooking the river, not as high as some but distinguished by a large notice, on which was painted in huge letters visible for miles: 'Churchill's Piquet'. Winston Churchill, then a young war correspondent for the *Daily Telegraph*, wrote a stirring account of a typical battle between the local Pathans and the British Army in 1897.

There was a ragged volley from the rocks; shouts, exclamations, and a scream. One man was shot through the breast and pouring with blood; another lay on his back kicking and twisting. The British officer was spinning round just behind me, his face a mass of blood, his right eye cut out. Yes, it was certainly an adventure.

It is a point of honour on the Indian frontier not to leave wounded men behind. Death by inches and hideous mutilation are the invariable measure meted out to all who fall in battle into the hands of the Pathan tribesmen . . . We all laid hands on the wounded and began to carry and drag them away down the hill.

I looked around to my left . . . Out from the edge of the houses rushed half a dozen Pathan swordsmen. The bearers of the poor Adjutant let him fall and fled at their approach.

The leading tribesman rushed upon the prostrate figure and slashed at it three or four times with his sword. I forgot everything else at this moment except a desire to kill this man. I wore my long Cavalry sword well sharpened. After all, I had won the Public School fencing medal. I resolved on personal combat *à l'arme blanche*. The savage saw me coming, I was not more than twenty yards away. He picked up a big stone and hurled it at me with his left hand, and then awaited me, brandishing his sword. There were others waiting not far behind him. I changed my mind about the cold steel. I pulled out my revolver, took, as I thought, most careful aim, and fired. No result. I fired again. No result. I fired again. Whether I hit him or not I cannot tell ... I looked around. I was all alone with the enemy ... I ran as fast as I could ... I got to the first knoll. Hurrah, there were the Sikhs holding the lower one ...

We fetched up at the bottom of the spur little better than a mob, but still with our wounded, while the tribesmen, who must have now numbered two or three thousand, gathered in a wide and spreading half-moon around our flanks ... The Colonel said to me, 'The Buffs are not more than half a mile away. Go and tell them to hurry or we shall be wiped out ...'

But meanwhile I heard an order: 'Volley firing. Ready. Present.' Crash! At least a dozen tribesmen fell. Another volley, and they wavered. A third, and they began to withdraw up the hillside. The bugler began to sound 'Charge'. Everyone shouted. The crisis was over, and here, praise be to God, were the leading files of the Buffs.

We bumped on in the heat and the dust to the Loweiri Pass (10,500 feet), which stands at the summit of a series of hairpin bends. The hillsides were green with cedars clinging to the steep rocks above the road, which reminded me of Nuristan. Whenever we met one of the huge, highly painted Pakistani lorries, which we did frequently, we had to stop at a well-judged spot to let it go groaning past. At the top we had a fleeting view of a snowy peak which I imagined was on the Afghan border and then we were zigzagging down to the floor of the valley from where we had an even more impressive view of Tirich Mir (25,230 feet), the highest peak in the Hindu Kush, a towering series of white buttresses, which do indeed look like a 'mass of frosted silver' as the explorer Lockhart saw them.

It was nearly dusk when, stiff and cramped, we came finally to Chitral, which sprawls haphazardly along the banks of the Mastuj River, a fast-flowing grey-green torrent bloated with melted snow. Masud's man in Chitral, Atik, lived on the far side, near the little airport, and we had some difficulty finding the house until Andy stopped some Panjsheris on the road.

Like all the houses in this part of the world, Atik's was surrounded by a high wall, in which was set a big wooden gate. After some delay, this was eventually unlocked by a man with a lantern and we drove into the inner courtyard where our friends were waiting: Ahmed Zia, one of Masud's brothers, Agha Gul, the piratical-looking arms runner who was Masud's chief of convoys, Khalili and Atik's brother, a dealer in lapis lazuli and Panjsheri emeralds.

We were also introduced to an American anthropologist, Whitney Azoy, a friend of Khalili's whom he had invited to come along. Whitney spoke Farsi and had once served as American cultural attaché in Kabul. I was not too happy about his presence but felt there was little I could do. A good deal of embracing and animated talk followed. Atik's wife had prepared a delicious dinner which we ate sitting on the dining-room floor, a position I always find rather uncomfortable as I have very long legs and am insufficiently supple to sit cross-legged, but the food was so good I forgot the discomfort. This was our first meal sitting on the floor, *à l'Afghane*, but I knew there would be many more to follow: it was as well to get into practice.

I had heard in Islamabad that the *mujahideen* in Mazar-i-Sharif, an important city in the north close to the Russian border, had recently suffered a big setback. When the Russians were digging foundations for a new headquarters, they had stumbled on, or rather fallen into, an elaborate tunnel system which the *mujahideen* had used to penetrate the city from the suburbs and carry out a number of daring raids. Then the Russians or the KHAD had captured a Hisbe commander and tortured him until he divulged the names of 123 *mujahideen*. This had paralysed the local resistance, I was told, because no one knew how many more people would be given away. I put this to Ahmed Zia, who said he had not heard of either event, but that he knew his brother, Masud, was in close touch with the Mazar group of Maulawi Alam, the successor of Zabiullah, the Jamiat commander who was killed by a landmine in 1985. He was said to have been betrayed to KHAD by a rival group, possibly Hisbe. It was typical of the worst kind of Afghan treachery – although no worse than the Campbells' treachery and their massacre of the Macdonalds in Glencoe – that narrow, tribal advantage is allowed to outweigh the national interest. On the other hand, Afghan clannishness has its advantages too. The arrest and torture of the Hisbe commander, while destroying the Hisbe organisation in Mazar, may not have totally disrupted the other groups in the city.

We slept on *charpoys* in the courtyard under a starlit sky, lulled by the happy thought that we had finally begun our journey after so many delays. Little did we guess that yet another infuriating and quite unforeseen obstacle was just round the corner.

Next morning, I changed a lot of Pakistani rupees into huge wads of dog-eared Afghanis, (two hundred to the pound) and purchased four saddlebags which turned out to be an excellent investment.

We left Chitral at eleven, and drove in two jeeps to Garam Chashma (Warm Springs), where you can apparently have a thermal bath, although I do not think many of the locals avail themselves of the opportunity: it was just as scruffy as I remembered it from four years before, but much busier, full of dark, poky shops and *mujahideen* eating houses. It is the main supply point for the northern route, but since the passes were not properly open, there were no horses to be seen. Last summer, according to Agha Gul, he had sent in 6,000 horses with arms and ammunition for Masud.

With Agha Gul as our escort, we drove up a very bad road for about eight miles to a spot where we were going to meet the horses and camp for the night well away from inquisitive eyes. It was a lovely day, the sky a pale clear blue with not a cloud in sight. We studied the mountains with interest: they were brown and bare with only the odd patch of snow. Progress was slow and it was late afternoon before we came to a water meadow with a small mill in the middle and the river roaring away beside it: it was both beautiful and, despite the noise of the river, very peaceful. Here we met the rest of our party: half a dozen horsemen, under the command of a jovial-looking bandit called Mullah Dhost, who confusingly was not a mullah, and half a dozen armed *mujahideen* as escort. They killed a sheep in our honour and cooked it, Agha Gul coming round with pieces of grilled liver on a stick as a special mark of favour.

The horses arrived late and the loading next morning was a protracted business. It always is the first time, with the horsemen cursing as they try to work out how best to balance a load of pieces of film equipment which are not just awkward shapes but also fragile. The process was considerably complicated by my insistence on using our brand-new Pakistani saddles and bridles which, being based on the English model, were unfamiliar. One horseman threw the bridle down in a rage when he failed to understand its intricacies. There was one hitch I had not foreseen. Afghan horses tend to be thinner and smaller than most saddle horses so without exception the girths were too long, and had to be supplemented by an Afghan girth. Now, Afghan girths do not work on the tongue and buckle system, but are looped through a metal ring and then pulled tight with a great deal of heaving and grunting, the horseman obtaining maximum leverage by planting his foot on the horse's belly. The final knotting is such an acquired art that only an Afghan could master it. To add to the confusion, the stallions were constantly trying to pick fights with one another – there was one mare present to about eight stallions. Apparently no Afghan can bring himself to geld a horse, it is contrary to his masculine *Weltanschauung*, I am told, as well as being economically unsound under Afghan conditions.

My heart sank as I saw I was being given the fieriest stallion to ride. He looked a beautiful animal, throwing up his head and blowing out his nostrils as he gazed at me with disdain. I was even more nervous when I was told that he was a *buzkash* horse, one specially trained to play the Afghan national game of *buzkashi*, a sort of rugby on horseback which is said to have been invented by the horsemen of Genghis Khan. Nowadays the 'ball' is a headless goat or calf: then, tradition has it, it was the torso of an enemy. However, despite my nervousness, I mounted without mishap and we were off.

CHAPTER FIVE

It was a wonderful morning ride up the valley, the river rushing below us, the track meandering between drystone walls and flanked by hedges and clumps of deep pink rugosas, purple vetch, a small blue flower like a speedwell, clover, and wheat and maize, both still green. There was a delicious scent from, I thought, the roses, but when I picked one it had no smell. As we crossed a water meadow, I saw several stunningly handsome yellow wagtails with rich lemon-curd heads and yellow chests and rumps. Curiously, I had never seen one before, although in 1982 we saw a lot of grey wagtails (which in fact are yellow and not grey). But having seen a yellow wagtail I now understood why the others were called grey.

I had gone to considerable lengths to smooth our final passage across the border, knowing from past experience that the Pakistani border police are prone to arrest journalists making their way into Afghanistan, as happened to Andy in 1984, or coming out of Afghanistan, as happened to me in 1982. I was quite sure that everything was going smoothly when we arrived at the base of Zidig Gol, from where we would climb the pass into Afghanistan, to find a friendly fellow in the uniform of a Chitrali Scout called Wazir, waiting to speed us on our way. He had had instructions by radio from Chitral or Garam Chashma to give us every possible assistance. A smart figure in his grey army uniform with red tabs, tapping his swagger stick on his leg, Wazir was seated under a tree on a broken-backed chair, which he promptly vacated and insisted that I occupy. His affability extended to ordering and drinking tea with us. Then he studied my map, which gave him a great deal of pleasure, and pointed out that there was a much easier route one valley farther along: unfortunately it was blocked by the presence of a big Russian post on the border, equipped he said with tanks, radar and a helicopter landing pad.

With him he had a tall, silent border policeman, Corporal Rahman Shah, known quaintly as the 'border holder'. After we had drunk our tea, and folded up the map, we shook hands with Wazir and Rahman Shah and started off up the mountain. It was a steepish climb in the heat of the day, leading the horses, but after the brow the mountain flattened out and we were able to mount again and ride across the grassy uplands that led towards the foot of the pass, itself hidden by a big mountain which, as Andy said, looked exactly like a giant's wingback chair. At about four we reached a pleasant alp and stopped to rest. The *mujahideen* lit a fire and were boiling the kettle for tea when, to our surprise, the lanky figure of the 'border holder', Rahman Shah, suddenly appeared, two henchmen with him. A long palaver started with Khalili and our headman, Mullah Dhost and, when they had finally grasped the purpose of the visit, Khalili translated for our benefit.

'He says that they have orders from the D.C. (District Commissioner at Chitral) to bring you back to the last police post where he is waiting to see you. They say he has come especially all the way from Chitral.'

I could hardly believe my ears. I had heard that these things had happened before to other, less well-connected parties, but that this should happen to us I found incomprehensible.

'But this is ridiculous. Rahman met us at the foot of the mountain with Wazir and knows we have permission.'

Khalili shrugged. 'He says he hadn't received the message from the D.C. then. Now it is different.'

I was damned if I was going to walk all the way down the wretched mountain again to satisfy the whim of some faceless bureaucrat. 'I'll write a letter to the D.C. explaining that we have the President's permission and they can take that down to him. He has heard of the President, I suppose?' I asked facetiously.

This was translated to Rahman Shah but he remained unimpressed. 'He says he has of course heard of the President but he has to take his orders from the D.C. not the President.' Rahman Shah permitted himself a little smile. Khalili explained. 'You know, these are simple people. To them D.C. is God.' He dropped the definite article in the Pakistani fashion.

'We'll see about that when I tell the President how we've been messed about. We'll see if he's God then.' I was angry and didn't like the way things were going. I tore a page from my notebook and started to write a strongly worded but as legible a letter to the D.C. as I could manage sitting halfway up Zidig Gol. The sun started to disappear behind the mountains and the temperature began to drop.

Dear District Commissioner,

    My two colleagues and I have the personal authority of the President, General Zia ul-Haq, to cross the border into Afghanistan to make a television report about the war there. I have just come from Islamabad where I met the President in State House. He has given orders that we should be granted every assistance. I should be grateful therefore if on receipt of this letter you will give instructions so that our journey may proceed as rapidly as possible.

I then added a last line which I hoped would strike fear into the heart of the accursed D.C: 'I shall be calling on President Zia on my return to give him a full account of our journey.'

The letter went off with one of Rahman Shah's men – two more had arrived in the meantime – and after a while they all decamped half a mile up the valley, presumably to show us that the way was blocked. We had nothing to do now except wait and have supper of sardines, cheese and tea; after that we slipped into our sleeping bags. It was going to be a cold night and I did not feel at all sorry for Rahman Shah and his men who had no blankets or sleeping gear as far as I could see. Perhaps it was discomfort that finally drove them to act, but in the middle of the night, when it was very cold, Rahman Shah and his men woke us up and said they had received another message instructing them to escort us down to the last police post where 'someone from Chitral is waiting to see us'.

This brought an angry refusal from all of us and Khalili was instructed to say in the vernacular to Rahman Shah, 'Bugger off and come back in the morning.'

This gave us a little peace, but they were back shortly after dawn, cold and hungry no doubt, clearly anxious to get off the mountain as fast as possible and return to the home comforts of Zidig Gol. Rahman Shah now tried another tack. If we refused to go back with him, he said, he would get into serious trouble with the D.C. We then discussed among ourselves over tea whether we should tell Rahman Shah that we were heading for the border and let him do his worst. This seemed an attractive proposition for a few minutes but we all realised that it would put the Afghans in an invidious position. Although our group of *mujahideen* easily outnumbered the border police and was armed with modern Kalashnikovs against their ancient Lee Enfield 303s, we did not want a trial of strength and certainly no shooting. This was Pakistan, we were guests, and even if we forced our way past the 'border holder' now, we would have to come back one day. I did not want to be arrested and have our film confiscated by angry Pakistani officials. So, suspecting that the whole thing was a charade, and angry that my attempt to circumvent precisely this sort of hold-up had failed, I reluctantly agreed that we should accompany Rahman Shah down the valley, leaving Mullah Dhost and the *mujahideen* camped out on the mountain. It was agreed that they would wait twenty-four hours. If we had not returned by then, they were to go on.

We descended the mountain in an hour and a half and found one of Wazir's men waiting for us at the spot where we had had tea the day before. I had decided that under no circumstances would we be forced to go back to Chitral, so I said I wanted to talk to the D.C. on the radio. A violent argument now broke out between the border police and the Chitral Scout and among the border police themselves, the finer points of which escaped me, but we finally got our way and rode off to the nearest Scout post where our friend Wazir was in charge.

He came to greet us, all smiles and embraces, sat us down outside his tent and ordered tea. We explained our problem in some detail, not forgetting to stress my connections with the President.

'You know, it very bad that D.C. overrule my military instructions. I have military instructions to give you every help to do your work. I am military man, you understand, so I carry out my instructions. I come to the foot of Zidig Gol to see you. I do everything I can to help, yes?'

I nodded. 'Yes, Wazir, you're a good man. We're grateful. I will make a point of telling the President you were very helpful.' His chest swelled with pride. 'But now, can we use your radio to send a message to the D.C.? I would like to talk to the D.C. myself.'

Wazir smiled. 'It is not possible for you, a civilian, to use the radio. It is for military only. But we will send a message for you.' He called over a man in civilian clothes and spelling my name out carefully I briefed him along the lines of my letter to the D.C. which I subsequently discovered had got no farther than the first police post. The plain-clothes man then went off to another part of the post, above which an aerial protruded encouragingly, to radio to Chitral. We sat and waited, drinking extremely strong, black tea, and not feeling very optimistic. Wazir was an enthusiastic conversationalist, telling us his home was in Mastuj, where there is a famous fort, besieged in its day by the British, and then going on to describe the highly sophisticated camera equipment he claimed to have in the post.

'Really, Wazir, why do you have camera equipment here?'

'We have to know what's going on. We have to keep an eye on things.' He smiled archly. 'I filmed you as you started to climb up the mountain. I filmed you with sound too. We have the sound of your voices.'

I looked sceptically at Noel and Andy. 'Really, Wazir? Sound as well? That's amazing.'

He looked pleased. Not wanting to spoil the story, I did not ask to see the camera. We talked instead about the Russian post at Topkhanna which he had mentioned the day before. 'It is a big post. The Russians have radar there, they have tanks and two helicopters. They have built a road to their side of the pass, which leads to Badakhshan' – a province in north-east Afghanistan which stretches to the Soviet border. 'So we have had to build a road on our side, too.'

'If we were able to take that route, we'd be in the Panjsher in four or five days' time,' Andy said.

'Is that the Anjuman Pass route?' I knew that was the easiest way to the Panjsher.

'Yes. Of course the Russians have another post there, so they have blocked the route at both ends, so to speak.'

While we were having lunch in the tent, we got word that my message had been transmitted to the army in Chitral and they were trying to find the D.C. Apparently some 'commander of refugees', according to Wazir, had spotted us on our way through and informed the D.C., who, not knowing anything about us, promptly ordered the police to detain us. We were still waiting for the D.C.'s answer when at 7.15, just as dusk was settling on the little post, there was a commotion outside. Peering out of the tent, we discovered to our amazement that no less a personage than Agha Gul had arrived, looking extremely tired but sporting an enormous grin of self-satisfaction. He had a border policeman in tow, who looked almost as pleased with himself as Agha Gul and who now delivered himself of the following message:

'The D.C. says you are free to go.'

We all gave excited cries, pumping Agha Gul's hand and bombarding Khalili for more information. At first, as Agha Gul reported *sotto voce* to him, who in turn interpreted for us, there was some confusion. 'Agha Gul has bribed the policeman to say he has a message from the D.C. But it's not true.'

'You mean there's no message from the D.C.?'

'Shhhh. Wait a minute.'

Five minutes later Khalili leaned towards us again. 'I was wrong. There is a message from the D.C. But someone told Agha Gul to bring a good *baksheesh* for Wazir. So he has given him thirteen hundred rupees and two hundred for the policeman.'

I examined the faces on the opposite side of the tent. Wazir was smiling broadly. So was the policeman. And Agha Gul looked like a man who had pulled off a difficult but very satisfying coup.

As if in anticipation, Wazir had commanded a slap-up dinner of chicken, rice, *dal*, and an omelette followed by small, sweet mulberries. It had been a tiring day and we went to bed soon afterwards, Wazir outdoing himself as the perfect host and insisting I occupy the place of honour, the bed inside the tent. It was too short and sagged in the middle, but I did not mind.

Wazir continued his three-star service next morning, bringing me tea in bed at six. Khalili found this an excellent joke, exclaiming several times, 'Bed tea, you know, this is very special honour. Bed tea, very very good.'

After breakfast, we all had a thorough wash in Wazir's bathhouse, the hot water arriving in a bucket from the kitchen: it was to be the last hot wash for more than a month. Feeling much refreshed, we finally said goodbye to Wazir and accompanied by Agha Gul, who was determined to make sure there should be no more hold-ups, rode up the now familiar valley to the base of the mountain. There we said goodbye to Agha Gul and started the climb, reaching Mullah Dhost and his patiently waiting party an hour and a half later. Andy, who had gone on ahead, was waiting for us with freshly brewed tea and after a brief rest we started off again, picking our way across several snowfields. My horse sank in to his knees several times but he struggled gamely on, even having the energy to try to mount a passing mare belonging to some Afghans making for the border.

We camped in a grassy hollow, made tea and ate some of our rations, but at five, as soon as the sun was off the mountain, it began to get cold. By eight, when I went to bed, the temperature was dropping fast and I needed bivvy bag, sleeping bag and all my clothes to keep reasonably warm. We must have been above 10,000 feet.

Mullah Dhost got us up at four, and I knew immediately that Wazir's hospitality, generous as it was, had been tainted: I had an acute pain in my stomach and an urgent need to go behind a rock. I just made it. But it left me weak and by the time we got to the top of the first steep gradient I was exhausted.

The rest of the climb was a slow purgatory, with my legs feeling like putty and my lungs like a leaky bellows. We laboured up a last long snowfield and near the top, on a flat stretch leading to the summit of the pass, I was able to mount my horse and ride the last half mile. There was a final steep snow ridge and we stood on the top of Zidig, 14,660 feet (4,500 metres) at seven. Khalili said, 'Welcome to Afghanistan.' As we waited for Andy, who had been filming our ascent from a nest of rocks above the pass, we saw, approaching from the opposite direction, a Nuristani farmer in woollen jacket and leggings, climbing up with a big slab of wood on his back. Khalili said it was a toboggan to speed his descent to the valley below.

'This is very clever. He can slide down very fast.' Khalili laughed happily at the ingenuity of it.

We made our way down first over a fissured snowfield, then over rocks and a zigzag, dusty, stony path which led eventually to a green, grassy, marshy meadow thick with alpine flowers including what looked like purple orchids. We finally came to a field knee-deep in clover adorned with a huge bush of dark pink gallica roses. At the bottom, reclining under a tree, were Andy, Khalili and Mullah Dhost. A tarpaulin was spread beside the stream and tea was being served out of the local headman's best cups. He was called Haji Matin, a splendid gnarled and almost toothless Nuristani, who stood for his photo like a Victorian patriarch, chest out and exceptionally serious.

Khalili explained: 'He says he has been praying to Allah to send him some guests and he is very, very pleased that we have come. He wants to invite us to a big lunch.'

'We can't really, we must get on. But thank him very much.'

Haji Matin received the news with what appeared to be acute disappointment.

Khalili said he was a devoted supporter of passing *mujahideen* and himself commanded a small detachment of local men equipped with 303s and a light machine gun. Haji and his men had not seen any fighting since the early days of the war. But the northern route which we were taking was vital for the supply of arms and ammunition to the Panjsher and the north and I wondered how long it would be before the Russians tried to block it.

After a long rest and some food which I couldn't really eat, we set off again at three and rode or walked for four hours to Peshawarak, a pretty little village built on both banks of a roaring river with some fine carved wooden buildings, notably the mosque. Hundreds of butterflies adorned the route, mainly yellow brimstones and green or grey hairstreaks, and a solitary hoopoe fluttered through the willows. I had heard a cuckoo when we were halfway up the mountain from Zidig Gol.

The Peshawarak authorities were not very hospitable, pleading poverty and wartime difficulties, although there was no evident sign of war, and being Nuristanis they had not been slow to levy taxes on the number of weapons brought in by the *mujahideen*. We were offered a bed on a nice piece of turf outside the village where we could enjoy the fresh air and watch the women of the village pass by, carrying loads of firewood.

I had spent the night in Peshawarak in 1982, on my way out

from the Panjsher. Then there had been a so-called '*koffi*' or tea-house in the middle of the village, next door to which we had stayed in fairly average squalor, the object of much local curiosity. At one point, an enraged Nigel Ryan had risen from the floor, on which we were all reclining, and shouted at the line of faces peering through the windows, 'Go away, you bloody people. Shoooh.'

They did, for a moment, but were soon back again to stare at us with a fixity which is so typically Afghan. In those days, the Nuristanis had seen very few foreigners and the northern route was only just being opened up. In the intervening four years, traffic had increased enormously and, generally speaking, to the displeasure of the Nuristanis. As they never tired of reminding you, they had been the first to start the *Jihad*, keeping the troops of the Communist government at bay on their Kunar border for a year or more. But the war had never penetrated to the heart of their mountain fastness and they had remained largely untouched by it. They seemed to me more than a little smug about their good fortune, not unlike another mountain people whom in some ways they resemble: the Swiss.

CHAPTER SIX

Physically, too, Nuristan is like Switzerland, being much the same size, spectacularly beautiful, mountainous and full of rushing rivers which could provide endless hydroelectric power. But unlike Switzerland it has no mod cons, it is sparsely populated and has a primitive economy. To travel through it today, seeing the long, crafty, iconic faces of the Nuristanis, who, some say, are descended from Alexander the Great's Macedonians, is to enter a kind of limbo: a neutral paradise surrounded by warring factions, but a paradise that resents the foreigner and makes him pay through the nose for any favour it grudgingly grants him.

The Nuristanis tend now to be a rather dour and unfriendly people who behave as if they had been dragged into the war against their will, and whose most fervent desire is that it and everyone connected with it should go away. There are exceptions, of course. One young commander in Peshawarak, called Mohammedzai, insisted, 'We are in the *Jihad*. We let the *mujahideen* pass through safely and we help them.'

When Eric Newby and Hugh Carless completed their 'Short Walk in the Hindu Kush' through Nuristan in the 1950s, they found a medieval society in which there were none of the trappings of modern civilisation and only one road. It is hardly less primitive today. Apart from the introduction of modern weapons, the Nuristanis still lead a life that belongs to another age, without electricity, television or telephones, without wheeled transport even; only the transistor radio has penetrated their seclusion. Newby and Carless found that few Nuristanis wore shoes, winter or summer. Now, a barefoot Nuristani is the exception. They all wear either their own excellent home-made leather boots and leggings, or, less attractively, cheap Pakistani boots and shoes. But in all other respects, the Nuristanis seem to have retained their independence and traditional habits. After all, it is less than one hundred years ago that they were forcibly subjugated by King Abdur Rahman, thus completing the unification of Afghanistan in

1896, and it was only then that they were forced to abandon their animist beliefs and were converted to Islam at the point of the sword. One of the sadder consequences was that they had to give up their cultivation of the grape for wine.

We rode off down the valley, the sun shining out of a blue sky and the river brawling along in full spate on our right. The meadows were full of alpine flowers: a purple plant like a sweet pea, tall blue cornflowers, purple orchids and dozens of smaller trefoils, speedwells, vetches and many others which defeated my meagre botanical knowledge. The steep hillsides were covered with evergreen cedars, which the Nuristanis fell by burning through at the base. We passed groups of locals making charcoal from the wood for the *sandali*, which although we did not see one sounded from Khalili's description something like a Spanish *brazero*, or brazier. In Afghanistan, the *sandali* is placed on the floor under a table which is covered by a thick quilt on which people sit and drink tea. At night the charcoal is heaped with ash to keep it hot. Khalili explained that it had a social function as well.

'Young lovers would get to know one another round the *sandali*. Lying there on top of it, the boy would touch toes with the girl of his choice and so they could show they were interested in one another.' Khalili laughed. 'In this way, in the long winter evenings by the *sandali*, love would blossom.' He spoke as something of an expert, we knew, because his wife was Nuristani.

We rode on past small fields, squeezed between the river and the mountain, protected by high, drystone walls, where only the women it seemed were at work. As we passed they would draw their veils across their faces, but not before we caught a glimpse of their features, old before their time, worn by toil and the harshness of their lives. I thought that they richly deserved any joy they might have found round the *sandali*. They never spoke, never smiled, behaved almost as if we did not exist. If they did recognise our presence, it was with the disdainful expression that the sanctimonious reserve for the sinners of this world. While they worked, their babies hung under the trees, suspended in conical baskets woven from goat's hair. Only the young girls were less *farouche*, darting surreptitious glances at us as we passed and giggling at one another. The men were slightly friendlier, stopping to look up from whatever they were doing, returning a salutation when they passed us on the track, an old rifle slung over their shoulder or, if they had been harvesting, with a great load of hay balanced on their back. Beside the river lay great planks of cedar, some shaped like doors, hewn by axe from a giant trunk. In clearings among the trees, or on a bluff above the river, stood small log cabins, idyllic in their remote tranquillity, each household virtually self-sufficient. Half-naked and usually very dirty children would come and peer at us with huge dark eyes.

In the late afternoon, we came down the hill into a village straggling along the river bank, with some large houses on our right. These were a town version of the log cabins, built of many parallel beams of cedar, plastered in between with honey-coloured mud, the effect being that of a many-layered cream sponge cake. A few yards farther on was the village square, where in 1982 an ancient Maxim machine gun was proudly displayed in one corner. It had disappeared and been replaced by a Russian Dashaka heavy machine gun, a standard *mujahideen* weapon. This was the centre of Barg-i-Matal, the capital of the self-styled Revolutionary Islamic State of Afghanistan, commonly known as the Daulat. The Daulat is really a joke, a postage-stamp-sized principality: but its inhabitants take themselves very seriously.

There was a slightly excitable air about the place and a large number of men were congregated on the far side of the square where I could see Mullah Dhost engaged in an earnest discussion with the village elders. Some of the old men had wonderful faces and I took out my camera to capture them. I had hardly raised it to my eye when a man in dark glasses with a wispy beard, who looked much more effeminate than the locals, reached out and half snatched it from me. I still had the strap in my hand and I yanked it back from him, at the same time giving him a shove and shouting, 'What the hell do you think you're doing?'

I was immediately surrounded by a group of Nuristanis who babbled excitedly at me, pointed to one side of the square and propelled me and Mullah Dhost, who had suddenly appeared at my elbow, in that direction. Resisting passively, I tried to walk as slowly and unconcernedly as possible. A few yards

47

farther on we came on Khalili, also hemmed in and arguing heatedly. Surrounded by Nuristanis, we were shepherded up some steps, towards a building which I suddenly remembered drinking tea in four years before. Then it had been described variously as a 'hotel' or '*koffi*'. Now it was the unofficial headquarters of the Daulat. As we walked up the steps, Noel appeared and said angrily, 'One of them tried to pull me off my horse.'

'Good God, what did he do that for?'

'I was right at the front and had nearly ridden through the village when a young bloke, I think he was some kind of commander, came belting up in a dreadful state, shouting. I paid no attention, and then he grabbed the horse and tried to pull me off. I told him to bugger off.'

We were ushered inside and to the same broken-down chairs along the wall that I had sat in in 1982, behind the same wooden tables. A dark-skinned man, clearly not an Afghan, started asking questions in English.

'Who are you, I must ask you?'

'Who are you?' I countered belligerently.

Before the man could reply, Khalili got up, walked over and sat himself down on the table in front of our questioner.

'You have no right to ask these people who they are.' He spoke with considerable force.

The man rounded on him. 'And who are you?'

'I'm an Afghan.'

'You're an Afghan? Prove that you're an Afghan.'

Khalili's eyes flashed. 'You dare to say to me "Prove you're an Afghan," you who are not an Afghan, to me who is an Afghan?' The attack was so passionate that the arrogant stranger was temporarily silenced.

Then the man who had tried to snatch my camera came in. He glanced round the room superciliously, plucking at his sleeves, whispering first in the other stranger's ear, then to three or four Nuristanis who sat in a row on the other side of the room, like judges confronting the accused in the dock. Another stranger appeared, olive-skinned, moist-eyed. All three had a kind of softness, a devious, conspiratorial manner that marked them out from the Afghans. 'They're Arabs,' someone muttered. We had heard that a number of Arabs were in Afghanistan with the *mujahideen*, the Koran in one hand, chequebook in the other. Whoever they were, they undoubtedly had the ear of the citizens of Barg-i-Matal.

A self-important figure came into the room and Khalili said, 'This is the commander.' One of the Arabs immediately leaned over and started whispering to him. The commander nodded his head several times and then turned to Khalili and gave what sounded like an order.

Khalili appeared to argue, using all the fluency of which we knew he was capable: he was not his father's son for nothing. This, however, appeared to infuriate the commander, who in a flash of temper pointed a finger at the door and shouted an unmistakable command. Khalili, outrage on his face but with as much dignity as he could manage, rose and marched out of the room.

It was clear we were about to be questioned. 'Let me do the talking,' I whispered as loudly as I dared. Andy was on my left, Noel immediately on my right and Whitney next to him. The commander now began the interrogation. It was an elaborate procedure. A ferrety-looking Nuristani sitting next to him first translated into Arabic; then the man who had tried to seize my camera, and who seemed to be the ringleader, rephrased the question, which was finally translated into English by the Arab who had tried to question us originally.

The first question was to Andy. 'What's your name and country?'

'Jim Fisher. From England.' Laboriously the commander wrote it in his book.

It was my turn.

'What's your name?'

'David Nicholas, also from England.' This was a private joke. David Nicholas, as the Editor of ITN, was an old friend. I looked forward to telling him I had taken his name in vain.

Back to Andy. 'What is your name again?'

'Jim Fisher.'

Back to me. 'Your name, what is it?'

'David . . . Nicholas.' I was not sure if they were trying to catch us out, or if the problem was bureaucratic.

On to Noel. 'Your name?'

'James Richardson, from England.'

Then, finally, to Whitney.

'John Conway. From England.' Whitney knew better than to say he was an American.

The names were now all in the book. The questions became more general.

'Have you heard of Daulat? Do you know this is an independent state?'

'Yes, we do,' I said.

'What is your profession?'

'We are businessmen.' I answered for everyone, but he turned to the others.

'All businessmen? What is your business in Afghanistan?'

I answered. 'We are on a confidential mission to see Commander Masud. I am a personal friend of Commander Masud.'

After the translation back into Arabic and Nuristani, there was some surprised muttering.

'What is your business with Commander Masud?'

'I'm afraid I cannot tell you. It is confidential. He has asked us to come and see him.'

'He has asked you to come and see him?'

'Yes. We are going to see him at his request.'

'You have your passports?'

'No, we left them in Pakistan.'

'When you left Pakistan you must have crossed through a border post?'

'Yes, but we were travelling with Jamiat, so we didn't have to show our passports.' This explanation was accepted grudgingly.

The interrogation changed tack. 'Why did you not get permission from our office in Chitral?'

This surprised me. 'But we did get permission from your office in Chitral. Mr Khalili has the document.' This caused equal surprise to the other side. Eventually, one of the Nuristanis put his head out of the window and shouted for Khalili. He came in, still angry, and without looking at us handed over the documents. The grubby pieces of paper were studied with great care and finally accepted as genuine. They had been examined before, apparently, when we arrived, but rejected for some reason. After a few more questions, the English-speaking Arab rose. 'You must forgive the questions. They are not meant in an unfriendly way. We have to be sure who is travelling through Daulat.'

Now that the risk of being detained and possibly sent back to Pakistan, which had happened to less fortunate travellers, had receded, I felt I could afford to be gracious.

'Of course. We quite understand.' But I thought the camera-snatcher looked disappointed, like a cat that has been deprived of its mouse.

As we strode as rapidly as possible out of Barg-i-Matal, just in case the commander and his friends should change their minds, Khalili burst into an angry tirade against the commander.

'I told him, "You are slaves of the Arabs and no slave can be a Muslim. If you come to Peshawar I will have something to say to you there. But here I say no more because I have guests with me."' We walked, talking out our pent-up anger, until the noisy rush of the river and the physical exercise eventually calmed us down.

'It's amazing that those three oily Arabs have got such a hold over the Nuristanis, of all people. They who are so independent,' I said to Khalili.

'It's the money. It must be the money.'

He explained. 'The old Amir of this area is a religious fanatic. He's a member of the Pan Piri sect, which is based in Pakistan. And they are an offshoot of the Wahabis, who come from Saudi. These people are crazy, these Wahabis. They see some *mujahid* praying and they tell him, "You are not a good Muslim, because when you pray you do not hold your hands in the right way," or some other nonsense. And instead of telling them to run away, they listen to them because they have money. It is really despicable. It makes me angry to see Afghans behaving like slaves.'

By now it was beginning to get dark, and we decided to stop at a *chaikhana* (tea-house) built above the river, near a bridge. I would have preferred to sleep outside, but the ground was either marshy or rocky and reluctantly I chose a *charpoy* on the open-sided first floor. After a supper of rice and goat which I found particularly unappetising, I lay down on the *charpoy* and, being exhausted, soon fell asleep. I have spent some of the worst nights of my life on *charpoys*. If you are tall, a *charpoy* is

51

doubly uncomfortable, since it sags in the middle and your feet and head stick out over the wooden frame at each end. In *chaikhanas*, the woodwork very often houses bed bugs and fleas which lie in wait to devour the unwary traveller. I awoke some time after midnight, bitten all over and feeling as if I was on a fire. I twisted and turned until dawn and got up feeling suitably wretched.

Next morning, after a breakfast of unleavened maize bread and tea, we rode south downriver, passing through the small town of Pul-i-Rustam (the bridge at Rustam), where in 1982 we had slept in the mosque very comfortably until the mullah kicked us awake at about four in the morning to make way for prayers. While the horsemen were loading up, I had played the local boys at Nuristani golf, which consisted of driving a twine ball about the size of a golf ball across a piece of flat ground, using a 'club' that was more like a hockey stick. To my chagrin one boy had consistently outdriven me. Now, I recognised the mosque and looked to see if any boys were on the driving range, but there were none about and the range had disappeared under a field of maize.

We made good progress along the King's Road, the best road I have seen in Afghanistan, although that is not saying much. Khalili explained it was built by King Zaher Shah in the Fifties or Sixties to open up Nuristan and link Barg-i-Matal with the provincial capital of Jalalabad, near the Khyber Pass. From Jalalabad, the main road runs through the Sarobi gorges to Kabul. You could drive from Barg-i-Matal to Kabul, in theory but not in practice, in five or six hours. I reflected it would be an ideal road for Russian tanks: they could take the independent state of Daulat in a morning if they were so inclined. But it would be like sticking your arm into a hornets' nest: they would get some very nasty stings from Nuristanis perched up on the cliffs above the road, taking pot shots at the advancing column. Holly oaks took the place of cedars and they are as prickly as their name suggests, although, incredibly, the horses manage to nibble round the prickles and eat the leaves. Mulberry trees lined the river banks, the fruit hanging thickly among the dark green leaves. Andy and Khalili explained there were four or five different kinds of '*tut*': white, grey-pink, black and a king berry, known as '*Shah tut*', the largest and juiciest.

Shortly afterwards we came to the border of Daulat and found a couple of young men sitting under a tree waiting to sign our travel papers. Bureaucracy had unmistakably arrived in Nuristan. We now left the main valley and turned up a steep, rocky gorge, down which the Papruk River foamed and cascaded with a sound like a cavalry charge, through thick clumps of silver birch. It would lead us, I knew, to Papruk Pass, which I remembered apprehensively as the highest and possibly most exhausting pass of all. I rode for a mile or so until even my game stallion was hardly able to heave me over the rocks which had tumbled down from the cliffs above and made an obstacle course which the horses had to clamber, slip and stumble across, sometimes cutting their legs quite badly. A trail of spots of blood often marked the passage of a convoy.

It was hot work as the climb got steeper and I let my mind run on, conjuring up visions of all the most delicious drinks to slake my thirst: cold draught bitter, flat but delicious, made by Shepherd & Neame, and served in a silver tankard at Royal St George's or in a glass at Rye, which are about the only places I ever drink beer; better still champagne – Bellinis, Buck's Fizz, or champagne cocktails. I thought of delicious, icy mouthfuls of green-gold Meursault and straw-coloured Sancerre. My body, meanwhile, laboured upwards, chest heaving, breath coming painfully, but leaving my mind on auto-pilot. Occasionally I had erotic fantasies and noticed that our stallions appeared to have them too – displaying enormous erections as soon as they saw a mare. I wondered if the cause was perhaps to be found in the Afghan climate or water. I also made all sorts of resolutions for my future life: things like getting a new set of Ping golf clubs, including the woods. I had played a couple of games in Islamabad with a set of clubs – the woods were not unlike Pings – borrowed from a man in the Embassy. I had hit the driver a prodigious distance, sometimes outdriving the young Pakistani assistant pro who made up our four.

As I struggled upwards I decided to play an imaginary round at St George's which I had recently joined. I got off to a very good start: 4, 4, 3, 4 (a very good four), 4, 3, 4 (a birdie), 4, 4. Out in 34. I started home 4, 3, 4, 4, 5 (level par) . . . but did not finish the round because a *chaikhana*, a rustic arbour with a canvas tent strung on poles to provide shade, suddenly appeared perched on a rock above the river. Noel and I stumbled into it gratefully and collapsed. Andy, whose fitness was a source of admiration and I regret to say envy, was wolfing down *nan* and *krout*, a kind of whey. We had just enough energy to drink copious cups of tea, mine liberally laced with sugar. It was 11 a.m. The flies were out in strength, and pestered us incessantly, but I did not mind them half as much as the vermin of the previous night, whose depredations were still making me scratch.

We had some of our own noodles for lunch, but they were a disaster, overcooked and tasteless. Afghans in general and Nuristanis in particular are not the world's greatest cooks. The *krout*, however, was good and there was plenty of tea. As we were digesting our meal, Mullah Dhost came and sat beside me. He was a genial, piratical-looking man, with something of the sergeant-major about him. He had a scar running from the bridge of his nose all along his forehead, the result of being kicked in the face by a mule. As our *chef de convoi*, he was supposed to look after our comfort but, as I discovered later, he and Khalili did not get on, and he eventually abandoned us to our own devices. He was an engaging rogue, like most good Afghans, and he had something he wanted to ask me.

'Mister, I want to go England. Or America. With you.'

'But I live in England.'

Mullah Dhost shrugged in almost Gallic fashion. 'OK. I come England. It not matter. Passport?' I realised he meant could I get him a passport.

'Yes. Mullah Dhost, I have a big garden at home in England. I have fruit trees, vegetables, lots of roses and other flowers too and I need a gardener.'

'Is that all?'

'No, I need a gardener-butler-chauffeur-groom.'

'Don't you need a cook or a barber?'

Everybody laughed. Mullah Dhost extended his hand, took mine and crushed my fingers. He grinned and jerked his head. It was time to move on.

CHAPTER SEVEN

Papruk village is perched on top of a mountain, the buildings clinging to the face of the cliff like house martins' mud nests. The steep path climbed in zigzags so close to the houses that I could have reached inside and shaken hands with the occupants, not that they would have welcomed such familiarity. Grubby children watched us struggle past, screaming at us or about us with voices as shrill as birds'.

A man came running after us, clasping in his arms a baby with an extremely dirty face. He thought we were doctors and was begging medicine for his sick child, but we could only pant at him, '*Doktor ne, doktor ne.*'

Still following, he repeated this querulously several times as if he could not believe it, and only then gave up and went back to his house. Most of the foreigners that Afghans meet are doctors, usually French doctors, so it was quite understandable that they should jump to the conclusion that we were doctors too. Since there are hardly any Afghan doctors in what the *mujahideen* call the 'liberated areas', which make up between eighty and ninety per cent of the country, and therefore no medical facilities, any foreigner is immediately bombarded with requests for medicines of any description. Robust-looking Afghans, who are undoubtedly among the hardiest people in the world, will as soon as they see a foreigner assume a hangdog expression and point to their stomach, head or any other part of their anatomy and beg for a pill to cure them. A few aspirins will work wonders even before they are taken, the happy recipient departing with a broad grin and the pain apparently gone.

We were not encouraged to linger in the centre of Papruk, a pretty little square shaded by some fine old walnut and mulberry trees, with a commanding view of the valley below. A group of greybeards sitting on a bench under the shadiest tree responded to my greeting by waving me on down the hill. As we descended, I regaled Noel and Andy with a description of the quarrel between Tom Murphy, my sound recordist in

1982, and Rahman, the senior horseman. They had been snarling at one another for some time, and the row came to a head at Papruk. We had all wanted to stop in the village to buy some food, but Rahman, who was slightly ahead with the horses and the other horseman Noor, insisted on bypassing the village and crossing the river. Tom shouted at him to stop, which Rahman ignored, and then hurled abuse across the water:

'Rahman, come back, you bloody fool.'

When we finally caught up with Rahman on the other side, he and Tom nearly came to blows. Rahman picked up a large stone the size of a 16-pound shot and, eyes popping out of his head, made a rush for Tom. I happened to be standing between them and grappled desperately with Rahman, who although much shorter than me was much stronger, and somehow managed to keep him off. Behind me, Nigel Ryan was restraining an equally angry Tom Murphy who was uttering dire threats of what he would do to Rahman when he got his hands on him. It was ludicrous in retrospect but seemed deadly serious at the time.

Afterwards, when we were back in Peshawar, Tom said, 'I don't know what got into me. I think I must have gone a bit mad. Maybe it was the altitude.' Possibly. It was also the end of a very exhausting, ten-week trip which at one point looked as if it would be a complete disaster.

After the bad night at the last *chaikhana*, I was anxious to find a good camping spot before it got dark, so that we could light a fire and prepare a meal. The area looked promising, green and sheltered in the lee of the mountain, and with the river on our right. As we rode beside it, my eye was caught by a bird like a large blackbird which emitted a liquid screech, flaunting its long tail by the water's edge. As I watched it, a big dark blue-green butterfly, its wings as lustrous as velvet, went swerving past at great speed. Ahead there was activity and shouting: Mullah Dhost was pitching camp, horses were being hobbled and tethered, and fires lit. It was a good place, dry and sheltered and we unrolled sleeping and bivvy bags and made ourselves as comfortable as possible.

I was reclining on my allegedly self-inflating mattress (what would Wilfred Thesiger think?), sipping a cup of tea, when I heard a commotion. About thirty yards away, a tough-looking lady dressed in the traditional Nuristani garb of baggy trousers, long flowered skirt and veil, was advancing towards us through the trees, gesticulating and shouting. Suddenly she bent down, picked up a stone and hurled it at one of the horses, just missing. She threw another. Missed. And another. This time it hit the horse with a thud and the beast whinnied in pain. Another stone came flying in our direction and I shouted, rather foolishly, 'Hey, what the hell!' She paid absolutely no attention but came on like an avenging fury.

Khalili jumped to his feet and called to Mullah Dhost to move the horses. Our *mujahideen*, looking sheepish, advanced cautiously under the barrage of stones. Their restraint was admirable. Not one of them shouted at the woman or remonstrated in any way.

'She's quite right,' Khalili said somewhat to my surprise. 'The Nuristanis consider all this grazing belongs to them. You may think because it's the mountain it doesn't belong to anyone, but it does. Every bit of grazing belongs to someone. You know, these people are vairy, vairy poor. They have nothing and if our horses eat it all, there will be nothing for them in the winter.'

A little later Khalili explained that the woman was furious because the horses were eating a particular plant, like groundsel, which is used to flavour tea and which the Nuristanis pick and sell.

Next day, Saturday, 12 July, was our fourth in Afghanistan; it was also exactly one month since we had left London. We did not seem to have achieved very much, and there was a daunting amount still to accomplish. But at least we were on the move, everyone was in good spirits and the sun was shining. We struck camp at 6.30 and walked for an hour up the verdant valley. There was no sign of the stone-thrower, but later we were to discover that our camp had been burgled during the night: someone had crept up in the dark and stolen a bag containing a small video camera, three three-hour videotapes, several video batteries, and forty rolls of film, all belonging to the two Jamiat cameramen who were just back from a training course in France. Khalili's stirrup irons and leathers, which for some reason he had removed from his saddle, had also gone. It was a disaster for the cameramen, as they would be virtually unable to function until everything had been replaced, and no one knew how long that would take. At home, the loss could have been made good in a matter of hours, but here it might take months. It was doubly disappointing for them because publicity has always been one of the weakest sides of the *mujahideen*'s war effort, and they were only just beginning to train cameramen and photographers.

However, we were to learn all this later, and for the moment I was enjoying the exercise and the beauty of our surroundings. Afghanistan is a birdwatcher's, indeed a nature lover's, paradise and I tried to keep a note of everything I saw. The first excitement was not long in coming. A small black bird flew out of a bush and darted across the river in front of me, revealing from the bright flame-coloured patch on its rump that it was a black redstart. A little later another small bird which I took to be a linnet, grey, with a pale bib, russet chest and longish tail uttered his plaintive call from the side of the path. 'I'm pleased to meet you, pleased to meet you,' the thin high-pitched voice repeated over and over again. Khalili said, 'We call it in Farsi *Hazar-Dastan*, which means "Bird of a Thousand Songs".' It sounded to me as if it had only one song, but repeated a thousand times over.

We now mounted and for the next three hours enjoyed what I think was the most beautiful ride of my life. We climbed steadily up the green valley with the snowy peak of Papruk standing out majestically in the distance, the V of the pass clearly visible. Everywhere, the hillsides were covered with an abundance of wild flowers: pale blue giant harebells, delicate, purple-blue geraniums, mock strawberry, celandines, wild parsley, what looked like a yellow lupin and banks and banks of dog roses, including the dark pink variety, as big as a domesticated rugosa.

On either side of the valley, snow lay deep in the corries, and snow bridges, their arches littered with rocks and earth, spanned the river precariously. In the small, stony fields groups of Nuristani women, working in family teams, weeded on their knees, while on the flat rooftops of the houses their men sat watching the world go by with rather surly expressions on their faces.

At half past ten we came to a jewel-green meadow with a lot of horses grazing on it and a *chaikhana* which we hungrily hoped could supply us with a late breakfast. As soon as my stallion scented the mares ahead, he started to play up, tossing his head and trumpeting his desire and giving every indication that he wanted to break into a gallop. My horseman, Abdi, gestured to me to shorten the reins, so I held him in tightly, and prancing and neighing we somehow reached the *chaikhana* safely. But as soon as I had dismounted and while Abdi was unsaddling him, he bolted, making a beeline for the mares and chasing them backwards and forwards across the meadow with Abdi, another horseman called Azimullah and his son in angry pursuit. Finally, after half an hour, Abdi caught him and gave him a walloping. The stallion had cut one leg quite badly in his amorous excursion and I had to hand over my valuable insect-bite cream to patch him up. The tube came back, as I knew it would, half empty.

I asked his name and discovered that Afghans do not give their horses pet names as we do, but only according to their colour and conformation: thus he was called Jerand, which means a bay with a white blaze. He also had three white socks. Khalili explained, 'If he had another white sock he would be a horse for a king. As it is, we say he is a horse for a merchant.' Everyone laughed, apparently finding this very suitable.

After lunch I sunbathed until it clouded over and a few spots of rain fell. With startling speed the clouds piled up, the mountains acting like a magnet, and within minutes there was a downpour which turned into a hailstorm. Luckily the *chaikhana* had a couple of tents, the gift it said on one of them of UNHCR, the United Nations High Commissioner for Refugees, and we huddled inside, drinking tea and eating *nan* made by our *mujahideen*. As the hail lashed the meadow, one of them started to sing folk songs. Khalili explained, 'He is singing about his beloved.'

> Learn from me how to love,
> Because I am like a moth,
> And you are like a candle.
> I burn myself, while my beloved
> Is still giving light to others.

The tune was extremely simple, two or three phrases repeated over and over again, and every so often the audience laughed at some witty sally.

It rained in the night and in the morning Mullah Dhost and some of the senior horsemen came for a discussion with Khalili.

'They say we cannot go on. The rain down here was snow up on the mountain and the horses won't be able to cross. It will be too soft.' It was infuriating to have yet another delay, but since we could not go against the advice of the horsemen and Mullah Dhost, we crawled back into our sleeping bags. At about eleven, a group of *mujahideen* arrived having just crossed the pass and said it was clear. 'Let's go then,' Andy said. We were all bored with the limited facilities of the *chaikhana* and it was miserably cold and damp. While we packed up, Andy set off ahead so as to film us crossing the pass. Then another group arrived, men from Yaftal in Badakhshan, the home village of Professor Rabbani, the head of Jamiat-i-Islami. This gave them a certain cachet and so their views were listened to with some respect. Their advice was entirely the opposite. They said it was too difficult for horses.

'We have to get Andy back,' I said. 'Quick.' Someone produced a whistle and blew a series of blasts, but by this time Andy was a tiny figure striding purposefully towards the foot of the pass. He disappeared from view. It was clear the whistle was a failure.

'Send a *muj*,' Noel advised. There was some urgent consultation and a *mujahid* was selected to go off in pursuit, on my horse. He went cantering off across the stony meadow, waving his whip above his head in approved *buzkashi* style. But Andy had been gone a good hour now and by the time the *mujahid* caught up with him, he was halfway to the top. In his place, I would have been furious, but when he rejoined us Andy was extremely understanding.

'Oh, it's all right, Sandy,' he said when I apologised. 'This is Afghanistan, you know.'

Andy said the pass had looked clear, but naturally he did not know what conditions were like on the northern side. Over lunch of soup made with bully beef and the remains of our Chinese noodles, now badly mutilated from being roped to the back of a horse, it was decided that we would leave early in the morning. Afterwards, Khalili and I strolled a few hundred yards to the top of the meadow to inspect a '*banda*', a small stone bothy surrounded by a drystone enclosure in which were about a hundred fat-tailed sheep and goats. Two grizzled Nuristani shepherds, one a deaf-mute, came out to greet us. The enclosure was deep in sheep and goat dung and the stench was so overpowering that although the vocal shepherd offered us a drink of fresh goat's milk, we both declined. The Nuristanis drive their flocks up from the valleys to the high pastures in the spring, spend all summer in their *bandas* making butter and cheese, and return to the valleys in the autumn. It is a lonely, primitive life which can hardly have changed for centuries. Less than a hundred years ago, Nuristani butter carriers would walk north to the Panjsher, strap a load of butter on their back, and then make the long return journey to Chitral, along very much the same route we were following, but travelling much faster.

When we returned to the *chaikhana*, there was another piece of bad news. Rabbani's men had been talking to Mullah Dhost and our *mujahideen* and they were all full of it.

'They say the Russians bombed Kantiwar two or three days ago. Sarwar Nuristani is expecting a Russian offensive which will block our route any day now.' After relaying this intelligence Khalili concluded, 'If this is true, it is bad news for us.' We agreed it did not sound too promising and I asked, 'Who exactly is Sarwar Nuristani?'

'He is a former general who lives in Pushal, which is north of Kantiwar. He has very close relations with the government in Kabul.'

'So he is on the side of the Russians?'

'Yes, they say he receives Russian arms regularly by helicopter from Kabul.'

Kantiwar was both the capital of Nuristan and also the name of the next pass after Papruk. If the Russians had bombed the town, it meant the war had arrived in the middle of Nuristan for the first time. To depress us even more thoroughly it started to rain again.

There had been one other piece of potentially disastrous news. Noel had received a report from Mullah Dhost about the elderly grey horse which carried our most precious cargo: the raw film stock.

'Do you know what happened yesterday? The horse fell in the river, with all the film on its back?'

'Good God. When did you find out?'

'The horseman arrived a little while ago. You know how he and his mate are always miles behind.'

'But is the film all right?' It was almost a cry of pain.

'Yes, fine. I unpacked it all and dried it out when you were out. The water hadn't got into any of the bags.' All our sixty-odd rolls of film stock had been meticulously wrapped in strong plastic bags against just such an eventuality.

'Thank God,' I said weakly. 'But how the hell did it happen?'

'Well, the horse fell off one of the bridges yesterday. I didn't see it. Apparently just fell off the bridge into the river. The trouble is you never know what's going on because those two are always way, way behind.'

We set off at five next morning. I rode for an hour or so across the meadow where Jerand had chased the mares so ardently the day before. Now, to restrain his impetuosity, Abdi walked in front of him, almost as if he were a dog at heel, and if he showed any sign of misbehaving, gave him a smart tap on the nose. There was another, last patch of vividly green grass, where we had originally planned to spend the night, and then the path started steeply up the mountain. Abdi motioned to me to dismount. He did not want his prize possession, which was worth a lot of money to him, overworked simply because an unfit foreigner could not climb mountains on his own. But generously, I thought, he pointed to Jerand's thick black tail, indicating that I should catch hold. I had often seen Afghans use this form of assistance so I accepted the offer with alacrity. Jerand was so strong that he hauled me up like a train, although faster than my legs wanted. Several times I was on the point of letting go, but the alternative was even less attractive, so I held on like grim death, forcing myself to believe that it was better to be rushed up the mountain under Jerand's power than to crawl up it slowly and painfully under my own.

There were some big patches of old snow, slippery in the

heat of the sun, and bits of ice from the previous night's storm. It was an exhausting business: perhaps fractionally easier than the first pass but only just. At one point, Jerand broke free from Abdi and despite the steepness of the slope hurled himself at another stallion.

'*Jang. Jang.*' Abdi shouted, trying to warn the other horseman that a fight was imminent. Too late. Both stallions rose on their hind legs and, screaming angrily, lashed out at one another with their forefeet, kicking and biting, in an extraordinary display of jealous rage, all the more amazing considering the exertion of the climb. Abandoning Jerand, I struggled upwards, providentially coming on Andy's grey mare, whose owner had stopped for a rest. Obligingly, he pointed to his horse's tail and invited me to help myself. As I reached out, the mare laid back her ears and swished her tail at me bad-temperedly, but once I had it in my grasp she made no more fuss and pulled me to the top where Andy was waiting. He had carried his camera all the way up to get shots of the final ascent, a remarkable feat that only someone of his fitness and determination would have attempted. Standing panting on the top, able to admire the magnificent view only with difficulty, I learned that the height of the pass was 14,850 feet (4,500 metres). Mont Blanc, Europe's highest peak, as opposed to a pass, is 15,782 feet (4,810 metres), less than 1,000 feet higher.

Going down, even on legs still rubbery from exhaustion, was a kind of bliss. The bleak mountain suddenly bloomed in a carpet of spring flowers, which had lain dormant under the snow and were now, miraculously, opening their faces to the sun: tiny little forget-me-nots, equally miniature buttercups, a purple-blue primula, thick drifts of blue geraniums and, beside a patch of snow, what I took to be a colony of gentians about to flower. Just below the summit we passed a pair of black redstarts which from the busy way they were hunting for flies and grubs appeared to be feeding young. Farther down the mountain, we passed a dozen common redstarts and in a bushy thicket a number of birds with russet heads and chests; perhaps they were what they call *Gul Sar* in Farsi: Flower Head. But the most surprising denizen of the mountain was a ginger-coloured marmot, about the size of a rabbit, which produced an ear-piercing whistle and then sat on its haunches inquisitively watching a stranger until he got too close, when it dived out of sight among the rocks.

The last part of the journey to the next village, Parun, brought a small shower of rain, causing the roses which flanked the path to give off a heavenly scent. We followed the river, sometimes high above it, the path running so close to the edge of the cliff that it was possible to look right down into the water boiling below. Finally, with the light fading, we came to Parun, an extended village built like so many Afghan villages between the river and the mountain, some of the houses clinging to the rock face. We stopped at the *chaikhana* on the edge of a pleasant meadow. The last time I had been in Parun, we had been invited to dine in a local headman's house. Now, the *chaikhana* had removed the need for the Nuristanis to extend the hand of hospitality: they could keep their distance from the strangers, and make money out of them too.

CHAPTER EIGHT

While we waited for supper, Khalili spoke about the *Jihad* or Holy War which the Prophet Mohammed first declared in AD 624. To find an equivalent in European terms, you have to go back to the Middle Ages, when the fervour of the Crusades, initially at least, swept the Christian world and even led to the launching of a children's crusade. Today, in a comparable example of youthful enthusiasm, Afghan boys of eleven or twelve carry Kalashnikov rifles and fight alongside their fathers against the infidel.

Khalili explained the rules. 'You see *Jihad* is automatic if there is an atheist government in power. As soon as Taraki came to power, religious leaders in Afghanistan declared *Jihad*. That was in May 1978. As you know, Taraki came to power in the Communist coup of 27 April 1978, the so-called Saur Revolution.

'*Jihad* embraces the whole Muslim world. All Muslims are obliged to take part in it by sending money, or demonstrating their support in some other way. Any writer or poet should write only about the *Jihad*. A merchant should work longer hours to make money for the *Jihad*. Not to take part in *Jihad* is a sin.'

The sun was sinking; the roar of the river seemed muted; perhaps it was only the effect of Khalili's eloquence.

I asked about the refugees. Was it compatible with *Jihad* to become a refugee?

'Yes, of course. You are allowed to migrate or emigrate if you cannot fight the enemy on the spot. But you migrate to prepare yourself and return to fight the *Jihad*. Also, anyone killed in battle automatically goes to Heaven and becomes a *shaheed*, a martyr.'

I had of course heard this, but had always presumed that educated Afghans did not believe it literally.

'Do you believe that yourself? That everyone who's killed in battle automatically goes to Heaven?'

'Yes, of course. Every Muslim believes that. I believe it completely.'

Mullah Dhost's piratical figure emerged out of the dusk, bearing a pot of tea to keep us going until the rice was ready.

'Afghanistan is now what we call *Dar-ul-Harb*, which means Place of War. That means that everything is military, but is based on religious grounds. Under *Dar-ul-Harb* there should be one source of order. As the Holy Koran says, "Hold the rope of God, all of you, and do not divide." In *Dar-ul-Harb* you can lie – to deceive your enemy – something that you cannot do in ordinary life.' Khalili gave a little laugh. 'You can also negotiate. That too is part of *Jihad*, as long as it is not from weakness.'

There was a stir as the rice appeared, mounded high on large plates, and everyone sat down in a circle, cross-legged. A boy took round a jug of water and a bowl and we all washed our hands, without the benefit of soap, wiping them on a greasy towel. The Afghans and Andy, using only the obligatory right hand, ate with silent concentration, taking a large handful of rice, kneading it into a ball and transferring it to their mouths in one movement. The trick lies in the way the thumb propels the ball of rice from the palm of the hand into the waiting mouth. I always find the operation difficult and a lot of my rice falls on the carpet. Afghans have the capacity to eat huge quantities of plain and rather tasteless rice and although Andy kept urging Noel and myself to do likewise, we both found it extraordinarily difficult. Only after several weeks of short rations, when hunger had increased our appetite, did we manage to eat enough to keep our strength up. I also find sitting cross-legged on the floor while eating extremely uncomfortble. All in all, I had to admit that I was singularly unsuited to travel with the *mujahideen*.

I glanced at Noel. He was obviously having similar difficulties, but keeping them to himself.

After the meal, and over tea, Khalili spoke about the people fighting the *Jihad*, the *mujahideen*.

'Only ten per cent of the old middle and upper classes are in the *Jihad*. The overwhelming majority of the *mujahideen* are peasants.'

'Like the army of Mao Tse-tung.'

'Exactly. They are simple people but they are very . . .'

'Hardy?'

'Yes, hardy, and they do not know the meaning of the word surrender.'

I reflected that I had never met a *mujahid* who would admit that such a concept existed, let alone one that would contemplate carrying out such an act. The talk turned to the *mujahideen*'s logistical problems.

'You know that, without horses, the whole of our supply system would collapse? For the Panjsher alone, this year, we need ten thousand horses.'

'That's an awful lot of horses. So how many do you need for the whole country? For all the *mujahideen*. A hundred thousand? Two hundred?'

Khalili shrugged. It was like asking how many grains of sand there were in the desert.

Agha Gul, Masud's chief of convoys, later confirmed Khalili's figure of 10,000 horses, but added that they would each make two trips during the short summer season, carrying in arms and bringing out lapis lazuli, a semi-precious stone mined in Badakhshan.

Khalili explained that the horsemen were also in the *Jihad*, under military orders. They get a set rate of about 4,000 Afghanis (£20) per *sear* (seven kilos) and a horse will carry ten *sear*.

Andy and I slept outside, in front of the *chaikhana*, sharing the field with several horses and one donkey, which sounded reveille as if it were the Last Trump. We were off again at seven, walking at a good pace, but all the same it took us an hour to leave Parun behind. Then we mounted and rode down the valley in the morning sunshine. Wild flowers were everywhere, and pied wagtails and sandpipers flitted between the little islands in the river, their plaintive voices embroidering its sonorous plainchant. The willows, silver birches and walnuts gave way to Scots firs and cedars, and the mountain of Mum, our next pass, rose in the distance. We stopped for a rest on a grassy river bank shaded by willows and poplars and I had just complimented Mullah Dhost on making the best tea of the journey when I discovered that we had used two-thirds of our tea supply in ten days, which seemed rather extravagant. But then the *mujahideen* had no thought for the morrow, being as improvident as they are generous. Afghan society, based on the village, is a communal one and the laws of hospitality, still rigorously observed despite the war, mean that most things are shared. No matter how poor, an Afghan would never dream of not offering a stranger his last piece of goat or *nan*. Equally, they are as liberal with your tea as they would be with their own.

In the afternoon, the sky grew black, it began to thunder and then, suddenly, the rain came pelting down. My kagool was packed on the back of another horse and not immediately obtainable, so I pulled on my Guernsey which was soon saturated. We sheltered for half an hour under a huge walnut tree and then made our way to a half-built house where the owner gave us wood and the *mujahideen* made a blazing fire. While we dried ourselves out, I urged Khalili to negotiate for some chickens which we saw running about below us. The young owner of the house seemed to be agreeable, asking how many we wanted. Looking round the hungry faces, and consulting the empty rumble of my own stomach, I said, 'Six. Can he manage six?'

The Nuristani gave a grin. 'He says it may take some time to catch them.' A little later the storm, which must have been the tail end of the monsoon, cleared and we set off for the base of Mum with the chicken question unsettled. I made a last try.

'Can you ask him to send them after us?' We planned to spend the night at an empty *banda* at the foot of the pass so as to get a good start in the morning.

'He says he will try.' I suspected that Khalili was tired of this conversation and was telling me what I wanted to hear and not what the Nuristani was really saying.

On the way, we came on an attractive young woman with three children, working in a field beside the path. She smiled and spoke to Khalili who immediately stopped. A lively exchange followed, ending up with Khalili giving the woman some money. She beamed and shouted her thanks as we rode off.

'Who was that, not a Nuristani surely?'

'No, she is a refugee from the north. I met her last year when I was passing by. She is a good woman, and although she's poor, she is always cheerful. You saw that. I gave her a little money to help her.'

We arrived at the *banda* to find Mullah Dhost in control, a huge log fire blazing and tea waiting. The *banda* was on a slope, half hidden among the pines, looking across at a great, frowning outcrop of rock which hung sheer over the river. We might have been in the Pyrenees or the Dolomites. The sky was beginning to show patches of blue. It was turning out to be a fine evening.

We were awake early and started off at five, trudging slowly up the path through the cedars. It was hard enough, although much easier than the first two passes: in fact, I remembered Mum as both the prettiest and the easiest of the five. After a steady three-hour plod, the last half hour or so above the tree line, we reached the top at eight and were rewarded with a superb view. In front of us lay the deep gorge of the Kantiwar River and then, beyond, range after range of snow-covered mountains, stretching to the horizon.

The previous time I crossed Mum, I had watched an Egyptian vulture, wings white against the dark green of the cedars, planing majestically above the river, but today, alas, the sky was empty. Last time, too, I had caught a glimpse of a golden eagle swooping on its prey among the trees with a ferocious rush of pinions. But there was no sign of the golden eagle either: indeed we were alone on the mountain until, approaching the first *bandas*, we met about a hundred unarmed Badakhshani *mujahideen*, travelling south to Pakistan for weapons and sweating as they climbed the steep path. Although Tajiks like the Panjsheris, who tend to be lighter-skinned and are easily recognisable by their '*pakuls*', the flat Chitrali hats with a rolled brim, Badakhshanis are usually darker and wear turbans. They looked a tough lot.

At ten we reached Mum, a collection of log cabins scattered across a high, sunny meadow with spectacular views of the surrounding mountains. So beautiful it might be an advertisement for Switzerland, Mum has a serene, otherworldly quality which struck me so forcibly the first time I saw it that the word Shangri-La came to mind. The inhabitants who gazed at us then with slow blank stares had had the simpleness of American hill-billies, but now I thought I detected a less friendly, slightly suspicious look in their eyes. The *chaikhana* where we had previously stayed the night seemed to have reverted to being a private house and we were directed round the corner to another house, reached by climbing an almost perpendicular, solid ladder hewn from a single tree trunk. Although it was not a proper *chaikhana* and he refused any payment, the owner gave us tea in new glasses, with the labels still on them.

Refreshed, we set off down the mountain towards the river and Kantiwar where, according to the man in Mum, an important *jirgah* (assembly) was being held to decide whether to declare war on Sarwar Nuristani, the former general said to be in league with the regime in Kabul. If battle were joined, Khalili pointed out, it could well block our route.

High above us, great pinnacles of rock towered over the cedars like ruined castles. On one, a flock of goats scrambled about with astonishing sure-footedness. The sun burned fiercely on the backs of our necks and the horses kicked up clouds of dust which choked our eyes, mouths and noses, covering everything wth a floury patina. Noel and I, who had fallen some way behind because of his bad knee, were extremely relieved to round a bend in the river and find the rest of the group camped beside it under the trees, Andy and Khalili absorbed in their diaries. Khalili had told me that he liked to write everything down for his wife, and Andy was also an assiduous diarist, committing his thoughts to paper in tiny, pencil script. I asked why pencil and he explained that a pen had once burst in his bag and covered his belongings in indelible ink. He looked relaxed and contented, puffing on his pipe while he wrote.

Whitney, Noel and I stripped off and had a thorough wash in the river. Although we chose a shallow pool and the day was very hot, the water was so cold it numbed the feet and made us gasp. I had just hung up my underpants to dry, wrapping myself rather inadequately in my scarf, when two Nuristani men arrived to give us the once-over. They sat down ten yards away, staring at me and my belongings with an intensity that I have never seen equalled anywhere else in the world. Finally, after ten minutes or so, satisfied presumably with what they saw, they opened up their conical wicker basket and produced from its depths a pile of maize *nan* and a bowl of *dugh*, a kind of yoghurt. The Nuristanis grow a lot of maize and make most of their bread from it. None of us liked it.

'Bloody Nuristani *nan*,' Andy would say. 'Tastes like sawdust.'

The *dugh*, however, was delicious and I greedily drank two cupfuls. After feeding us and having a brief chat with Khalili, the men repacked their basket, one of them slinging it on his back like a rucksack, and departed. Even in Nuristan, where they obviously have reservations about the passage of so many *mujahideen*, Afghan generosity is inescapable.

At five, when the heat of the day had cooled, we saddled up and rode up the smiling valley, past fields of tall green maize and ripening wheat, reaching Kantiwar at seven. Although the view is more impressive from the other side, the town perched on its hilltop, rather like a village in Tuscany, is still a fine sight. The timbered houses cling to the slope and on the very top, commanding the whole valley like a medieval castle, stands the impressive bulk of the *Q'ala*, a big fortified house which used to belong to Khalili's wife's family.

A lot of horses were tethered outside a building in the middle of the town and we could see their owners in the courtyard, the first arrivals for the *jirgah*. Someone said three hundred were here already, with another seven hundred expected. Accommodation and food were going to be difficult, Andy warned us. We rode across a big common to the walls of the *Q'ala* and dismounted. Then hurrying, so as not to attract too much attention, I supposed, we were led towards a group of houses on the far side of the common where Haji Ghafoor, the headman of Kantiwar, lived. Andy explained that on his last visit he had stayed with Haji, but because of the *jirgah* we would have to stay elsewhere this time. Our lodging turned out to be a rather cheerless and dirty house, but I was too tired to care, gratefully subsiding on to the dusty carpet. Haji Ghafoor's number two, a friendly-looking man called Khalim, came to welcome us and had a long talk with Khalili. They talked about the *jirgah* and the problems posed by Sarwar Nuristani.

'Khalim says there is a fresh risk that we may get stopped going through Sarwar's territory.' This was a couple of days' march to the north.

'That's not very encouraging. What would happen if we did get stopped?'

Khalili put the question to Khalim. 'He doesn't know. But he says Sarwar is in touch with Kabul – what I told you – and they supply him with arms by helicopter.'

'What worries me is that if the KGB is, by any remote chance, looking for us and we do get stopped by Sarwar's people, we may end up in Kabul. That wouldn't be funny.'

No one disagreed.

'Can you ask Khalim how great does he think the risk is?'

'He does not know.'

'But can't he give us an estimate? Is it a big risk in his view or not?'

Khalim shrugged. 'He says it is the Will of Allah if you will be stopped or not.'

And with that rather metaphysical answer we had to be content. We would hear what Haji Ghafoor had to say tomorrow. It was now nine o'clock and there was still no sign of any food. I was so exhausted I unrolled my sleeping bag on the roof and went to bed hungry. Before falling asleep I listened to the BBC's World Service on my Sony shortwave. They were talking about South African sanctions, and Malaysia had just announced it was boycotting the Commonwealth Games in Edinburgh. It all seemed very remote from our problems.

Next morning, coming down from the roof where we slept, I slipped on the rickety wooden ladder and trying to save myself cut a deep gash in the top of a finger. It bled profusely but Andy, who had done a medic's course in the army, bound it up expertly. After breakfast Haji Ghafoor came to call, a fine-looking man with an aquiline nose and a big bushy beard. He had led the Nuristani *Jihad* in the early days of the war and had about him the stamp of authority. He expressed himself forcibly about Sarwar.

'He must be driven out of Nuristan. He is an agent of Kabul and the Russians. We have called the *jirgah* for this reason, to decide on the action that must be taken.'

'Do you think the *jirgah* will vote your way?'

'Yes, the great majority of Nuristanis want to put a stop to Sarwar's activity.'

Khalili was sceptical, arguing that if Sarwar was a Russian puppet as they said, the Russians would never allow him to be pushed out. Khalili has a combative streak and he taunted

Haji. 'You want to get rid of Sarwar, but you can't even provide security on the road from here to Chamar.' Chamar is the entry to the Panjsher Valley.

Haji's voice rose excitedly. 'Carter couldn't provide security for his own ambassador in Kabul.' (Adolph 'Spike' Dubs had been shot by Afghan police, advised by Russians, in February 1979, when they stormed the hotel in Kabul where he was held after being kidnapped.)

Haji calmed down and said that the Pushal area dominated by Sarwar should be the joint responsibility of Badakhshan, the Panjsher and Nuristan. Khalili agreed, since the arms convoys to the north depend heavily on this route. Andy thought the Russians were interested in getting Sarwar to do their dirty work for them. 'If they can get Sarwar to block the route, they don't need to send in their own troops.'

I asked if Haji was willing to face the consequences of doing battle with Sarwar. 'If he attacks Sarwar, the Russians will bomb Kantiwar and the rest of Nuristan. Is he ready for that?'

'Yes. He says they started the *jihad* and they are ready to continue the *jihad*.' Haji had said it proudly, with a lift of the head and a flash of the eyes, as if he resented the implication that the Nuristanis might be less brave than any other Afghan.

All this was academic, however. We had to decide whether we were going to push on or, what was to me unthinkable, turn back.

'I personally think there is a very slight chance of us being stopped and an even slighter chance of Sarwar arresting us and sending us to Kabul. But it's there and we have to consider it. What do you think?' I looked at the others.

Andy took his pipe out of his mouth. 'I think we have to go on, Sandy.' His blue eyes were untroubled.

Noel agreed. 'We can't go back now.'

Whitney, however, who had been showing increasing concern about the Sarwar threat, said, 'Can I ask you something, Sandy? Would you let me join your team and go in as a journalist?'

'That's not the problem, Whitney. The difficulty is the passport. You have an American passsport and if we do get stopped and taken to Kabul, saying you are a member of the team won't help. After all, you were a diplomat in Kabul and if they discovered that I think they would be extremely suspicious.'

Whitney had already thought of that. 'I can't afford, as a former diplomat, to run the risk of being captured. So, very reluctantly, I'm afraid I'm going to have to leave you and go back.'

It was bad luck, but I think he made the right decision.

CHAPTER NINE

With typically Afghan courtesy, Haji Ghafoor and Khalim escorted us to the top of the hill and after warm embraces for Khalili and Andy, and handshakes for Noel and me, watched us depart down the steep hill to the lower part of the village. The little square, overhung with enormous walnut and mulberry trees, was deserted. We followed the river, fast-running and greeny-white with melted snow, forced at one point, where the path had been swept away, to climb to the top of the cliff which hung vertiginously above the rapids. Three hours' riding at a good pace brought us to the village of Chaman which overlooked a wide strath richly sown with wheat and maize. Andy knew someone called *Kaka* (Uncle) Musa there and we turned up a stony path between drystone walls to his house, only to find him away. His wife, however, lent us a kettle and we brewed some of the last of our precious Earl Grey. It tasted like nectar. I lay down in the meadow above the house to write up my diary.

> Very beautiful, tall with grass and clover, decked with wild orchids, forget-me-nots and a profusion of other wild flowers. Butterflies galore – tortoiseshells chasing one another, what might be green or grey hairstreaks and a yellow brimstone. The profusion of butterflies everywhere is no doubt thanks to the absence of all insecticides. Being Friday, the women aren't in the fields (all day yesterday, from six to six, they weeded the wheatfields outside our house in Kantiwar), but one woman was doing her washing in the stream beside the meadow.'

We left *Kaka* Musa's at about midday in hot sunshine, crossing first the lush green meadows of Chaman, then, as we forged on upriver, travelling through a desolate, empty landscape. In late afternoon, at the end of the valley, we crossed the river and climbing up steeply eventually reached a group of *bandas* perched on a small plateau at about 12,000 feet. Several wild and hairy Nuristanis in charge of a large flock of fat-tailed sheep and goats wanted the exorbitant price of 500 Afghanis (£2.50) for a bowl of milk, which we declined. The plan was to camp here and then make an early assault on Kantiwar Pass in the morning.

The horsemen soon had a fire blazing and kettles on the boil, but these arrangements did not include us, apparently because the simmering feud between Khalili and Mullah Dhost, of which I had not really been aware, now came to the surface. Khalili set up a rival camp in a small sheep pen about a hundred yards away. Our only helper, Mirza, a young *mujahid* who had worked in Iran for a year and bought a pair of jeans with part of the proceeds, went to forage for sticks for our own fire.

It was now about eight and I was cold, hungry and tired. Khalili sat with his back to the wall of the sheep pen, busily writing his diary.

'What do you think we should do about food?' I asked him.

No reply. Khalili remained deep in his diary. I turned to Andy.

'Andy, what do you think? Are we going to get any food, or should I go and fetch some sardines?'

'We'll probably get some rice later, Sandy. *Inshallah*' (God willing). Andy laughed. Discomfort and lack of food hardly troubled him.

'Noel, are you hungry? Would you like something?'

'Wouldn't mind some sardines, or cheese.'

Deciding that Mirza's fire might take a very long time to materialise and seeing no other prospect of sustenance, Noel and I got stiffly to our feet and trudged up the hill in the dark to where our men, surrounded by the baggage and the horses, were happily eating *nan* and drinking tea by their fires. I found the saddlebag containing the food and retrieved two tins of sardines, one of bully beef and the last of Nigel's lifeboat biscuits. As I rummaged about in the dark, one of the Nuristani shepherds came and watched with predatory intensity. This made me nervous about the big bundle of Afghan money I kept wrapped in a plastic bag in my grip, along with my clothes. But I was reassured when one of the horsemen helped me to zip it up, patting it reassuringly and pointing to himself to show that he would look after it. Noel and I set off down the hill again and had a cheerless supper with Andy.

Mirza had disappeared, so there was no tea, and Khalili was still writing his diary. At nine, I unrolled sleeping bag and bivvy bag and despite the rockiness of the ground lay down with real pleasure. I was asleep within a minute and apart from slipping down the hill every time I moved, managed to stay warm and dry despite a light fall of snow.

It was only next morning that I discovered how eventful a night it had been. Andy told me that late in the evening, no rice having materialised, Khalili had gone up to the horsemen's camp, and, finding them regaling themselves with no care for the rest of us, had kicked over one of their cooking pots. Mirza had finally managed to produce tea at around midnight.

Noel had had an equally exciting time.

'I woke up in the middle of the night to find someone had thrown some blazing sticks right beside me. I thought at first the whole place was on fire. One red-hot piece of stick landed nine inches from my face. I could easily have been burnt.' These were presumably the embers from Mirza's fire which he had hurled into the dark before lying down to sleep in the narrow confines of the sheep pen. Noel has a pithy Birmingham accent and although he clearly thought he had fallen among lunatics he made it sound as if it were all a joke.

Starting at five in the morning was no joke, however. It was miserably cold and there was no tea. I chewed a piece of dry *nan* and one of Nigel's biscuits and started off on foot up the first steep ridge. At the top it levelled out to a plateau and Abdi appeared with Jerand, whom I mounted gratefully. Small, light hailstones began to fall. After half an hour or so we came to a lunar-like stretch of broken rock: some of the slabs on which the horses slipped and stumbled were twenty yards across. Abdi turned and pointed at the ground.

'*Bombard, bombard.*'

It looked as if a meteor had crashed on the rocks, streaking them with the white stress marks of violent impact. Then I remembered. The Russians had attacked the previous summer, dropping several bombs. This one had landed right on target: on the path. Farther on, we passed the skeletons of three or four horses sprawled among the rocks, their hide stretched taut over their bones, sightless eyes turned to the sky, the casualties of the arms trail. We reached the top of the pass,

16,500 feet up, at 6.30. A few yards farther on, where the rock rose sheer above the path, memory seized me by the throat. It was exactly here, travelling in the opposite direction four years before, that two of our horses had slipped off the path and nearly fallen to their deaths.

This time, no such disaster befell us as we hurried to get away from the exposed area of the pass. The path ran along the steep flank of the mountain, and we saw some vivid signs of the previous year's earthquake: rocks had been shattered and huge boulders which had split away from the mountain hung precariously above our heads. Despite the early sun on our faces, it remained cold until we were well down and then suddenly there were the flowers and butterflies again. A magnificent black redstart, surely one of the handsomest of birds, made my heart beat joyously instead of painfully as it had done on the way up. Then came a small flock of very tame snow buntings, plump birds with a black stripe on the wing. You expect a snow bunting at that altitude, and they are beautifully camouflaged, but not a black redstart with its striking red and black plumage. I wondered why we were not seeing more lammergeier vultures, which were almost common in 1982. There was no shortage of food for them, in the shape of dead horses; perhaps Soviet air activity had driven them away.

We now came to the checkpoint at Do Ab (Two Rivers) which had caused so much heart-searching and was the cause of Whitney's turning back. No one actually stopped us, but since there was a *chaikhana* opposite, we halted for tea and *nan*. While we rested in the shade, a number of local worthies armed with Kalashnikovs came to inspect us, engaging Khalili in conversation. Andy cast a professional eye over the weaponry.

'These are Russian-made, not Chinese or Egyptian. They must have come from Kabul.'

Khalili confirmed this. 'Yes, these people belong to Maulawi Rezak, a very religious old man who controls this area. They say that Maulawi Rezak is a friend of Sarwar Nuristani, and the Maulawi gets the guns from Sarwar.'

I was surprised. 'How can a religious leader like Maulawi Rezak be a friend of someone like Sarwar, who is an ally of the Communists in Kabul?'

'You see, he is a very nice old man and he believes Sarwar

when he tells him that he takes arms from the Communists but that he doesn't necessarily believe in their policies.'

'Perhaps it's true and Sarwar *is* taking the Russians for a ride?'

'Nobody believes that apart from the Maulawi. You heard what Haji Ghafoor said.'

Khalili walked across to the stone-built guard post to talk to the commander. When he came back he said, 'He wants us to go to Pushal and have a rest for a couple of days. We are invited.'

'Is that where Sarwar is?'

'Yes, his headquarters.' We looked at one another. 'Don't worry, I told him it was very kind but we are in a hurry. I think he meant it nicely. But as soon as you have drunk your tea, we should go on.'

We all agreed with that. In fact I thought we had already spent too long in the *chaikhana*. On the other hand, Khalili had told them who we were and there was little doubt that the name of Ahmed Shah Masud of the Panjsher carried a lot of weight, even in Nuristan.

We had passed a family of refugees halfway down the mountain, two young couples and several small children struggling up towards the pass; but we now met about a hundred more, from Badakhshan in the far north-east, walking along in single file. Because of the checkpoint, we had decided not to carry the cameras openly, but to leave them out of sight on the horses, so we could only watch as the pathetic column, made up mostly of old women and children, came trooping past us. Some of the old ladies were in their seventies and looked exhausted, having probably crossed Chamar Pass that morning and been on the road for about ten hours. The path was so narrow that we had to stand to one side and let them go past. It was also very muddy and they kept slipping, but there were no complaints, they just kept plodding along. The smallest children were strapped to the backs of donkeys, two to a donkey in some cases, or carried piggy-back by their fathers, brothers or sisters. Khalili stood watching them go past with tears in his eyes.

I was angry that we had missed getting pictures of these refugees, since the continuing flight of the civilian population, running at about 7,500 a month to Pakistan throughout the summer, was going to be a key element in the film. But we were helpless, since the cameras were a mile away, and it merely confirmed what I already knew: that filming in Afghanistan is both a lottery and a nightmare. Even someone as fit and strong as Andy could not carry a camera weighing thirty pounds all day, every day, and it was impossible to know when a sight like this would present itself. In fact it was to take us nearly two months to get our sequence on refugees, and although very good, I do not think the pictures were quite as moving as what we had just seen: possibly because the refugees we filmed were crossing the last pass into Pakistan on their way to safety and looked comparatively cheerful.

The general jumpiness about Sarwar and the long arm of Kabul was demonstrated by the advice that we should avoid the next *chaikhana*, because, it was said, the long-haired owner had a radio and spoke some strange language: he might even be a Tajik from across the border in the Soviet Union, it was rumoured. Accordingly, when we got near the *chaikhana*, Andy, Noel and I were instructed to contain our thirst and walk past quickly, heads averted, just in case the man was a spy. Andy and I did so without difficulty and although we saw the ruffian with black hair to his shoulders standing outside, he was looking the other way. However, he did spot Noel and chased after him, pestering him to stop and drink tea. But Noel, face averted, strode manfully on. Khalili, however, as an Afghan was able to stop and play the role of special investigator. His report was illuminating.

'I think he is a good man. He is not a foreigner, but a Nuristani. He used to work in the Intercon in Kabul and even speaks some English.' Khalili's currant-bun eyes glinted at the thought of the simpletons who had peddled these rumours.

'What about the radio?'

'I saw his radio. It is a small Sony shortwave, just like yours. His food sounded vairy good, much better than most of the other *chaikhanas*. Rice, chicken, eggs . . .'

Noel, however, was not convinced. 'If he's not a spy, what's a man who used to work at the Intercon in Kabul doing running a *chaikhana* halfway up a mountain in Nuristan?'

'Maybe he was homesick,' I suggested.

Unfortunately we spent the night at another *chaikhana* where the food was well below the standard claimed by the long-haired one.

Next morning the horses had to ford two rivers. The film horse, the elderly grey, was nearly swept away by the current on the first crossing, and emerged exhausted and with badly cut legs. The second crossing was almost as hazardous. Fortunately, we were able to cross by footbridge. The man who owned the grey hoisted the heavy saddlebags which contained our sixty rolls of film on to his shoulder as if they were a sack of feathers and strode across.

We walked for a couple of hours, crossing several more extremely precarious-looking bridges, too narrow for horses. These bridges usually consist of two or three long, springy tree trunks, trimmed by an axe and lashed together with rope but often without a handrail.

As we rode, climbing gently, the warm sun drew a delicate scent from the dog roses, one species of which was a deep buttercup yellow. My eye was caught by another flower, tall and shaped like a red-hot poker, but yellow. One of the Jamiat cameramen came up to me holding something in his hand. It was a baby redstart, brown and fluffy, its bright eyes staring back at us without apparent fear.

'Let it go,' I said. He opened his hand and after a moment's hesitation it flew off rather shakily, managing to keep airborne for thirty yards before landing on a rock, where it sat looking very pleased with itself.

Two young, wild-looking Nuristanis now appeared and seeing we were foreigners made a beeline for us. They carried Kalashnikovs, like everyone else in Afghanistan, and although probably perfectly harmless had such a *farouche* air that I could not help feeling a trifle nervous. They tried to engage me in conversation, but with my five words of Farsi this was rather a one-sided business. I guessed they wanted to know where I came from.

'Englistan.'

'Ah, Englistan?' Much chattering and eyeing of horse and equipment. Where was I going?

'Panjsher.'

'Ah, Panjsher. Ahmed Shah Masud?' More talk in Nuristani

81

and predatory looks. I took a picture of them with my camera. They laughed and swung their Kalashnikovs from one shoulder to another, throwing back their long black hair. They were powerfully built but lithe, and walked with an animal grace. Having exhausted my Farsi and their interest, they changed direction and went loping off into the distance.

We came to an escarpment, and the river, which had been meandering along quietly as clear as glass, now went leaping down over the rocks to a wide meadow of close-cropped, emerald-green grass.

I thought there seemed to be rather a lot of skulls and bones scattered about and I suddenly realised that this was the killing place. Two years before, a party of refugees trekking south had just crossed Chamar Pass when Russian jets spotted them and dive-bombed the convoy. Forty were said to have been killed or wounded, most of them women and children. A few rough gravestones stood on the hillside, scraps of green or white cloth fluttering on poles in the Afghan fashion, and in the springy green turf one big bomb crater and several smaller ones were still clearly visible. In that still lonely spot, I could hear in my imagination the sudden howl of the jets as they came hurtling down the bare valley and sense the panic they must have caused among the terrified refugees. I could hear the children screaming and the terrified neighing of the horses. Looking at the smaller craters in the meadow, I guessed the jets had probably used rockets as well. Then, as I remembered from my own experience in the Panjsher, they would have climbed away steeply into the blue sky, leaving behind the broken, bleeding bodies of the refugees and their animals. Some of the skulls looked too big for horses, more like those of camels, but I did not see how one could get camels over these passes.

Edward Girardet of the *Christian Science Monitor*, travelling in the opposite direction towards the Panjsher, was on the scene a day later and wrote a graphic report for his newspaper. The publicity produced a rare apology from the Russians and the Afghan government: they said they thought the refugee column was an arms convoy and so they attacked it. If true, that would suggest poor target identification by the Russian or Afghan pilots especially as the refugees were heading south, to Pakistan. Much more likely and chilling is the thought that for

Russian pilots in Afghanistan, any target is fair game. In Vietnam, the Americans used to define any area deemed to be under Communist control as a 'free fire zone'. Since the Russians and their Afghan allies control hardly a single acre of Afghanistan outside the cities and their own bases, the whole country is for them a 'free fire zone'. Indeed, riding through that meadow at the foot of Chamar, and adding to it in my mind a hundred other stories of massacres and atrocities by Soviet troops in Afghanistan, I was forced to conclude that as invaders every bit as ruthless as Genghis Khan or Tamerlane, the Russians were prepared without the slightest compunction, but without publicity, please, to bomb the whole Afghan nation into oblivion.

CHAPTER TEN

At the foot of the Chamar Pass, we stopped at a *banda* for a rest and whatever food we could get: it turned out to be *dugh* and milk and we gulped it down hungrily. As we sat there, enjoying the sun after the morning's walk, one horseman approached Khalili and an earnest conversation took place. Khalili looked grave.

'Bad news. The film horse, the white film horse is dead.'

'Dead? Good God! When did that happen?'

'This morning. A few hours ago. This man has just come with the news. You saw it after it had crossed the river and its legs were all bleeding? It looked very tired then, very sick. A little time after that it just lay down and died.'

After a moment's pity for the poor horse, practicality returned. 'Where's the film?'

'They have put it on another horse. They're bringing it now.' We looked back down the valley but in that desolate landscape nothing moved.

Every *banda* has a couple of dogs, big, sand-coloured mastiffs with cropped ears and a savage pair of jaws. The shepherds are proud of them, although they treat them roughly. The Afghan way of disciplining any animal, including a dog, is to throw a stone at it. These mastiffs are quite unlike Afghan hounds, those silky-haired aristocrats you see on the streets of London and New York, bred as royal hunting dogs, but which I have never seen in Afghanistan.

As we were leaving, one of the *banda* dogs which had been lying down while its master chatted to Khalili suddenly rose and made a silent run at me, like a collie, body close to the ground and jaws ready to snap. I saw it coming and froze. At the same moment the shepherd shouted and flung a stone which hit the dog in the ribs with a thump. The dog howled and lay whimpering on the ground while its owner berated it and everyone else laughed.

'If you hadn't stopped, it would have bitten you,' Khalili said, satisfaction in his voice that I had had so narrow an escape.

Noel and I set off first, hauling ourselves slowly up the first steep flank of the mountain, conscious of the fact that the top of the pass was somewhere far above us. After a quarter of an hour, I stopped for breath and saw the owner of the now deceased grey film horse and his friend coming slowly up to the *banda*, driving in front of them a feeble-looking chestnut which was now carrying a double load and hardly able to put one foot in front of another.

Khalili and Andy caught us up. I pointed at the trio below. 'That horse is never going to get over the pass with that load on its back. It can hardly carry it on the flat.'

Khalili, to his credit, had anticipated this problem. 'I have arranged with two of the Nuristanis from the *banda*. They will carry our film over the pass to Chamar. I have given them one thousand Afghanis (£5) each. They will bring it, don't worry.' Noel and I looked at one another. They were better men than we were. We would need all our energy to get ourselves over the pass, let alone carry a load of film stock on our backs.

Chamar turned out to be a horribly long and exhausting climb and Noel and I were almost the last to reach the top at four, collapsing gratefully on a rock in the knowledge that we had now surmounted the fifth and last pass leading to the Panjsher. We took photographs of one another but it was too cold to linger, although we did have time to admire the great snowy pyramid of Mir Samir, 19,880 feet, and reflect gratefully that we did not have to climb it. A green lake like a flawed emerald lay on a plateau at the foot of the pass and just beyond, where the soil was damp, a mass of beautiful pale purple flowers like primulas, but only half the size, pushed up between the stones: it looked as if someone had scattered handfuls of amethysts on the ground. It was hard to believe that anything could flourish here, yet a little farther on, an even smaller version of it gladdened the eye. It is wonderful what a little deprivation and hardship can do: the senses become sharper, one's appreciation of things is heightened and a few clumps of a little purple flower can cause a pang of pure pleasure.

Crossing a tangle of broken rocks we were halted by a piercing whistle. It was so loud and so unexpected that for one panicky moment I thought we had stumbled on a Russian patrol.

Noel and I stopped and peered among the rocks.

'There it is,' Noel said. 'Look. Sitting up as bold as brass.'

A bright orange marmot was sitting on its hind legs watching us carefully. Then, as we moved, it suddenly turned and dived into a hole in the rocks, disappearing as abruptly as it had appeared.

We had been walking for a long time and I was beginning to feel tired. 'Where the hell are the horses?' I grumbled. Suddenly there they were, with Abdi and Azimullah sitting on the rocks beside them, obviously in a bad temper. We could only imagine half the conversation that followed, but it must have been along these lines.

(*Them*) 'Where on earth have you been? We've been waiting for hours and it's getting bloody cold.'

(*Us*) 'Why the hell did you disappear? We could have been riding all this time. We're both bloody tired.'

(*Them*) 'You should have come by the direct route, like everyone else.' Abdi pointed his whip angrily at the mountain.

(*Us*) 'We didn't know the route, and anyway it looks far too steep.' We knew Andy was planning to come down by the *direttissima*, but then he was like a mountain goat.

Huffily, Abdi and Azimullah held the horses for us while we mounted and then rode off at a fast pace, leaving us to follow as best we could. Noel's horse was painfully slow and he soon dropped well behind. It was now bitterly cold and the last few miles were miserable, brightened only by a bird which might have come from Paradise instead of that rocky desert: a Güldenstädt's redstart, amazingly handsome and brightly coloured, with a jet-black head, a snowy white cap, black and white on its back and chest and bright red underneath. It made me think, rather illogically, of a cardinal. This sumptuous creature's mate was dowdy by comparison, being a pale lemony colour.

At seven, cold to the bone, I saw a big outcrop of rock on the left of the river and knew that the *chaikhana* we were making for was opposite, although still out of sight behind the shoulder of the mountain. We crossed a soft, marshy meadow and there it was, a cluster of stone *bandas* built against the cliff, smoke from the cooking fires rising to welcome us. The *chaikhana* owner, a former Dashaka gunner who had been badly wounded, rushed out full of smiles and held my horse's head while I got stiffly down. I found Andy, Khalili, Mullah Dhost and a number of Panjsheris sitting in a *banda*, its roof open to the sky. Andy was smoking his pipe, looking pleased with life.

To my rather testy question about how long he had been there, he gave a puff and said affably, 'Oh, a couple of hours. How about a cup of tea, Sandy?' Noel arrived a few minutes later and stretched out beside me. He too was stiff with cold. A young Panjsheri *mujahid* sat opposite us, his feet bare.

'Aren't you cold?' I asked, my teeth almost chattering.

He looked at me pityingly and said in Farsi, 'No, not a bit cold.'

It was good to be in the Panjsher again, after twelve days of hard walking, even if it was more like winter than high summer.

Just as we were settling down for the night, Khalili announced we were moving to a more comfortable spot, a cave used by the lapis merchants, where we would be dry if it rained. Reluctantly, we got up and, stumbling in the dark, carried our belongings to the cave which turned out to be so small and so full of lapis that there was really nowhere for the four of us to sleep. So after more discussion with the *chaikhana* owner, we moved to yet another *banda*. This proved to be not only less windproof than the first, but extremely stony under-foot and, after trying in vain to find an area six feet by three where I could unroll my sleeping bag without a rock sticking into my kidneys, I gave up and resigned myself to an un-comfortable time; although I was dressed in shirt, trousers, Guernsey sweater and socks I was cold all night.

Next morning, over tea and *nan*, Khalili held a council of war.

'First, the good news. The two Nuristanis arrived in the night with the film, and I paid them their money. The horses have already left for Chamar, taking the film with them.

'The next thing is that since we are now near the Panjsher we must take care for the jets.' He pronounced it 'jits'. 'So I think it is better if we walk to Chamar, carrying the cameras with us. Just in case.'

'Has there been any bombing recently?' I asked.

'They fly over every other day. You never know when they

come. I think it is better too if Andy and I go first and you and Noel come half an hour after. So we leave some distance between us.' I thought this was all rather pointless since I was quite sure the horsemen would have gone together in a bunch as they always did. But I knew it was done for our safety, so we did as instructed, starting only when Andy and Khalili were tiny figures in the great sweep of valley that descended to Chamar.

If it had not been for the weight on our backs of the camera, which Noel carried, and the sound gear, which I carried, it would have been an enjoyable seven-mile stroll; but after an hour or so the straps of the rucksacks cut into our shoulders and the sharp edges of equipment dug into our backs. Despite the concern about Russian jets, the sky remained silent and innocently blue. The only things that flew were wagtails, flitting from rock to rock in elegant undulating sweeps and so yellow, Noel said, they looked like canaries.

The mighty bulk of Mir Samir was now well behind us, but big mountains, still with plenty of snow on them, rose on both sides, and ahead of us, at right angles, we could see the far wall of the Panjsher.

I remembered Chamar well for the large, imposing *qarargah* (*mujahideen* headquarters) that stood on a bluff overlooking the river where we had spent the night in 1982, before starting our journey across the wilds of Nuristan. To my surprise it looked exactly the same, and if it had been bombed, no damage was visible. Round it, fields of short-stalked wheat and barley ripened slowly, heavily infiltrated with wild sweet peas and yellow mustard. Flowers grew in profusion beside the path and along the edge of the fields.

Andy and Khalili were established in a big room, the floor covered with a large red and black carpet and thick cushions round the walls. The local *mujahideen* commander, a plump, affable man, greeted us courteously and introduced another quiet, bearded man, who, Khalili said, was in charge of military supplies for the valley.

'They say that as far as they know Masud is not here, but the commander has sent a message to Dasht-i-Raiwat to find out. We should get a reply by this evening.' We had been told by some Panjsheris we had met on the road that Masud had arrived in the Panjsher after an absence of ten months, and we thought he might have come to meet us. I hoped then that the information was wrong, because I would rather see Masud in his new operational area, organising the north.

The horsemen now appeared with all our baggage which they piled in a corner of the room, the saddles and bridles in one heap, the precious film stock and the rest of the camera gear in another.

Abdi and Azimullah came to shake hands and say goodbye. I said to Khalili I would like to retain their services. They were good men, with good horses, but Kahlili had other ideas.

'There is no food for them here, so they will go to another village just a few minutes away.' That meant at least five miles. The owner of the late lamented grey stood before us, looking deeply dejected. Although we had no contractual obligation, I had already offered to give the man something for the loss of his horse.

'How much do you think I should give him?'

'As you like. Anything.'

'Well, what do you think? Ten thousand? Twenty thousand?'

'Twenty thousand Afghanis (£100) would be very generous.'

'What does a horse like that cost, to buy? Sixty thousand Afghanis (£300)?'

'Something like that. It depends, you know, on how good a horse.'

I rummaged in my grip, took out the plastic bag with the money, and counted out twenty thousand Afghanis in dirty, dog-eared notes; some were stuck together with Sellotape.

'There you are.' The horseman took the money hesitantly, almost reluctantly, with both hands, a nice Afghan gesture which suggested that the gift was one of overwhelming generosity. He stammered a speech of thanks, and withdrew, half bowing.

'He says that thanks to your generosity his family will now survive. Your gift makes all the difference between living and dying.'

While counting out the twenty thousand, it had occurred to me there was less money than there should have been in the plastic bag. One of the Badakhshani cameramen offered to count it for me.

'How much should there be here?'

'About a hundred and forty-nine thousand. I started with two hundred thousand and we've spent about fifty-one thousand.'

He counted rapidly, making a clucking noise and then counted again.

'There is only seventy thousand here.'

'Is that all? Are you sure?'

'Yes, I have counted twice. Seventy thousand.'

'That means we are eighty thousand short.'

The cameraman looked startled. Khalili, hearing the end of the conversation, became excited.

'You have lost eighty thousand?'

'Yes, approximately.'

'How did it happen? Are you sure? You haven't got it in your other bag?'

'My rucksack? No, I carried it all in this plastic bag, in my grip.'

'Please check. It is very important.'

I unpacked my small rucksack to please Khalili, although I knew there would be no money there. 'No, I'm afraid not. I kept it all here. It must have been stolen either the night we slept at the foot of Kantiwar, at that Nuristani *banda*, or else another night when we camped beside the river. I unpacked my grip that night and the horsemen saw where I had all the money. Entirely my fault, I should have kept it in my rucksack. Damn stupid of me.'

Originally, there had been enough notes to fill a briefcase: if I had put them in my rucksack there would have been practically no room for anything else.

'You think it was the horsemen?'

'Well, they looked after our bags, Noel's and mine.'

'Mutt and Jeff,' Noel said. 'They were always miles behind everyone else. They would have had plenty of time to open the bags and help themselves.'

Khalili was puzzled. 'What did you call them? Matt . . .?'

Noel laughed. 'Mutt and Jeff. Characters from a cartoon at home. The one whose horse died and his mate.'

'I will tell the commander and we will have those two men searched and questioned.'

'It might not have been them. It could have been one of the Nuristanis.'

'No, those two men were responsible for your bags. If they have taken the money, we will get it back.'

I thought that would be unlikely. But I knew how highly the *mujahideen* valued honesty and what a slur they would consider such a theft. Not only was it an offence against a friendly foreigner and guest, but it also impugned the *Jihad*.

'Ah well, it was my fault and it only represents a loss of ...' I worked it out: '£387.50.'

I spent a delightfully lazy afternoon, listening to Chopin's Second Piano Concerto on my Sony Walkman. Andy told me it was really his First, but that Chopin had lost part of it on a journey across Europe and by the time he had reconstituted it he had written his next one. Hence the First became the Second, and vice versa.

'The Larghetto, Sandy, he wrote for a lady he admired. It's very beautiful, the slow movement.'

A young *mujahid* came in, carrying a Kalashnikov, shook hands all round and sat down opposite Khalili.

'This boy, his name is Nabiullah, is eighteen years old. He has been a *mujahid* since he was seventeen. He took part in the Pushghour operation – when Masud captured an Afghan army post farther down the valley, taking 400 prisoners and killing the Afghan army commander and two Russian colonels. That's where he got his Kalashnikov. Before that, for three years, he acted as a courier and a helper for the *mujahideen*. His parents lived at Shawa, halfway down the valley. Now they are refugees at Parian, the next-door village.' The young man looked very young, but proud that we were talking about him.

The day drifted on, punctuated by Andy's demands to the cook, who was also the *qarargah* clerk, for pots of tea. The conversation turned to attempts by the KGB and the KHAD to assassinate Masud.

'Two, three years ago, a high-ranking KHAD officer was briefed to assassinate Masud. This man, Kamran, was given four months' training by the KGB, a pistol with a silencer and several ampoules of poison. Before he started his mission, he was taken to see Babrak Karmal, who was then President, and a number of very high Russian officers. They promised him, if he succeeded to kill Masud, two million Afghanis (£10,000), a house in a good part of Kabul, a new Volga car and a trip abroad.

'Now, this KHAD officer had been to school with Masud and had been a friend of his. He told his wife about the mission and she said, "Now is your chance to do something for your country. You can't go, but let me go to Masud and warn him." So Kamran's wife comes to the Panjsher, in disguise, and tells Masud the whole story.

'Then he comes himself, according to the plan, is taken to Masud and they greet one another like long-lost brothers. He tells Masud about the two other teams that had also come to the Panjsher and they were all captured. Later Masud sent Kamran to Pakistan and from there he went to Germany, where he now lives.'

'I'm sure the KGB would like to talk to him.'

'Yes, he is frightened that the KGB will kill him. He was a brave man.'

Next day, after the commander had produced his best breakfast of crusty *nan*, butter and yoghurt, which we ate by scooping up the latter with chunks of the former, I went down to the river to have a much-needed wash. The water was icy, taking my breath away as I went under. It reminded me of cold baths at school, although the purpose was different: they were intended to wake boys up in the morning and freeze their libidos: now I merely wanted to get clean. I was sunbathing among the wild lavender and willows when my reverie was shattered by the sinister drone of an Antonov reconnaissance plane. I remembered the sound and the air strikes that usually followed so vividly that although I could not see the plane I scrambled hurriedly into my clothes.

After lunch, with no word from Masud and anxious to start filming, we set off to interview a big tough-looking man called Issa, a machine-gunner who had shot down three helicopters during the Pushghour operation, despite having only one eye. By a strange coincidence we had met him four years before and even stored our camera gear in his house at Shawa. A few weeks later he had been wounded in the eye by a mortar splinter,

Travels with the Mujahideen

walked to Peshawar and then by a stroke of luck had been sent to the Walter Reed Hospital in Washington where they operated and gave him an artificial eye. He was now in charge of a Dashaka post above Chamar.

Getting to Issa's mountain proved a short but very Afghan journey. Issa's brother came to fetch us at the *qarargah* with a horse, on which he loaded the camera equipment. We walked due west down the valley and forty minutes later arrived at a village. Good, I thought, plenty of light. But where was Issa? The brother pointed to a mountain to the east, in almost exactly the direction from which we had come.

'We'll have to go there,' Khalili said, his face a mask.

'But why have we walked all this way if we have to walk all the way back again? It's crazy,' I said.

'Let's go,' Khalili said, cutting short any further protests.

'What about the horse?' I asked, but no one was listening. Apparently the brother and the horse intended to remain here in the village. With nothing else for it, Noel shouldered the camera while Khalili and Andy strode on ahead. I kept offering to take my turn but Noel steadfastly refused. Forty minutes later we arrived at the foot of the mountain and scanned the heights: Issa was a tiny figure halfway up. By now it was after five and we all knew that by the time we had climbed up it would be dark. We stood there in indecision for a few minutes. Then someone said, 'He's coming down,' and there he was with his team, leaping from rock to rock with the dismantled gun on their shoulders.

Issa's tale of derring-do began about three weeks before the attack on Pushghour.

'It was being supplied only by air and I was able to get a position on the mountain close to where the helicopters came in to land. Two took off one day, one close behind the other. As they came past me I opened fire, shooting hundreds of rounds into each. One crashed, then the other, and both burst into great balls of fire.

'Then, just before the big attack, Masud called together all the commanders and said, "Who can stop helicopters landing at Pushghour?" There was silence and then I said, "I can, on condition that I have a cave made by a rock drill in a strategic position and unlimited ammunition."

'Masud said, "Agreed," and gave orders to drill out the cave where I wanted it.

'One or two days before the battle I was in my position when a helicopter approached, flying straight for Pushghour. I waited until it completely filled my sights and then I let it have it, hundreds and hundreds of rounds. It started to catch fire and crashed outside the camp. We captured the pilot, co-pilot and ten Afghan army officers.

'Now they only supply Pushghour by road, once every six months, with a heavily armoured convoy.'

After capturing the base and destroying it, Masud withdrew and eventually the Afghan army reoccupied it. It seemed to me a very expensive exercise to hold on to a base that could only be supplied with such difficulty and which served so little purpose. Chamar was only thirty or forty miles from Pushghour and yet it might have been in another world. Yet the Russians had no real choice. To abandon Pushghour, or any other base, would be an admission of failure.

CHAPTER ELEVEN

A small lapis convoy of five horses each carrying ten *sear* (70 kilos) arrived from the north next morning, and unloaded behind the *qarargah*. The commander, holding a small piece of the dark blue stone in his right hand like a talisman, went to inspect the shipment in his role as the revenue officer.

He explained that the country's five lapis mines were in the hands of the *mujahideen* and that the total annual traffic was worth 300 million Afghanis (£1.5 million). All the traffic came through Chamar and Masud levied a tax of between five and ten per cent on it: five per cent for local traders and ten per cent for outsiders. The commander was reluctant to put a figure on the total revenue, but even at five per cent it must have been 15 million Afghanis, about £75,000 a year, and was probably more like £100,000.

The value of the stone depends on the grade. The commander explained that there were three grades, the best fetching more than £200 a kilo in Pakistan. At this stage it was merely a bluish lump of rock, but when cut and polished, mainly by craftsmen in Hong Kong or Germany, it emerges as a magnificent dark blue stone much prized for rings, necklaces and bracelets.

We were becoming increasingly restive at the lack of any word from Masud, but at lunchtime a messenger arrived with instructions for us to go immediately to Parian, a few miles down the valley. In Afghanistan, all such messages demand 'immediate' action.

'What exactly does the message say?' I asked Khalili.

'It just tells us to come as soon as possible to Parian, to the house of the commander there. I think maybe Commander Masud is on his way to see us.'

'Good news. That would be wonderful.' Everyone was excited by the prospect of an imminent meeting.

The Parian commander's house was on the side of a hill overlooking the village, a neat conglomeration of mud-walled houses, honey-brown in colour, all with flat roofs and a few with simple balconies. The village was surrounded by fields of wheat and barley just turning from green to gold and one field of tall, dark green beans. Commander Najmuddin was a handsome man with a good voice and plenty to say for himself. He installed us in the end room of the house, reserved for visitors, with a carpet on the floor and cushions round the walls. It was clean and comfortable. Male friends or visitors would come in from time to time for a chat and a cup of tea, and as often as not food. We soon discovered that Najmuddin's wife was an excellent cook and she won our hearts the first morning by providing a large dish of chips for breakfast. Chips may be of minor culinary importance at home, but in Afghanistan they are the height of gastronomic luxury. But we were never able to thank the commander's wife for the huge meals of roast lamb, *kofta* (meat balls) and yoghurt she provided day after day, for we never met the good lady. As is the custom in Afghan villages, the women live apart in what is in effect the harem, and when they do venture out they are always veiled. They would never dream of speaking to a stranger, let alone an infidel.

The person who looked after us, bringing us our food and pots of tea, was a lad of about twenty, a nephew of the commander's and a near deaf-mute. His story, as told by his uncle, was a remarkable one.

'He was playing with some friends in Kabul when he was about nine or ten. They were kicking a ball about and one of them kicked it too hard and it went into a graveyard. My nephew went to retrieve it and as he ran into the graveyard, he saw a dead body lying on the ground.

'The ball had rolled right beside one of the corpse's hands and it seemed to him that he had actually to pull it away from the dead man's hand, almost wrench it away.

'That night he had a fever and a nightmare, and he dreamt that the dead man was chasing him and shouting at him, "Why did you come and disturb me? Why did you come and wake me from my sleep?"

'In the morning, the boy was dumb and after several days he still couldn't speak, so his parents took him to hospital. He was there a long time and it was only three years ago that he got his hearing back, but only partly, as you can see.

'You know, the extraordinary thing is that he was a very good Dashaka gunner, but I had to bring him home here because he was unreliable. Being so deaf, he couldn't hear the planes when they attacked, or the cannon and rocket fire. He cried when I took him away and he had to leave his Dashaka behind.'

There was an old single-barrelled gun hanging on the wall of the room and one day the boy took it down, speaking in the strange, jerky accents of the deaf.

'He's going out shooting pheasants,' Andy joked. A few minutes later there was a loud bang and the excited jabbering of the marksman. We went outside and found that he had killed a bird like a thrush or an oriole which until a few minutes before had been filling the copse below the house with joyful sounds. I was horrified at this wanton killing of such an innocent creature, but the boy was beside himself, holding the bird up for everyone to see.

That evening it was served up to Khalili as a first course, although its sad little naked body hardly produced more than a couple of mouthfuls. He generously offered to share round his delicacy but the rest of us tactfully declined.

During the day Khalili sent two more messages: one down the valley to the Panjsher commander, who maintained a radio link with Masud; the other by messenger to Takhar Province to the north, where Masud had been operating for some time. They said it would get to him by next morning, but I thought this was over-optimistic.

'Do you really think it will reach him by tomorrow?'

'*Inshallah.*'

I had been told that Masud had an efficient radio network and that sending messages to him and getting a reply would not be too difficult. But, as nearly always in these situations, not just in Afghanistan, what sounds eminently practical sitting in a comfortable chair in someone's house with a glass of whisky in one's hand turns out to be a very different proposition when put to the test in the wilds.

I was fascinated by the apparent contradiction in the situation in the Panjsher. Here was a valley that had undergone nine or ten major invasions in the past seven years. Each time, between ten and twenty thousand Soviet and Afghan troops, supported by hundreds of tanks and armoured personnel carriers, had swept its length and breadth, burning and looting. In the last couple of years, the Russians had actually bulldozed whole villages. They now occupied three bases at Anawa, Barah and Rokha at the bottom of the valley; while the Afghan army held three more at Tawakh, Rahman Khel and Pushghour. Yet neither the Russians nor the Afghans patrolled outside their bases and there was no attempt to pacify the local population. It was purely a holding operation. The *mujahideen* were able to move freely round the bases, which they attacked from time to time, as well as in the upper valley, where there was no Soviet or Afghan army presence, apart from aerial patrols.

We were woken by one: two MiGs, fully loaded with bombs and rockets, went over on a routine mission, flying up the valley from their base, probably Bagram. Twenty minutes later they were back again, flying low enough to make plenty of noise in what was obviously a show of strength.

One of Najmuddin's lunch guests was a former mayor of Parian. He said, despite the occupation of the lower valley, there were still eight to ten thousand families (40–50,000 people) in the Panjsher, as compared to 20,000 families (100,000 people) before the war. 'Many of them now live high up in side valleys or in the upper valley. In Parian alone there are 2,500 families, that's about 12,500 people. Many are refugees from the lower part of the valley and some are forced to live in caves.'

One day I had my beard trimmed by a refugee barber from Rokha, the main town of the Panjsher before it became a Russian base. He and his large family lived in a cave on the far side of the mountain facing Najmuddin's house. To do his rounds must have meant a daily walk of ten or fifteen miles. After clipping the straggliest bits of my beard he shaved my throat with a blade so blunt I cried out in pain. Looking hurt at what he took to be criticism of his professional skill, he asked Khalili what was wrong.

'Hasn't he got a sharper blade? That one is sheer agony.'

With a look that meant no Afghan would dream of complaining about such a trivial affair, he changed the old blade for one that was marginally newer. I gritted my teeth and endured the

torture in silence. His charge was 50 Afghanis (25 pence).
Khalili explained that he had a wider repertoire.

'He can do more than just cut beards, you know. He is
dentist too. He is vairy good at pulling teeth, this old man. And
he is surgeon, too. He can amputate legs and arms and do many
operations.'

'I think I'll just stick to a shave,' Andy said.

Over tea at the end of the meal, Khalili summed up the
situation. 'The commander says it is really a stalemate, mili-
tarily, in the Panjsher. But the real problem for us is the civilian
population. The bombing has made life extremely difficult for
them. If they all leave, then it becomes much more difficult for
the *mujahideen* to remain. Because if there are no civilians,
there is no food. Also if all the families go to Pakistan the
mujahideen worry about them, and how to feed them.

'The Russian tactic is to drive the civilians out and Masud's
is to keep them here. But that needs money. We badly need
humanitarian aid, that's to say, money for food, as well as, or
even more than, for Stingers and SAMs.'

These were pleasantly lazy days in which we were not
required to climb a mountain and I had time to read and listen
to my tapes: Chopin, part of Rossini's *La Cenerentola* and an
abbreviated version of *The Marriage of Figaro*. One afternoon,
after a delicious lunch of mutton with apricots, yoghurt and
spinach, prepared by Najmuddin's wife, we listened to a tape
recording of a *mujahid* singing about the last King of Afghanistan, Zaher Shah, who was deposed in 1973 by his cousin,
Daoud, and now lives in exile near Rome. It was in the form of
a folk song and Khalili translated it verbatim:

> 'You have none of your family fighting in Afghanistan,
> Only the brave are here, you are
> Enjoying life in Italy.
> Wind of the morning, go tell Zaher Shah
> There is no *halwa** for you in Afghanistan.
> The graves of your ancestors are here,
> But there will be no grave for you in Afghanistan.'

There was another song about the Afghan army.

---

* *halwa*: sweetmeat.

'Why do you not join the people?
Why do you help the enemy . . .?'

A bit later we had another visitor, a young Russian deserter from Moldavia, formerly part of Romania which the Russians annexed at the end of the Second World War. Khalili introduced him and we spoke in French, although his command of the language was somewhat erratic. His name was Leonid Volku, aged twenty-one, from the village of Shinoshika in the district of Chimishliya. His father was a shopkeeper and his mother the principal of the local school.

I asked how big the village was.

'We have eighty families in our village, that's about four hundred people. There is only one Communist. She has a car. When I was called up to do my military service, I was trained on Strela 10 missiles. They are very big and weigh between two and three tons. It has its own radar and lots of buttons to guide the missile to its target.'

'What's the point of having anti-aircraft missiles in Afghanistan when the *mujahideen* have no aeroplanes?'

Leonid laughed and turned the palms of his hands up in a very Latin gesture.

'How do you spend your time here?'

'I live with the *mujahideen*. I am now a Muslim, I work in the *qarargah* at Parian, a few miles farther down the valley, mainly in the kitchen.'

'What sort of service did you see in Afghanistan?'

'I was mostly at Bagram air force base. I was in hospital there and when I got better I worked for one of the Russian doctors. Two years ago in 1984, at the time of a big offensive against the Panjsher, Panjsher Seven, they brought a hundred and eight dead Soviet soldiers into the hospital morgue. I know the exact figure because I worked there. There were many wounded too. They flew them into Bagram from the Panjsher by helicopter.

'Later I was sent to the Salang' – on the main road from Kabul to the Soviet border, the scene of many ambushes. 'When they told me I would have to do the rest of my service there I decided to get out. So one day I walked out of the camp and met some *mujahideen* and they took me with them.

Eventually I came here to Parian.'

Leonid said he had made a couple of broadcasts for Radio Liberty and indicated he would like to do more. I also got the impression he would like to settle in the West. He struck me as being anxious and unsure of himself, by turns frank and suspicious. I felt sorry for him, cut off from his home and family.

'It's a big step you've taken. Presumably you can never go home.'

'I think maybe in a few years' time I can go home. I would like to see my family again, one day.'

I asked him if he knew of any Russian officers who had defected.

'Yes, there was one. He was quite young, a lieutenant. Masud liked him. I didn't trust him. He told me his plan was to get to Pakistan and then to go to the West. I know he was KGB. I'm sure he was sent to find out everything about Masud and then to go to Pakistan and from there he would have come back here.'

'How would he have done that?'

'Once he got to Pakistan, he would have gone to the Russian Embassy and asked for asylum.

'I think Masud became suspicious of him. He tried to escape once. They brought him back. He tried to run away again. The second time they shot him.'

It was now Saturday 26 July, our sixth day in the Panjsher, still with no word from Masud. At seven, two Russian MiGs flew up the valley, returning very high shortly afterwards. At nine, two more circled high over Parian and then went off in a leisurely way towards Chamar, black specks against the blue summer sky. Ten or fifteen minutes later they came back with a roar, heading down the valley to their base at Bagram or Kabul.

In the absence of anything more active to do, I finished reading Eric Newby's *A Traveller's Life*, which I enjoyed enormously, especially the descriptions of his cycle rides through France to Italy, punctuated by huge provincial meals washed down with litres of wine for less than one pound. I wrote out my interview questions for Masud again and even composed a bad verse about Parian:

Parian's fields ripen in the summer sun.
The wheat is still green, the barley half gold,
The village lies below, so peaceful, calm.
The jets roar by and the air is cold.

An old man with a spade walks through the wheat.
Gossamer seeds drift by on the light breeze.
Parian means 'fairies', but I think the jets
Have frightened them away, over the hills.

I thought of various ways of spending a perfect day. In this
dry, mountain landscape, the idea of a swim in the Mediter-
ranean was immensely attractive: perhaps in Hydra, along the
rocky coast from Kamini to Vlichos, where there are a couple
of delightful *tavernas*.

Or a day in the south of France, staying at a friend's house
near Grasse; going to the sea for a swim and then having lunch
at some small restaurant on the way back: lots of *fritures de
poissons* and fresh fruit, accompanied by copious draughts of
white wine, something like the Provençal *'blanc'* they used to
serve in jugs in L'Aterbéa in Saigon, pretending it was tea or
lemonade to avoid customs duty.

I looked at my watch and realised it was nearly twelve o'clock
on this sunny, very slow-moving and boring Saturday. God, I
thought, I could do with a drink. After some thought I decided
a glass of champagne would be best, if only because it was not
hot enough for a gin and tonic.

The next day, Sunday, the long-awaited message from
Masud arrived. Khalili read it hungrily and then translated.

'Commander says he has twice been on the way to the
Panjsher to meet us and twice has had to turn back because he
had information that a big offensive was about to start in
Takhar. He asks us to send our whole programme to him as
soon as possible so that he can make all the arrangements.'

I thought the request for our programme strange, but I
merely said, 'Our programme is to get to him as quickly as
possible and interview him. Once we talk to him we can work
out what else we can do.'

Khalili knodded. I had discussed this many times on the way
with Andy and himself. Our original plan had been for Andy
and me to make the documentary on Masud, with Khalili

coming with us as escort and interpreter. But Central had suggested we should take Noel with us: he was not only an experienced documentary cameraman, but extremely anxious to come. Andy, it was agreed, would concentrate on the battle photography. We had discussed at great length how we would ensure we had action footage in the film. In a guerrilla war with few set-piece battles, this is always difficult to guarantee, especially if time is limited. Accordingly, Andy had proposed that as soon as we reached Masud and had interviewed him, he and Khalili would leave us and head for either the Salang Road, where he was virtually sure of being able to film an ambush – he had done so with spectacular success three times before – or to some other target selected by Masud. My response had invariably been that while as a general plan I did not disagree, the final decision must wait until we had talked to Masud.

Najmuddin went off to find horsemen for our journey north (Abdi and Azimullah were said to be not available) and when they arrived, one of them pointed to me and said, 'I took him to Chitral four years ago.'

I looked hard at him. 'It can't be Rahman. It must be Noor.'

He beamed happily. 'Yes, it is Noor.' I felt I had just been reunited with an old and valued friend. Once the horses were loaded, Najmuddin led us at a smart pace down to the *qarargah*, where we had tea with Leonid hovering in the background.

An argument developed about our route, the full implications of which only became clear later. One man was especially vehement, saying we must go by the mountain behind the *qarargah* rather than by the more direct route down the valley to a place called Do Ab (Two Rivers: there must be a thousand Do Abs in Afghanistan). Possibly the reason we were so unceremoniously hustled off, after so many days waiting, was that at 8.30 that morning two MiG 23s had flown over and bombed, it was thought, Chamar Pass. They were big explosions – echoing heavily in the still air – possibly 1,000-kilo bombs.

It was now midday and very hot and we sweated as we climbed a series of grassy slopes beside a small clear stream. After an hour we stopped for a rest and another argument developed about the route.

Andy questioned the advice we had been given, arguing that

it would have been better to continue down the valley to Do Ab before turning north to Khawak Pass.

What irritated me more than the futility of the argument was that we now discovered Khalili had not sent a reply to Masud's message, although it had called for a swift response.

'I thought you sent a message this morning, before we left the commander's house?' I said. Khalili made no answer. I was really more surprised than irritated, because I knew Masud's discipline was strict and not to reply to his message seemed a strange lapse. We started climbing again, stopping after another hour or so at a Kuchi tent. Kuchis are nomads and, unlike other Afghans, their women go mostly unveiled. There were two small children and three women in the tent, one older and two about twenty. The prettier one half drew her veil across her mouth when she saw us watching her. The man invited us to sit down and have some food which we declined, but accepted tea. A long-tailed sheep and a calf shared a manger made of branches in one corner and a fire burned smokily in the middle of the tent.

The man, darkly handsome in a blue coat and aged about forty, told us that the Kuchis were no longer able to follow their traditional pattern of migration, which used to take them all over the country and into Pakistan and Iran with little heed for national borders.

'The Russians bomb us, when they see us moving with our flocks of camels and goats. Many people have been killed. Now we move only short distances. Life is very difficult now, many people have been killed.'

As if to emphasise his point, the sudden roar of two jets made the women gather up the children in their arms. The MiGs flew down the Panjsher, at about the same altitude as ourselves, probably returning to base after another strike, perhaps on Chamar or farther north, in Takhar.

CHAPTER TWELVE

The argument about the route had upset Khalili and in the heat and exertion of the climb his mood grew blacker. By the end of the day, he was hardly speaking to us. He evidently resented us having doubted his judgement and was probably hurt that his friend Andy had disagreed with him. I resented being made to walk in a huge loop unnecessarily, as I thought, and blamed this piece of apparent incompetence on Commander Najmuddin, much as I admired his wife's cooking and his powers as a *raconteur*.

As we slogged up to the top of the pass at 14,000 feet, having started at 9,000 or 10,000 feet in Parian, I recalled Najmuddin's tale of the last stand of Abdul Wahid, one of Masud's commanders who, when I first met him in 1982, had just lost a foot clearing Russian mines. He had come to England and my friend Peers Carter, formerly British Ambassador in Kabul, and I had paid for him to have a new foot fitted at Roehampton. He spent several months in London with another *mujahid* called Abdul Azim, who had lost an arm, and we became good friends. Abdul Wahid was a fine-looking man, tall and dignified, and he stole the show when he appeared on 'This is Your Life' in 1983. Eamonn Andrews's peroration went, 'In 1982, Sandy Gall went to Afghanistan to make a documentary about the war. While he was there he met Abdul Wahid, who had lost a foot in the fighting. He arranged for him to be brought to Roehampton Hospital and have a new foot made. And tonight, to say thank you in person, we have flown Abdul Wahid ...' The stage doors opened and in walked Abdul Wahid, looking bemused. As the applause mounted, he walked towards me and embraced me three times, Afghan fashion, shook my hand and said, 'Thank you.' It was an emotional moment for both of us and the climax of the show.

I knew that in 1984, after his return home, he had been captured by the Russians and taken to Kabul where he had been tortured and made to denounce Masud and his former comrades. It must have been a bitter experience. He was also paraded before Western television cameras, appearing in a farcical propaganda film shown on Channel 4 called 'Kabul Autumn'. In it, he was obliged to say that he no longer supported the cause of the *mujahideen*. I squirmed for him as I watched. He looked haggard and exhausted and it was quite plain to me he did not believe a word he was saying.

The story of Abdul Wahid's capture is worthy of an epic poem and I hoped that perhaps one day Khalili *père* would write it. I only have my notes of his son's running translation of Najmuddin's account.

After he came back from England Abdul Wahid was anxious to take up the *Jihad* again and he carried out a number of successful actions. He proved he could fight as well as ever with his new leg.

One day he was in Parende [a side valley] in a cave when the Russians found out where he was. They had been looking for him ever since he came back. Abdul Wahid had eight *mujahideen* with him. The Russians tried to force them out of the cave. First they brought a helicopter and fired rockets. Then they brought up a Dashaka or a Zigoyak and fired round after round at the cave, but still they couldn't dislodge the brave defenders. Then the Russians tried to lower some of their men by a rope from the top of the cliff, but they shot them and they fell to the ground. Abdul Wahid and his men fought with grenades and Kalashnikovs and a pistol. They fought for two days until they ran out of ammuniton. The Russians called on them to surrender, saying that they would not be harmed if they gave themselves up. Otherwise the Russians said they would storm the cave and kill them all. So they surrendered one by one: Abdul Wahid was the last to give himself up.

The Russians made them line up at the foot of the cliff below the cave. Suddenly without warning three of the *mujahideen* ran to the edge of the cliff and jumped to their deaths in the river below. They tied up the rest of them, but that night two more of the *mujahideen* escaped, despite having their hands tied. One of them left his boots at the edge of the river and next day the Russians found them and thought he had committed suicide too.

They took away Abdul Wahid's leg so that he couldn't escape and he and the other three were taken to Bagram and then flown to Kabul where they were tried. Abdul Wahid was sentenced to twenty years' imprisonment and the others to nineteen and eighteen years respectively. Abdul Wahid and the others fought heroically, but when their ammunition ran out, there was nothing they could do.

After the pass we walked all afternoon and evening, for mile after mile. At one point, where the track led across emerald-green meadows, we saw a number of exploded 'butterfly' mines, small, plastic anti-personnel devices which are designed to blow off a hand or foot and have caused numerous casualties in Afghanistan, especially to children. I imagine that someone had collected a number of them and detonated them here. We passed two totally deserted villages and finally, at around eight o'clock when it was getting dark, we stumbled into a third. This was deserted too, except for a *qarargah* in a dilapidated house. The village had been heavily bombed two years before and the *mujahideen* were the only people left.

I lay on the floor until they brought in some unappetising-looking rice which Noel and I only picked at. Andy and Khalili, being made of sterner stuff, ate determinedly, obeying Andy's maxim: 'It may taste bloody awful, but you have to eat the stuff to keep your strength up.'

Khalili had gone very quiet and the atmosphere was chilly. Suddenly he said to me, 'You'll go down to Do Ab tomorrow?'

'Oh, is that the plan?'

'That's your choice.'

'What are you going to do?'

'I shall go on to Khost and hope to meet Masud by tomorrow night.'

I thought it was unwise for us to split up, but Andy and I both felt strongly we must send a message to Masud as soon as possible, and that could best be done by radio from the Panjsher. There is usually a point at which the arrangements break down on this kind of expedition and that point had been clearly reached. It was also plain that Khalili was determined to go his own way. I wondered if we should see him again. 'You will send the message to Masud? Saying that our first priority is to see him, our second to film a military operation and our third to film refugees?'

'Of course. I will send it tomorrow morning and I will try and reach Masud himself in Khost tomorrow night, *Insh-allah*.'

Noel and I went to sleep outside on a flat roof, not fancying the flea-ridden aspect of the *qarargah*, which was in any case overflowing with recumbent *mujahideen*. We were up early and left on empty stomachs at five: Andy said Khalili had departed at about two. As we marched down to Do Ab in the half-light, a couple of jets roared overhead, going north. Noel, who was some way behind, reported that he heard them drop one bomb. We hoped it was not on the pass Khalili was making for. In the soft light of morning, the mountains had the gentle texture of a watercolour but farther down the valley became steeper and just above Do Ab, as he was crossing a patch of scree, Noel was hit on the knee by a falling stone. Andy and I were a few hundred yards ahead and did not see it, but when Noel limped in to the *chaikhana* where we were sitting half an hour later, he said he had glanced up the slope in time to see a rock, possibly dislodged by a goat, come spinning down towards him. He tried to dodge it but misjudged the distance and it struck him full on his bad knee.

'It hit me so hard I thought my leg was broken. I collapsed beside the path. It was so painful I came out in a muck sweat. I had to sit there for twenty minutes before I could go on.'

Noel already had a damaged cartilage in that knee and on the journey in had found walking downhill painful. Andy and I were worried that he was going to be unable to continue. We had three horses – Khalili had taken one, with my old friend Noor – but they were just enough to carry our equipment. If Noel did not recover, we would have to get another horse.

After tea and sweet, hard biscuits, Andy said, 'We'll go to the Do Ab commander's house. He's a nice bloke and we can stay with him for a couple of days, until we get a reply from Masud.'

The commander was not at home, but while we were waiting for him our horsemen arrived and said Khalili had told them we should advance them 5,000 Afghanis (£25) for food for the horses. Khalili had agreed a price of 30,000 Afghanis (£150) for the trip to Khost, which had seemed a lot to me at the time, and this demand so early in the trip seemed exorbitant. However, in the absence of Khalili or any other escort, we were on the point of paying up when Commander Khalilullah arrived. He immediately took charge and after reading Khalili's letter, which he had given to our horsemen, told them, 'No, give the money back. You'll get paid when Khalili returns.'

After some argument they accepted reluctantly, but we were to have constant trouble with them about money. The two older men would, I think, have been manageable on their own, but the youngest seemed always to be egging them on to demand more money.

Andy now came into his own as *chef d'équipe*. Since he was the only one of us who spoke Farsi he had to deal with Khalilullah and the horsemen, and without his determination we might never have reached Masud.

While Andy and Noel slept, I read Eric Newby's *Slowly Down the Ganges* – thank God for Eric Newby! – which I enjoyed not least because his trip, in its different way, seemed just as ghastly as ours. Newby's boat kept grounding and had to be manhandled through the shallows by him and his recalcitrant boatmen, who kept changing, usually for the worse. If for boat you read horses, for boatmen, horsemen, and for shallows, mountains, our fates seemed identical.

In the afternoon, with nothing to do, I counted my money like a miser. We had only 65,000 Afghanis (£325) left, which seemed alarmingly little, since we were paying the horsemen 30,000, almost half, one way to Masud. Andy was very reassuring.

'Don't worry, Sandy, when we get to Masud he'll lend us as much as we need. You can always pay him back in Chitral.'

I knew this was good advice but I remembered how short of money we had run last time. Not surprisingly, the war had caused a high rate of inflation; food was three or four times as expensive and the cost of horses had at least trebled since 1982.

In the evening the horsemen returned, wanting more money to buy barley for the horses. They also brought a radio message from Masud which had been forwarded from Safed Shir. This said, 'Come to Khost immediately.'

'I think we should leave tomorrow at four in the afternoon,'

Andy said. 'That will give Noel most of the day to rest and it will be cool by then. We'll be at the *qarargah* at Chowni by seven or eight and cross the pass in the dark. Just in case there's any bombing.'

Commander Khalilullah agreed, but the horsemen wanted to leave at one in the morning, thus ensuring, as Andy pointed out, that we would be crossing the pass in broad daylight. Finally they were persuaded to accept Andy's plan, and as a sweetener I paid them 900 Afghanis to buy food for the horses for two days.

In the morning Andy and I went shopping with the commander. Do Ab consists of a number of stone houses built against the rockface, which gave them some protection from bombing. A wooden bridge spanned the river which foamed below the half-dozen shops, all apparently selling the same things. The one the commander took us to stocked cloth from Japan, Russia, India and Pakistan, which had either been taken from an ambushed convoy or acquired in a more conventional manner in Kabul. Thus, despite the Russian occupation, trade persists and flourishes even in the Panjsher.

Andy and I bought a *kala*, a local suit, each consisting of baggy trousers (*tumla*) and shirt (*peran*). The shopkeeper said they were made in Kabul of wool and they were certainly warm. He and his friends, who sat in the shop drinking tea, were all from Dasht-i-Raiwat, the emerald centre of the Panjsher. They all seemed to be emerald merchants and did not take much persuasion to produce a few samples. Most of the stones were quite small, almost chips, but the shopkeeper displayed his gold ring, containing an emerald the size of a pea.

'Do you know how much it's worth?'

'No idea, but I'm sure a lot.'

'Guess.'

'I can't.'

'For this I pay one and a half million Afghanis (£7,500).'

I thought the stone had a big flaw, but said nothing. Some of the emerald men are reputed to be very rich, as are the 'blue men' who deal in lapis.

Fortunately Noel's knee, which Andy had bandaged, was much better and he was able to walk to the Chowni *qarargah* in a brisk two and a half hours. The horsemen, who had grumbled at having to stay in Do Ab, saying there was nothing for their horses to eat there, were still loading up with maddening slowness as we left the village.

At the *qarargah*, we dined off some unspeakable goat and started off, the horses in front, just after ten. There was no moon, only starshine and the light of our torches, and before long doubts about the skill of our guides began to grow. At this point the young horseman took over, saying he knew the way, and we followed him blindly for another hour until it began to dawn on us that he was as incompetent as he was unpleasant.

The older men rounded on him, cursing him with real anger until he was practically in tears. I felt almost sorry for him. It was now midnight and we were completely lost halfway up a large mountain. We blundered on in the dark, until the furious barking of a dog told us a Kuchi tent was somewhere near. Eventually the owner appeared, remarkably civil for a man made to get out of his bed at two in the morning.

I was exhausted and declared to anyone who cared to listen, 'Why don't we stay here for a few hours and go on when it's light?'

Andy was listening to the four-way conversation that was taking place in the darkness against the continued barking of the dog.

'The Kuchi says we can't stay here, Sandy. He says they may bomb in the morning, so it's better if we go on.'

My heart sank, like a schoolboy who's told he has to do another hour's prep, and although I did not believe what the man said about bombing, I was in no position to contradict him. (My instinct was right: when we reached Khost they said Khawak had not been bombed for a long time.) I suspect the Kuchi simply wanted to get rid of us, thinking that if we were spotted from the air near his tent, he and his family would be bombed too.

The Kuchi came with us for a short distance to make sure we were on the right path and then wished us Godspeed. Reluctantly we returned to the task of ascending this hateful mountain; I do not think I have ever loathed a mountain as much as Khawak. Every time we breasted what we hoped was the *kotal* (pass) it turned out to be a false crest, a disappointment that is familiar to everyone who climbs mountains, but no less frustrating for that. The fifth or sixth time this happened I nearly cried with exhaustion and frustration. Noel kept plodding along with admirable tenacity and Andy tried to encourage both of us by repeating, 'It can't be much farther, we must be nearly at the top.'

But Noel and I were less of a liability than the wretched horsemen. They were moving more and more slowly, as if in a dream, and Andy kept swearing at them to drive them on.

'Come on, you bloody bastards, move. *Birra, birra ...*' When the rough edge of his tongue failed to produce the desired effect, either in English or in Farsi, Andy raised his fist to the recalcitrant trio.

'You see this, you lazy sods. If you don't get a move on, I'll give you a right good thumping.'

On the top of the mountain, in the half-light, with his blue eyes snapping, Andy was a formidable sight. But the horsemen seemed to have fallen under a spell. As the climb grew steeper, one man, the only one who wore a turban, lay down on the ground when his horse stopped, closed his eyes and started to fall asleep. Exhausted as I was, I stood behind him, shouting, '*Birra, birra!* Come on, get up!'

He opened his eyes, yawned, hauled himself slowly to his feet and even more slowly climbed after his horse. The horse stopped again ten yards higher up. Turban lay down again, closed his eyes and drifted off.

'*Birra, birra!*' I shouted, anger overcoming exhaustion, and he sat up as if he had been kicked. Slowly Andy and I drove this motley crew to the top of the pass, but such was their sloth that we did not reach the *kotal* until half past four, well after first light. We were thus at the most vulnerable point of our journey, on the summit of the pass, at dawn, a favourite time for the Russians to make an air strike. Despite this, the horsemen insisted on stopping at the top for a rest, so we pushed on down as fast as Noel could walk. The northern slope had much more snow and we found ourselves in the middle of a huge amphitheatre of naked rock streaked with snow, an extremely forbidding place at five in the morning. But amazingly, only a few hundred yards below the pass, we came on some tiny yellow flowers, then a scattering of dwarf buttercups and finally, farther down, a tiny blue flower growing on little green mats. I pulled a few to study them and they looked like miniature sweet peas. Crossing a patch of snow, I noticed the footprints of a wild cat, and flocks of small birds with white flashes on their wings rose in the air as we approached. The last stretch of the mountain consisted of a series of rocky steps and then we were down on the flat.

After a few more miles, the valley widened and we came to a big Kuchi encampment. Noel and I, feeling extremely foot-sore, took off our boots and bathed our feet in an ice-cold streamlet while an old man with a beautiful face and manners to match came to meet us with a pot of tea and a bowl of *dugh*. As we sat there, a *mujahid* arrived bearing a message from Khalili dated the previous day. It read:

> Khost,
> Larwan.
> 29 July 1986
>
> Dear Sandy,
> Everything is all right, Jan Mohammed was waiting for us. Commander himself is anxiously waiting to see us. I am on the way to see him. I got his written message that since 8 days he was waiting to see me. You can come with Allah Mohammed. After 16 hours you will reach Commander Gadda's house in Larwan.
> Hi to Andy and Noel.
>
> Masud Khalili.
> The way for the horse is not good. Reduce your film if you can. Otherwise get two horses for your film. Don't load them on one horse. Come directly to Commander Gadda's house. If other thing I want to tell I will send it through radio.
> All the best.

We had been walking for twelve hours and it was all I could do to cover another couple of miles to the next *chaikhana*. I managed it by putting my mind in neutral and letting my legs function like automata. Even my back was sore, although I was not carrying anything. The ebullient *chaikhana* owner, a Panjsheri who knew Andy, showed us to a bothy and brought us tea.

Through the open door I noticed two small birds, smaller than a hedge sparrow, with bright red caps on their heads, like a firecrest. The valley here was wide and beautiful, although uncultivated, and the road was busy with dozens of horsemen and donkey drivers moving south to pick up arms in Pakistan.

The over-friendly *chaikhana* owner proved to be a robber, and I was cross that the young *mujahid* Khalili sent to accompany us, Allah Mohammed, allowed us to be charged 2,300 Afghanis (£12) for our overnight stay.

The road to Khost was lined with blue cornflowers and tall flowers with dark pink trumpets, and the fields were alive with birds: linnets with handsome red chests, wheatears, which are everywhere in Afghanistan, and what looked like greenfinches. A large group of Panjsheri refugees were living in huts like African *rondavels*, built of grass and reeds. We reached the village of Darra Deh in two and a half hours and nearly missed the man who was waiting for us: the fabled Jan Mohammed of whom Andy had spoken so much.

We were just about to leave the village when a mullah saluted us and invited us to his house for tea. It turned out to be a school and the room which we were ushered into was soon filled with about twenty young student mullahs, who sat and watched us politely and smiled when I produced my camera and took their photograph.

While we were having tea, a big man smiling broadly erupted into the room and threw his arms round Andy, embracing him like a brother. This was Jan Mohammed, the former licensee of the National Hotel in Kabul and Masud's friend and quartermaster. He pretended to be upset.

'Why you take so many days to reach here? I, Jan Mohammed, wait here many, many days. Too much days I wait here.' His grin belied any real anger, but the student mullahs, watching with fascination, were not entirely sure.

'Why did you not give this idiot Allah Mohammed proper instructions? We nearly went on. He didn't know where you were.' Andy pretended to be equally cross.

Jan Mohammed clicked his tongue in annoyance. 'You blame Jan Mohammed, I teach you big lesson.' He raised his fist and Andy made as if to strike back. The head mullah, an elderly man who had sat aloof at the end of the room, looked faintly disturbed while the young mullahs goggled in disbelief.

'Come on,' Jan Mohammed said. 'We go to my house now.'

Jan Mohammed, who was staying in a house belonging to a Panjsheri, told the horsemen to unload our gear and take themselves off. When we told him about their performance on Khawak Pass, he was shocked.

'These horsemen very bad men. Why Khalili not stay with you?' He clicked his tongue disapprovingly.

Andy unpacked one of his bags and presented Jan Mohammed with a small black case. With the concentrated excitement of a child, Jan Mohammed opened it and took out a large shiny Seiko chronometer, its big diving rings glowing luminously in the dark room. We all exclaimed in admiration.

A beautiful smile spread over Jan Mohammed's honest features but for once he was lost for words. 'Andy,' was all he could say, 'Andy.' Then, not knowing what else to do, he rose and embraced him with a ferocious hug.

Despite his happy exterior, Jan Mohammed's story was a grim one, typical of hundreds of thousands, perhaps millions of Afghans. His family came from the village of Sangana, in the Panjsher. I told him I knew Sangana. 'I stayed there for several days in 1982, when Masud was there. We spent several days together. It was a lovely village.'

'Yes, it was a lovely village. We had a house there, with a beautiful garden, full of grapes. Very good grapes.' I remembered that the grapes had been at their best that September.

'Well, there are no more grapes in Sangana. You know what the Russians did to Sangana?'

'No.'

'They bulldozed it. Two years ago, after the big offensive, they came with their tanks and knocked down all the houses. They bulldozed them until nothing was left. No houses, no gardens. Nothing.

'They took my father and poured petrol over him and set him on fire. They burned him to death. Four of my brothers have also been killed, fighting the Russians. Another brother is in prison, in Kabul. Ah, they very bad people these Russians. Very bad people.'

Jan Mohammed had brought another message from Khalili. It said:

Garmaba,
Khost.
29 July

Dear Sandy,

Salam, Monda Nabashi [Peace, may you not be tired].

I told everything to Jan Mohammed. He knows what to do. I am going to reach that MAN, Inshallah. Up to now everything is superb. Commander is waiting for us. I think he will give us more than three days to be with him. He has instructed everyone on the way. I am sure Jan Mohammed with his perfect English will be a great help to you.

Best for you, Andy and Noel.

Regards
Masud Khalili

Andy teased Jan Mohammed. 'I didn't know you spoke perfect English, Jan Mohammed. Where did you learn your perfect English?'

'You shut up, you . . . Andy bastard. My English maybe not very good, so now we speak only Farsi.'

After tea and raisins, the horses were loaded up and we started down the valley, Jan Mohammed setting a cracking '*mujahideen*' pace between the clumps of tall white hollyhocks and banks of sweet-smelling wild lavender that bordered the wheatfields. At one point, where the track ran along the bank of the river, a strong smell of decomposing flesh made us hold our breath and hurry on: the corpses of several donkeys and horses, the victims of a recent Russian air raid, lay scattered on the stones. We passed more Panjsheri refugee families as well as a steady procession of horses and donkeys loaded with supplies, heading for the Panjsher. In the early evening we turned off the road and climbed a path to a big new house set in walnut trees among fields of wheat. This was Commander Gadda's house where we were to stay the night.

CHAPTER THIRTEEN

Commander Gadda was not at home, being away with Masud, but we had the run of his house, which had two attractive features: a balcony shaded by a huge walnut tree, and off one end of it a small bathroom, a rare luxury in Afghanistan. In our two months' journey it was the only one we were lucky enough to come across. Before supper, the former licensee of the National Hotel ('Very nice hotel, in Chickeny Street, in bazaar') stoked the boiler until the small, wood-panelled room was as hot as a sauna. We took it in turns to bath before supper. It was a wonderful relief to wash away all the dirt and sweat with soap and hot water, despite the awkwardness of the operation: you had to hold a tinful of hot water above your head and let it splash over your body on to the wooden floor. The whole experience qualified as one of the preliminary stages of Paradise and I came out feeling refreshed in body and spirit, almost self-righteous in my clean new suit from Do Ab. We slept on the balcony, listening to the stamping of a fine grey stallion immediately underneath. This was Masud's personal charger, and, according to Jan Mohammed, so fast it could outrun a jeep.

The sun was still behind the mountains at five the next morning when we left, the colours of the landscape unusually soft, like a pastel drawing. Men were already winnowing the wheat on the threshing floor below the house and farther down the valley they were harvesting and bringing in the sheaves piled high on their backs. Muscle power is the basis of farming in Afghanistan, whether human or animal. Passing two men on a threshing floor, I tried to describe to them through Jan Mohammed how at home the whole process would be done by a machine. Although I do not know if the concept of combine harvester got across, they grasped the general idea with less difficulty and disbelief than I would have expected, although their laughs meant they knew such things were a million light-years away from their own experience. Apart from anything else, most fields in Afghanistan are so small and stony

117

that even the simplest mechanisation would be difficult. On the other hand, the marvels of modern technology are no secret to even the simplest Afghan peasant, since he sees them daily in the shape of Soviet high-performance jets and helicopter gunships.

Soon the valley widened, with large honey-brown *q'alas* (farmhouses) standing among clumps of walnut trees, their dark green foliage making pools of deep shade. The whole impression was one of peace and plenty, almost 'a land flowing with milk and honey'.

There was a sense of spaciousness which I had never seen in Afghanistan before and also a sort of brooding calm which made me think of the secret world of the Mekong Delta, with its endless rice paddies. In the Mekong, with the Americans, I always felt alien. Here at least we were not outsiders.

Jan Mohammed said one of Masud's captured jeeps would meet us at the next village, another Do Ab, so we arrived with high hopes just as the Friday market was getting into its stride. Jan Mohammed was anxious we should not be exposed unnecessarily.

'Many spies in Do Ab. Plenty bad people. We go quickly.'

He hurried us past a string of little stalls to a walled meadow surrounded by poplars, pausing only to order breakfast. The owner of the meadow, a courteous old man, dispatched his son with a *kilim* and a quilt for us to sit on. Shortly afterwards a large, smiling stall-keeper and two boys arrived bearing tray-fuls of food. They spread before us, like an emperor's feast, several melons, lamb kebab on skewers hot from the grill, small, round *nan*, spring onions, whole cucumbers, apples and lots of tea.

We were reclining happily, digesting this delicious meal, when two Russian jets made an ill-timed appearance, causing Jan Mohammed to jump up agitatedly and hurry us away. He was taking no chances that we reached Masud in one piece.

'What happened to the jeep?' Andy asked.

'It came at six o'clock, waited for one hour and then went away again.'

Jan Mohammed decided we should get clear of Do Ab just in case the Russians, knowing it was bazaar day, chose to bomb it. He led us to the outskirts and then disappeared briefly on some errand. While we were waiting, a *mujahid* presented me with a small round fruit indicating by sign language that I should sniff it. I did and it smelt like a melon, although it looked like a rubber ball, was the colour of a ripe peach and was apparently inedible. Khalili told me later it was called an 'Istanbul', or alternatively, 'The smell that comes from handling', and 'the melon of the father of the stupid'. The more you handle it, the stronger it smells.

After Jan Mohammed's return we crossed the bridge to the north of the town, meeting a stream of men on horses and donkeys going to the bazaar, and walked for a couple of hours until midday. The heat being intense, we stopped under some trees and Jan Mohammed went off in search of tea.

After only a couple of days I was much impressed by Jan Mohammed. He was the perfect fixer, guide, diplomat and friend.

'He's a wonderful chap, thank God we've got him to arrange things, Andy.'

'He makes the best chips in Afghanistan. Wait until you taste those.'

'Can't wait,' said Noel. 'Fish 'n' chips'd go down a treat.'

Jan Mohammed came back with a smile. 'This man who lives here is miller, yes? He very good man. In five minutes bring tea. Good, yes?'

'Five minutes?' Andy pretended to grumble. 'Why so bloody slow, Jan Mohammed?'

'You bloody Andy. No tea for Andy. Tea for Sandy and Noel. No tea for Andy. You bloody man.' Jan Mohammed grinned and cast a surreptitious glance at his new Seiko. He was inordinately proud of it and kept touching it and showing it off to all his friends.

A flash of yellow in the tops of the trees above us caught my attention and I watched until one of the birds, the size of a big thrush, made a rapid sortie from one tree to another, revealing itself as that most gorgeous of creatures, a golden oriole. Earlier, a hoopoe had swooped across the road, its barred cinnamon and cream plumage and striped crest making it look like an escapee from some exotic garden.

These small pleasures were interrupted by another row with the horsemen, whom, now that the jeep was expected, we were

119

anxious to be rid of. After doing my sums, I calculated that I owed them 27,600 Afghanis, being the balance of the original 30,000 agreed by Khalili and Commander Najmuddin, after deducting advances.

They complained bitterly, apparently arguing that they should get 30,000 clear, as well as expenses.

'Jan Mohammed, please tell them that they can take it or leave it. If they don't like it they can go and argue the toss with Khalili.'

'I tell them this already. These men too expensive. Thirty thousand too much.'

'Well, that's what we think. Also, they have been extremely bad horsemen, they were a disgrace on Khawak and they won't get another penny out of me.'

While this was going on, the jeep had gone past in the direction of Do Ab but it now reappeared, heading towards us with about twenty people clinging to it like flies. It stopped below us and Jan Mohammed ordered everyone to get off. The horsemen brought our bags in a last surly act and we stowed them and ourselves aboard.

The jeep, which was riddled with shrapnel and bullet holes, had been captured in Kunduz. The driver was a splendid character called Gul Ahmed, who with his rugged features and spade beard looked exactly like Asterix the Gaul. He was Masud's driver and we remembered one another from the Panjsher four years before.

'Khenj,' he said, 'I remember you at Khenj.' I remembered him too and we shook hands.

He and the mechanic, Jan Mohammed and a turbaned mullah got into the front and we squeezed into the back. As we drove off I was overcome with a ridiculous sense of pleasure and superiority. After walking and riding for more than three weeks over some of the roughest country in the world, it seemed nothing short of miraculous to sit in a self-propelled vehicle and be conveyed like a lord along a relatively smooth road in well-sprung comfort. It pleased me greatly to see horses and donkeys take fright and go skittering across the road as we approached; the same reaction that greeted the first cars on our roads at the turn of the century.

The country was flat and barren, almost like a desert, but it was a remarkably smooth and enjoyable ride, as if we were going on a picnic. This impression was heightened when we stopped at a *chaikhana* beside the river, complete with samovar and carpets spread under the trees. We ate succulent white melon (I could see why Persian poets compare the breasts of their lovers to ripe melons), tomatoes, cucumber, cheese, *nan* and tea, most of it provided by Jan Mohammed. Afterwards, the mullah led the *mujahideen* in prayer, and then we climbed into the jeep and drove away.

I found travelling across this empty landscape exhilarating, not only because of the wonderful comfort and ease of our progress, but because I kept thinking that at any moment a Russian jet could come hurtling over the mountains and shoot us up. But the sky remained empty, except for two large lammergeiers spiralling slowly on stiff wings high above us. However, a few miles farther on, as we drove deeper and deeper into the mountains, we passed an overhanging rock face. Asterix pointed and said something to Jan Mohammed, who turned to explain.

'You see that rock. Gul Ahmed sometime hide the jeep there. One day some Russian jits fly over, they see the jeep and they shoot racket. Look! Look! You see?'

There, clearly visible, like sledgehammer blows on the rock, were the marks where the rockets had struck, harmlessly as it turned out.

The valley grew steadily narrower and finally the road petered out at the foot of a cliff. Thinly camouflaged among a few straggly trees was a second jeep. Fifty yards beyond, a narrow opening, tunnelled into the side of the mountain, led to an ammunition dump. Alongside, in a sort of lean-to, we found Khalili and the local commander. Khalili got up to greet us, all smiles.

'You had a good trip? You got my letters? Good. Good. Sit down and rest, you must be tired.'

'Any *chai*?' Andy asked. 'We're thirsty.'

'Yes. I will ask one of these boys to bring it.'

Half an hour later, while we were having our tea, four jets came over and circled the base. They made one or two dummy runs, dropping anti-missile flares; it looked as if they were going to start bombing, but after ten minutes or so to everyone's surprise they flew off. The commander, a doctor called Abdul Rahman, said the base had been heavily bombed a month ago, but the ammunition dump, being right in the heart of the mountain, was untouched.

That evening Jan Mohammed excelled himself, providing a large plateful of fish and chips for dinner. The fish were trout, straight out of the river, crisply fried and eaten whole with the fingers. I think it was the best meal I have ever eaten.

The doctor commander said we were still a day and a half's march from Masud and so next morning, after a plate of porridge cooked by Jan Mohammed, the equipment was loaded on to donkeys and we set off on foot. The donkeyman said that jets had bombed another *qarargah* farther up the mountain the day before, probably the same ones that had circled over us. To save a three-hour detour by the bridge, the commander suggested we ford the river about half a mile downstream. As I watched the two *mujahideen* who acted as guinea pigs being almost swept away, I was not sure this was a particularly good idea. But the decision was taken out of my hands.

'Come, Sandy Gol,' Jan Mohammed ordered. 'You come with Jan Mohammed, we go first.'

Linking arms like Greek dancers, trousers tucked up and carrying our boots round our necks, we entered the water. It was icy cold but there was no time to think about that. Halfway over, it suddenly became a foot deeper and the current much stronger and if it had not been for Jan Mohammed's brawny arm, I am sure I would have fallen. The rocks were extremely slippery and I staggered about like a drunk, desperately trying to keep my footing. What worried me was that I would bring down Jan Mohammed to whom I had entrusted my camera, but he got us both safely across and I was able to stand rather smugly on the bank watching the antics of the others. A *mujahid*, whose feet must have been like leather, waded back again and brought over Khalili, Andy and Noel, all hanging on to one another like a chorus line. We climbed a steep hill above the river and turned up a narrow valley, coming after an hour or so to a small village where most of the houses had been burnt.

'You see this house and this house. Look, all houses burnt.

Russian commandos come here by helicopter looking for Masud. When they not find, they burn whole village.

'Last winter Masud give training courses here. Seven hundred commanders and group commanders come from all over the north; from Badakhshan, Kunduz, Baghlan.'

We stopped at what had been his headquarters, a small stone-built house with a miniature parade ground in front of it. Opposite, on the other side of the stream was the entrance to a cave, and when a little later the jets appeared, high over the valley where we had spent the night, we all moved closer to the cave. They circled twice, again dropping anti-missile flares in what seemed to have become a routine manoeuvre. By 1984 or 1985, most *mujahideen* groups had Russian-designed SAM 7B anti-aircraft missiles and by late 1986, although we did not see any, the first American Stingers had reached Afghanistan and claimed several successes. The Russian pilots must have been fairly confident against SAMs, since it was their own weapon and they knew the counter-measures: but the Stinger was a much more sophisticated missile and Russian pilots were nervous of it.

During the whole journey we saw hardly any helicopters, the *mujahideen*'s explanation being that as their weapons had improved, helicopters had become more vulnerable and were being used less as gunships and more for carrying troops, particularly special forces.

By lunchtime, the jets were back, up to eight of them, climbing high in the blue sky and diving steeply into the next valley, called Anjiristan, where, according to Jan Mohammed, Masud used to spend a lot of time. The rumble of the bombing sounded like the crash of distant thunder. Despite this distraction, Jan Mohammed produced an excellent pilau of rice and raisins. As we ate, we watched eight lammergeiers soaring effortlessly against the mountain opposite, their superb control a joy to watch. I was particularly glad as I had begun to think their numbers were in decline; certainly there had seemed to be many fewer in Nuristan: perhaps the increase of traffic over the passes there had driven them to remoter areas like these. At any rate their presence here seemed to explode my tentative theory that they had been frightened away by the bombing, since by all accounts this area had had a lot of it in the past year.

After lunch while we were dozing in the shade, more SU25s appeared and apparently struck at the base where we had spent the night, as well as at Anjiristan and one other area. I began to wonder what had happened to the donkeyman, who had had to make a long detour via the bridge, but just as we were becoming really worried a man came by on a donkey and said that he had stopped in the village below us and that all was well. Jan Mohammed was as relieved as the rest of us, which endeared him to me even more. He was an entertaining companion, full of titbits of information.

'Sandy Gol. My friend, Gulai Dar, he often speak of you. He often say, Sandy Gol, he very good man.' This was flattering, but also good news. Gulai Dar had also lost a foot and had gone through the same process at Roehampton as Abdul Wahid. But he had been more fortunate and had gone on to do brilliantly as Masud's commander at Chemal Warda, near Rokha, where I first met him.

'He fight very good. Very brave *mujahid*. Kill many Russians,' Jan Mohammed said with admiration in his voice.

'And his leg. Can he manage with his artificial foot?'

'Yes, he run and fight very good. Gulai Dar very, very good commander.'

We set off again in mid-afternoon, when it was cooler, walking up the valley until dusk when we stopped under a huge umbrella pine just outside a village. The villagers came to inspect us, bringing tea and later food: rice with a bit of chicken for us and a whole goat's head for those with stronger stomachs.

Just before dark, the SU25s were back again, the low sun flashing off their silver fuselages as they climbed and dived steeply in their destructive ballet. Everyone watched in silence, knowing precisely what it must be like for those who were underneath. We wondered why Anjiristan had taken such a pounding for the greater part of the day: was it that news of our passage had reached the Russians via the spies that everyone talked about? Or was it entirely unconnected, based perhaps on some wider strategy of keeping Masud's supply lines under intermittent attack? These are the questions that you inevitably puzzle over as you travel across Afghanistan. There are hardly ever any certain answers, although sometimes various probabilities present themselves. In this case, as we spread our sleeping bags out of the way of the *mujahideen* and villagers, busy with their evening prayers, there seemed to be no obvious conclusion.

We slept where we dined, as Dr Johnson recommended, although not for the same reason and not for very long. Mindful of the threat of more bombing, Jan Mohammed roused us at two to make an early start on the pass.

For some reason Noel and I became separated from the rest of the party and found ourselves following Khalili up a series of steep grassy ridges a long way off the main path. Jan Mohammed, who must have started behind us, eventually caught us up and, after much whistling and shouting, steered us back to the right path.

'This very easy path, here. We have small rest and then we climb to the top.' This sort of understanding of the difficulties lesser mortals have climbing their terrible mountains marked Jan Mohammed out as a man of great sensibility. Most *mujahideen* cannot comprehend that anyone should find walking up a mountain anything other than the simplest and most natural thing in the world. Although they constantly use the words *Monda nabashi* (may you not be tired), it is a state none of them ever seems to experience personally. Under Jan Mohammed's encouragement, we reached the top of the pass a few minutes later, just as the sun began to warm the rocks ahead.

We descended slowly, matching our pace to Noel, whose damaged knee made walking downhill more painful than climbing up. The easy pace gave me plenty of time to observe, just below the pass, several clumps of beautiful dark blue, trumpet-shaped flowers, which I took to be gentians; then came prickly cushions of pinks, like sea campion; tiny white flowers shaped like stars, and finally a dark purple flower. We crossed several long screes and on one grassy spit between them put up a hen partridge and about ten young just able to take wing. Although they flew only a short distance, going to ground among the grass and rocks, they were so well camouflaged that we were unable to find any of them. The mother went through all the well-known decoy tricks, trailing her wing as if it were broken and limping just ahead of us until she judged her family was safe, and then suddenly rocketing into the air under full power.

At the bottom of the slope, two dark-skinned men carrying old British Lee Enfield .303s sat on a rock watching our progress with polite amusement. They talked to Jan Mohammed while Noel and I walked on, later catching us up with the easy stride of hill men.

'They say they want us to go to their *banda* for breakfast.' Jan Mohammed pronounced it break-fast, in the literal manner. 'These people called Gujers. They live in mountains. They very good men.'

From the valley below came a faint shout: Andy, Khalili and several *mujahideen* were waving from the far bank of a fast-running river. One of the Gujers scrambled down the hillside to try to persuade them to join us but they either could not ford the river or found the climb too stiff, and so we temporarily went our separate ways. The Gujers led us to a kind of arbour perched on the top of a cliff overlooking the river, just below their village. They brought carpets and cushions and after a considerable time a delicious breakfast of *nan* which we dunked in melted butter, tea and boiled sweets in lieu of sugar and finally a bowl of *dugh*. Two small boys sat and watched us with big, blank, expressionless eyes. Jan Mohammed pointed to one of them.

'You see this boy? His father killed by the Russians when he looking his goats on the mountain. Commandos come by helicopter to Shasdarra, big mountain over there. Bang! Bang! Shoot this boy father dead. He do nothing. Just looking his goats.'

We left our Gujer friends and set off along the hillside in the full noonday glare. The country was bone dry, with the river rushing several hundred feet below us, and the juniper bushes and wild thyme gave off a strong aromatic smell, which reminded me of Greece. The path swooped down steeply like a dust-slide to the river and there, in a small encampment of refugees from Khanabad, farther north, we found the others camped under a tree eating *tut* and drinking tea. The refugees, who were living in makeshift *rondavels*, and can have had very little for themselves, brought us more tea and *tut* and some apples as well.

We walked for another couple of hours, stopping beside the river to rest and bathe our feet while the mullah, Khalili and Jan Mohammed washed and prayed. It was still very hot, as we were much lower now, but in another mile or two we reached the *qarargah*, a couple of unprepossessing shacks in a hot and dusty ravine, just off the main valley. While we waited for the local commander, they brought us tea, and one of the *mujahideen* travelling with us, a young man returning from leave in Kunduz, produced some thick home-made wheaten biscuits and, with that Afghan generosity which never ceases to amaze me, unselfishly offered them round. The commander appeared a little later and announced that Masud had not arrived yet which I considered to be good news, as I was worried that the bombing might have made him move off.

I asked Jan Mohammed if we could go down to the river to wash but the commander said in case we were seen by people on the road it was better to use the stream above the *qarargah*. This fear that we might be 'seen' always irritated me but I carried out instructions, only to find that the stream at its deepest point was all of six inches. I dammed one section and was just starting to wash my underpants, socks, and trousers when Jan Mohammed appeared and took over, pounding them on a rock in a highly professional manner. I told him that washing another man's smalls went beyond the call of duty. I do not think he understood but he beamed happily.

Next morning after a luxuriously late breakfast, two *mujahideen* arrived and conferred with Jan Mohammed and Khalili who announced that 'Masud is on his way', although it was not clear exactly what that meant. Noel had spent a long time getting the camera ready when Jan Mohammed, who had been gone for half an hour, reappeared.

'Sandy Gol. After you finish tea, we go down to see Masud.'

'Do we take everything with us?' I pointed to all our gear.

'Yes, everything.'

Noel, swearing very quietly, had to dismantle the camera and pack it in a rucksack while the rest of our equipment was loaded on to the donkeys. We left the *qarargah* at eleven. It was very hot; the clouds were building up and the wind was rising. It looked as if we might be in for a storm.

We had only gone about a hundred yards when we met a

sweating *mujahid* and a rapid exchange ensued with Jan Mohammed.

'After lunch we go down.'

'You mean we stay here now?'

'Yes, eat something here and then go down later. Masud not arrive. They clean place for him.'

'You expect him to come tonight?'

'Yes. But many people want to see Masud. Too many people, all time. Masud ver busy. Masud ver tire.'

So we turned and trudged back to the *qarargah* while Jan Mohammed, with the donkeys following, went down the valley to find out exactly what was happening.

After lunch, we walked down to the village; it was full of Masud's advance party, but there was no sign of him. Jan Mohammed beckoned us to one side.

'This place too many people. We go much better place. You ready?'

So for the third time that day we loaded our equipment up again, retracing our steps almost halfway to a small house standing above the road: this was to be our new home. It had only two small rooms, one of which was locked, and a crude verandah. Jan Mohammed explained that the owners were away, at their *banda* in the mountains.

It was dusty and without shade but we made ourselves as comfortable as possible; and then, around six, with the valley already in shadow, Andy announced, 'Ahmed Shah is coming.'

CHAPTER FOURTEEN

Masud came striding up the path below our house as if he did not have a care in the world, accompanied only by Jan Mohammed and a young assistant: surprisingly there were no bodyguards. He looked exactly as he had done when I last saw him four years before, a spare figure, shoulders slightly hunched, with the same springy step and the same quick intelligent eyes.

He came towards us smiling and shook hands with each of us in turn.

'Vous allez bien? Le voyage n'était pas trop difficile?' He said he thought I was looking well, which pleased me.

We went inside and he gestured for us to sit down on the carpet beside him. At first we talked in French, which he speaks with a good accent and confidently, if not always very grammatically. Then, to bring in the others, I switched to English with Khalili translating. My first impressions were that he was in good health and even better spirits, his mind just as quick and incisive and, contrary to what Jan Mohammed had said, not a bit tired. With only an occasional interruption to see someone or for prayers, we talked from six until eleven o'clock. Even Jan Mohammed's excellent dinner of chips and fried meat hardly interrupted the flow.

Masud began by describing what he was trying to achieve in the north.

'You know there are four stages. First of all there was the preparatory phase which is now over. The second phase consisted of organising the *mujahideen* both in the mountains and in the plains.

'The third phase is the offensive stage, which we are in now, and finally the fourth stage is mobilisation. That means the general mobilisation of everyone in the country. We are not yet ready for the fourth stage, it will take time.

'Generally speaking, we have completed the programme for basic training in the five provinces, that is Baghlan, Kunduz, Takhar, Badakhshan and Mazar. These provinces are now able to operate independently.'

'If you gave an order, to be carried out in the north, would it be obeyed?' I asked.

'Yes.'

Masud then talked about a battle at Khelab, in the same province of Takhar where we now were.

'About 150 to 200 Russian commandos were landed there by helicopters. Against them we had only about twenty to twenty-five *mujahideen*. The battle lasted for several days and we inflicted very heavy casualties on the Russians.'

'How many?' I asked Khalili.

'It is hard to say exactly how many, but very many, including a Russian officer. This officer was lying there on the battlefield and the *mujahideen* wanted to go and bring back his things for Commander Masud, but Commander Masud told them it was too dangerous and not to do it. But one or two of them did it all the same, and they brought back the map case belonging to this officer and gave it to the commander.'

Masud had the leather map case with him and he opened it and drew out several heavily annotated Russian maps. There was also a grey exercise book which he took out and gave to me.

'Thank you very much. Is this the officer's diary?'

'No, it probably belonged to someone else and we just put it in here to keep it safe. You know about the Pushghour operation which we carried out last year?'

'Yes, we heard a lot about that. It was by all accounts a great success.'

Pushghour probably ranks as Masud's biggest victory of the entire war. Not only was Pushghour in the middle of the Panjsher Valley, only a few miles from three Soviet army bases, but it was within easy range of Soviet bases at Bagram and Kabul. Masud's success, right under the noses of the Russians, must have been a tremendous encouragement to the *mujahideen* and a serious blow to the morale of the Afghan army, as well as to the Russians themselves.

Masud drew a map and showed exactly how the attack was carried out. It was another example of his meticulous planning. Khalili added a gloss of his own.

'Commander discussed various plans and finally he adopted the plan put forward by a young *mujahid* from the area. He suggested that the *mujahideen* cross the bridge over the river

This young mother from Kunduz, near the Russian border, had just arrived in Pakistan. She said the Russians had bombed her village and taken away all the men, including her husband, and most of them had been killed.

Two very young refugees from Badakhshan, in the north-east. To reach Pakistan and safety, they had trekked for weeks across the Hindu Kush, some of the roughest country in the world.

Our convoy at the top of Kantiwar Pass, 16,500 feet, on the main arms route to the north. The Russians bomb it from time to time – the white marks on the rocks show where one salvo landed.

Threshing wheat in the traditional manner. The oxen are yoked together and driven round and round in a circle, urged on by the young man with the whip.

My sketch of the *Qala* at Kantiwar, the capital of Nuristan.
A mud-brick fortress, it dominates the valley for miles around.

Noel and I near the top of Papruk Pass, 14,850 feet, on our return journey. Andy persuaded us to try the *direttissima*, which turned out to be quite a steep scramble.

One of the Masud's captured Russian jeeps, which went well despite being full of bullet holes. Passengers included (left to right) the mullah, Andy (in turban), Noel, a hanger-on, the mechanic, me and Jan Mohammed.

Masud gives some raw recruits a lesson in infantry tactics. His emphasis on training and discipline, as well as his strategic grasp, set him apart from other guerrilla leaders.

Despite the demands of the war, Masud found time each day to study the Koran with the mullah. The mujahideen pray five times a day, and are excused only in battle.

Abdul Azim, one of Masud's top commanders, who can still shoot straight thanks to his Roehampton arm. He is always in the thick of the battle and even Masud says he is a 'hard man'.

Masud, with Andy (right), Noel and me. It took us a month to reach him, travelling for hundreds of miles mainly on foot or on horseback and climbing eight passes of up to 16,500 feet.

Test firing Masud's new Chinese BM12, which can loose off twelve rockets in rapid succession. The projectile is on the left of picture.

A direct hit on one of the five government forts at Farkhar. Masud's men captured the post after a stiff battle, taking more than one hundred prisoners.

just beside the base at night and then infiltrate the base. They did this and when the infiltration force was established inside the camp, the main force outside started the attack. The two operations were so well synchronised that they captured the base very quickly with about four hundred people of the garrison.'

But Masud was more interested in describing his next operation, an attack on another base near Farkhar, about twenty miles north.

'This is the last in a series of *garnesions*, Soviet and Afghan, which extend from Khanabad to the east. It is heavily protected by minefields and machine-gun posts and has a garrison of about three hundred Afghan army soldiers. We will attack it with nine groups, each of about thirty men, which is more than strictly necessary, but some of them will be relatively untrained. What is very important about this operation is that for the first time we will have groups drawn from all over the north, under one operational command.'

I said excitedly, 'We would very much like to film that. Andy can film the actual attack on the ground and we would be with you. Would that be possible?'

Masud nodded. 'Yes, of course.'

He then turned, with remarkable frankness, to his long-term plans. First he drew a rough sketch of the north-east.

'This area is very strategic, because you have one road running from Kabul north, through the Salang, to the Soviet border. Then you have another road, running from Kabul east, here, to Jalalabad near the Pakistani border.

'Dividing this whole area you have the Hindu Kush. So you have three areas: One: the area north of the Hindu Kush. Two: the area south of the Hindu Kush and bordering Pakistan. Three: Kabul.

'I have virtually completed my work in this area, north of the Hindu Kush. Shortly, I will be concentrating on the area south of the Hindu Kush. And finally, I will turn to the third area, Kabul itself. This will take time. We are not ready for that yet.'

It was impossible not to be impressed by his energy and determination. I remembered that he had told me four years earlier how he planned to move out of the Panjsher, exporting his guerrilla war, as it were, to the north-east; 'carrying the war to the enemy's bases', as he put it. Well, it seemed he was well on the way to doing just that.

'Kabul must obviously be the ultimate target,' I said. 'How much of an organisation have you got there?'

'We are very strong in Kabul. We have an infrastructure there already. But we are not ready to mobilise it yet. We have a lot of work to do first.'

We were all feeling sleepy and Andy and Noel excused themselves and retired to bed on the verandah outside. Masud, who did not seem at all tired, began to question me about Pakistan in general and about President Zia and General Akhtar, then head of military intelligence, in particular.

'I saw President Zia before I left Pakistan and he told me that unless the Russians agree to withdraw their troops "within months if not weeks" – those were his words – there would be no agreement and no return of the refugees. I think he personally is as committed to the *Jihad* as ever. But a lot of people in Pakistan are tired of the war and would like a settlement.'

Masud digested this without comment.

'They say they would like to help you. If only they knew what your plans were, they would try to help you. But they say it's impossible to find out what you're doing and what your problems are.'

'They are welcome to send a delegation to see what we are doing at any time. I have always told them that. But I will not send them details of my operations. They have asked for this in return for sending us arms. But this I will never do. We tell no one what our plans are in advance.'

I asked him about the state of the civilian population.

'The Russians have bombed the north very heavily because of our operations and our training programme. Khanabad was the most recent example, but there has been a lot of bombing all over the north. The Russians have also deliberately destroyed people's crops and the irrigation systems. So the population is facing famine. The dilemma is that because of the bombing and the shortage of food, many civilians want to go to Pakistan as refugees, or to the towns where they will come under government control. This is what the government wants.

'I and all the other commanders in the north have given

orders that they are not to leave their villages, but if we tell them to stay, we must give them money to buy food. And we are very short of money.' Masud turned his palms upwards to demonstrate the enormity of the problem facing the *mujahideen*.

I began to feel my eyelids drooping and I had to force myself not to yawn. The evening ended on a more optimistic note, with Masud describing enthusiastically how a *mujahideen* commander in Baghlan City, surrounded by Russian and Afghan army posts, managed to survive by using a network of underground tunnels. Masud showed me on his map.

'Look. You can see here. The Russians are in this factory, an old sugar factory. They have people here, and here and here.' The posts were marked in red on the map. 'But the commander uses tunnels that go right under the city to attack them, sometimes here, sometimes here . . .' Masud laughed.

I got up and shook hands. 'I must go to bed. Thank you for a very fascinating talk. I've enjoyed it very much.' The others were already asleep and I unrolled my sleeping bag beside them while Masud and Khalili went up to the flat roof above us. It was a beautiful, starlit night, the little valley utterly peaceful. The war might have been a million miles away.

Next morning, while Masud and a number of his *mujahideen* were having what appeared to be a Koranic lesson with the mullah, I had a cheerful reunion with Abdul Azim, whom I had last seen in London, and who was now one of Masud's top three commanders. He said he was having problems with his artificial arm and, taking off his jacket, showed me what was wrong.

'The arm is too heavy, and when I walk a lot it pulls on my shoulder and makes it sore. Also this part here does not work very well.' He pointed to a button which allowed him to flex the arm. 'Sometimes it does not work. This is important because I need it to fire my Kalashnikov.'

Abdul Azim squatted down, holding his Kalashnikov between his knees, and tried to flex his arm. He suceeded after a couple of attempts. Then, with his artificial hand round the barrel of the gun, he fired a couple of shots at the mountainside opposite. He gave a grin. 'It's all right if I am not in a hurry.'

I said he would have to go to Peshawar and see our prosthetist. 'He will either be able to make the necessary adjustments, or possibly even make you a new, lighter arm.'

Abdul Azim smiled. 'I will try. It depends on Masud.'

When Abdul Azim lost his arm, his legs were badly wounded by mine splinters and the scar tissue was extremely itchy. Sometimes when the itch was uncontrollable, he told me he had had to get his men to hold him down by force.

Gadda, Masud's number two, was standing listening to all this. Khalili explained that he was almost blind in his right eye.

'Two years before, in the Panjsher, Gadda was involved at close quarters in an attack on several Russian tanks. He and his men had destroyed all of them except one which fired at Gadda. The round exploded on the ground in front of him and blew grit and dust in his eye.' It looked now as if he had a cast in that eye and I wondered if it was not too late for treatment.

Masud spent the rest of the morning hearing petitions and complaints, rather like an MP conducting a clinic in his constituency, except that he combined political and military matters.

First came an old man, with a beautifully combed white beard, who complained that some of the young men in his village were behaving 'like hooligans'. Masud smiled as if to say we were all young once, but he wrote out a letter warning them to desist.

'Don't be caught with this letter. Najib' – the new Communist Party leader – 'is cruel.'

'I trust in God,' the old man said.

'Babrak' – Karmal, the ousted President – 'was better, he had pity on the old.'

'Don't mention their names to me.'

Masud finished writing. 'Be careful. Everything is in this letter.'

Then Gadda raised a question about taxing local traders. Masud's system of levying a flat rate of five per cent on everyone in the Panjsher was obviously being extended to the rest of the north. Gadda wanted to know if they should differentiate between local traders and outsiders who passed through occasionally.

'Yes, five per cent for the locals, ten per cent for the others.

134

I told you once before ... What you should do, when they bring their goods in, ask them how much they used to pay and decide on a price.'

A man sitting listening interjected, 'May God make the man who cheats at this time go blind.'

Finally, there was a more difficult encounter, with the Jamiat commander from Shomali, east of Kabul. He was not afraid to criticise Masud to his face, saying that he had promised him military assistance but had failed to deliver when they desperately needed it.

Masud listened with exemplary patience, repeatedly asking, as the commander digressed, that he come to the 'heart of the matter'. After he had given his own version of the incident, Masud addressed a little pep talk to the assembled audience.

'From the lowest to the highest in the revolution, everyone should understand, we don't play politics like the others. We should know where we get our income and where we spend it ... who's honest and who's dishonest ...'

We had lunch together and I recalled that Masud had always been a sparing and choosy eater, picking out bad bits of rice and putting them to one side. But he was not at all choosy about his table companions. Anyone could sit beside him and share whatever was available. Masud also enjoyed intelligent or at least lively conversation throughout the meal; not always the case in Afghanistan, where the simpler brethren tend to fall on their food without ceremony, exchanging few words until the dishes are empty.

Prayers followed, and then another session with the Koran. Afterwards Masud disappeared, either for a rest or more private discussions, and we whiled away the time taking odd shots and drinking tea until evening prayers, which we wanted to shoot.

Just before sundown, Noel and I installed ourselves on the flat roof of one of the houses which was the chosen spot and waited for the mullah to give the call to prayer. Unfortunately he chose to do this from an adjoining flat roof, so we failed to get it on film. He would have to be asked through Khalili to change his routine.

Masud and about fifty *mujahideen*, including newly arrived commanders from various provinces who were congregating for the coming battle, walked up to our roof and stood in two long lines. The mullah stood in front of them, and started the ritual which, although I have now seen it dozens of times, never fails to move me. Most of these men were simple peasants, many of them young, in their teens or early twenties, and yet there was about them a sort of nobility as they submitted themselves to a faith that has given them the strength to fight for seven years against a superpower quite prepared to destroy them and their families, their homes and even their country; a faith that could move mountains.

'*Allahu Akbar* . . .' God is Great. There is no God but God . . '

After prayers, two or three young men sat on the roof and intoned the Koran to themselves, rocking slowly as they sat cross-legged, while two older men cleaned their Kalashnikovs in preparation for the impending operation. Just as we finished filming, Masud invited us to join him on an adjoining roof. He made me sit beside him and asked if I would like coffee. I said I would and he started to make it. First, he placed a large spoonful of sugar in a glass, a large spoonful of dried milk – made in Ireland, I saw to my amazement – then a spoonful of instant coffee and, adding a small amount of weak tea from the teapot, stirred the mixture to a paste, finally filling the glass with more weak tea. The result was delicious, with no taste of tea. While he was doing this, the young man who acted as his assistant and bodyguard, a relative from the Panjsher, was making Masud a cup of coffee to the same recipe.

We discussed our plans for filming the attack on Farkhar. I wanted to be absolutely sure we understood one another.

'Our plan, since we have two cameras and two cameramen, which is very unusual, a real luxury, is that Andy should be with the main attacking force, wherever you decide to place him, maybe with one of your senior commanders like Panna, while Noel and I stay with you in your command post. Is that possible?'

'Yes. I will be on top of a hill, directing the battle by radio. All my commanders have walkie-talkies, so we will be in touch throughout the entire operation. You will be able to see and hear everything.'

'Good, that's marvellous. I want to make this the best documentary to come out of Afghanistan.'

'*Inshallah*. You can also film my sand-table briefing, and my final briefing to all the commanders. You will also be able to see the arms and ammunition arriving in the next few days, and the various groups, although there is some problem with the Panjsheri group. They may be delayed. So the operation may be a day or two late, although it would be dangerous to delay too long.'

We walked back to the house, where the resourceful Jan Mohammed had managed to find the ingredients for another tasty dinner, including by unanimous demand his speciality of chips. Andy, however, was not feeling well, and had a large and painful-looking boil on his hip. Unfortunately we had no lint to draw the poison out.

'I've brought the bloody stuff with me on every other trip and never needed it and now, when I don't bother to bring it, look what happens.'

Jan Mohammed came to inspect and suggested the Afghan remedy of a hot onion. He went off, selected a large onion and placed it in the embers of the fire. When it was burning hot, he cut it in half and applied it to the boil. Andy gave a yelp of pain.

'Hey, you butcher, watch what you're doing . . .'

'This very good medicine. Jan Mohammed very good doctor.'

There were more curses and gasps of pain from Andy and then Noel bandaged him up. The only encouraging thing was that Andy would be able to have a few days' rest while we waited for the arms and the other groups to arrive. If we had been on the move, it would have been much more serious.

Jan Mohammed had recruited two villagers to help with the cooking and fetching of water and supplies. One, Ibrahim, sported a Davy Crockett hat and was always cheerful, although Khalili discovered that a large number of his family had been killed a month before in a Russian air raid. Ibrahim was anxious to tell his story on camera.

'The Russians were bombing another valley. The *mujahideen* escaped and came to our village and we gave them food. Next day, the planes came and bombed our village.' Ibrahim had not been in the village at the time, but hurried back when he heard about the bombing.

'One man who was not at home lost five children and his

137

wife. We removed their bodies and five or six more, making ten or eleven plus my brother and his wife, thirteen altogether.

'A lot of animals, God knows how many, had been killed or wounded. I was so sad I couldn't speak. We collected them all. My other brother called Mullah Malen, he wasn't at home but three of his children were lying there, they'd been hit by shrapnel. We carried them out and took them all to the doctor. We also took my other nephew, Nassir, and my cousin Manan to the doctor too.

'While I was searching around, I saw that my sister-in-law had also been killed. We took the bodies outside and at night we buried three in one grave, four in another. It was a terrible sight. May God never let this happen to any Muslim.' Here Ibrahim's composure cracked and he gave a sob.

Ibrahim said he would arrange for his cousin, a shepherd, who had been wounded in the leg, to come from his village to talk to us. A couple of days later, Abdul Manan arrived in his best blue cloak, limping on a stick. Like Ibrahim, he told his story in a matter-of-fact way which made the details all the more terrible.

'The women were heating the milk. Two aeroplanes went over very high. We said nothing would happen but there was danger. They went away but two black aeroplanes all of a sudden dived and dropped their bombs.

'There was a lot of smoke, it was dark as night and we couldn't see one another.

'I was hit and fell down. I couldn't see anyone; it was like night time; and everyone was worried about his own safety. They bombed for quite a long time. They bombed and bombed. I thought my leg had been blown off but it wasn't, although I was bleeding a lot. I tried to move, I couldn't; then I fainted. I thought no one would rescue me and later a child came and told me his father had been killed; a seven-year-old brother and his mother had also been killed.'

CHAPTER FIFTEEN

There now ensued a period of waiting for the donkeys carrying the arms and ammunition, and for the various groups of *mujahideen* from the different provinces. After a month's hard walking we were all in need of a rest, especially Noel. His knee had given him a lot of pain and it must have taken considerable courage and will-power to keep going over such dreadful terrain. Also, after so much travelling, he and Andy were anxious to strip and clean their cameras, the sound gear and the rest of the equipment and make sure everything was in the best possible working order. The next two weeks would be crucial for the documentary.

So there was time to wash ourselves and our clothes in the shallow stream above the house and to observe the slow rhythms of the Afghan countryside, little changed despite the war. The *kaka* (literally uncle but used to denote any old man) who brought us our milk was now reaping the field of rather sparse and spindly wheat opposite. He used a short-handled sickle, gathering the cut stalks in the crook of one arm and making little piles as he went. His son, who wore a splendid pair of home-made boots with pointed toes, like Turkish slippers, gathered up the cut stalks and tied them in sheaves in the old-fashioned way, with a 'string' of half a dozen stalks. Farmers used this method in Scotland when I was a boy.

On the mountain above, two small children were trying to drive their flock of goats down to the valley for the night. One particularly disobedient group defied them and the more the little girl and her even smaller brother, who looked no more than five, chased them up the steep, shaly slope, the more the goats raced ahead of them, enjoying the game. Eventually, an elder brother came to the rescue, running nimbly up the scree and with a few well-directed stones cut off the recalcitrant beasts. Once the leader was turned, the whole lot went leaping down the mountain helter-skelter, amazingly sure-footed.

The old man put away his sickle and led his donkey, which had been grazing peacefully in a corner of the field, to the stable

139

for the night. For some reason, the little girl was still climbing about on the side of the mountain, although the goats were all down at the foot now, and the cooking fires were beginning to glimmer in the dusk.

Jan Mohammed appeared with a knowing smile and beckoned me over. In a bowl, freshly gutted, were a dozen brown trout, their speckled silver sides still gleaming from the river.

'Jan Mohammed, you're a genius. What are they, trout? They look like it.'

'I do not know name in English, but they ver ver good to eat. You see. I cook for tonight, with chips. Is good?'

'Very, very good. Jan Mohammed, fish and chips would be the most perfect meal I could imagine. For this, name your price. Anything.'

Noel was equally enthusiastic. 'I said fish 'n' chips would be the perfect supper. Just like Harry Ramsden's in Yorkshire.'

Andy took me aside a little later. 'I tell you one thing that Jan Mohammed would like, Sandy.'

'What? Another watch?'

'No, he's all right for watches. But he'd like your radio. The Sony. Ahmed Shah's got one and so it's a bit of a prestige thing as well.'

'Well, he can't have it now, but when we leave, provided . . .'

Andy grinned. 'Provided what?'

'Provided he keeps coming with the fish and chips.'

'I'll tell him. I'm sure he'll do his best. He really wants that radio.'

Supper was the culinary high point of our trip so far, equalling if not excelling the fish and chip dinner at the ammunition dump in Anjiristan. Jan Mohammed fried the trout in a light vegetable oil, so crisply that I ate the whole fish, head and all. Andy only ate one or two, knowing perhaps how enthusiastic Noel and I were about them, filling up with rice instead. We had expected Masud for dinner, but he arrived late, at about ten, having been held up by various supplicants anxious for his ear.

He sat down and began asking me questions, with Khalili translating. Jan Mohammed brought him some supper which he had kept for him, but Masud ate little and without interrupting the conversation.

'What does the West think of Babrak's replacement by Najib?'

'Well, no one is very sure what it means, but one view is that Babrak was old and tired and also possibly sick as well. There have been reports lately of him not looking very well.'

'No, that's not the case. I have a report from a student who was at a meeting with Babrak, after his replacement, and Babrak told the students, "They say I'm old and sick, but do I look sick?"'

'There's another view that Babrak was too closely identified with the old guard, Brezhnev, Andropov and so on, and that Najib is a Gorbachev man.'

'Yes, maybe, except that Najib, since he took over, has been repeating the same old policies. He has come up with nothing new.'

Masud's dark eyes appraised me, his aquiline nose gave him an almost Semitic look; it was a mobile, sensitive face, the face of a thinker as well as a man of action.

'Is it part of the Geneva process?' I asked. I was referring to the proximity talks between Pakistan and the Kabul government, with Señor Diego Cordovez, the United Nations' Assistant Secretary General, acting as intermediary. They began in 1982 and as late as 1987 were still deadlocked on the question of the timetable for a Soviet withdrawal.

Masud shrugged. The Geneva talks did not impress him. 'Do you think the Russians will make concessions to America, Europe, China and Pakistan and hope to persuade them to forget Afghanistan?'

'I don't think so, because even if they did, it wouldn't affect the United States Congress. It's interesting that both Houses of Congress, the House of Representatives as well as the Senate, have consistently supported the Afghan Resistance. They've even increased the amount of money the administration's set aside for covert aid to the *mujahideen*. No, I don't think they would forget Afghanistan. Nor would Europe. Mrs Thatcher is very conscious of the Afghan War. Anyway, I don't think the Russians are given to making sweeping concessions on anything.'

'Do you think the Russians will withdraw from Afghanistan? What is the war costing them? Can their economy sustain it?'

'I don't really know, but if I was to guess I would say around two or three million dollars a day,* compared to something like five million dollars a day for the Americans in Vietnam twenty years ago. But whatever it is, it must affect the Soviet economy, which is under enormous pressure anyway. Then there's the question of casualties. Whatever they are, that must affect opinion at home, in Russia. But let's assume the Russians do want to withdraw. How would they do it? What would happen to the Kabul government?'

Somewhat to my surprise Masud said, 'Yes, I think the Russians do want to withdraw. In fact, when I discussed the possibility of a truce with them in 1983, one officer said to me, "We want to withdraw, but how do we do it?" I said "Go out, the same way you came in."' Masud had agreed to a Russian offer of a year's truce in the Panjsher when he was desperately short of arms and ammunition.

'How do you think a future government of Afghanistan would be constituted? Presumably it would have to be neutral, and not hostile to the Soviet Union?'

'There would have to be some sort of elections, under international supervision. The Afghans would have to choose their own form of government.'

'But surely the Russians would only withdraw if they could leave a Communist government in power in Kabul. After seven years of fighting, after all the money they've spent, all their casualties, they can't just walk out, leaving the *mujahideen* to take over, can they?'

'No, I agree that they want to leave a Communist government behind them. But that is not acceptable to us. So the war will go on.'

It was nearly midnight and I was beginning to wilt, but Masud seemed as fresh as when he arrived and eager to go on. The other thing that I found frankly astonishing was his ability to relax. There was no sign of strain, despite the coming battle

* The IISS (International Institute for Strategic Studies) estimates $15 million a day (April 1987). The Americans estimated $40 million a day at the height of the Vietnam War.

and the multifarious problems he had to cope with. He began to talk about the difficulties the Russians had in Afghanistan, unable to rely on the Afghan army or even the Communist Party.

'There are dedicated Afghan Communists who are in touch with me and who assure me they support the *mujahideen* because of the way the country and the population is being destroyed. These people are or were committed Communists, who sincerely believed that their policies would improve the lot of their fellow countrymen. But they did not expect the Russians to behave in the way they have, committing atrocities, bombing the civilian population, killing people, burning people and so on.

'If the Russians were not here, the Afghan army would stage a *coup d'état* straight away. I'm sure of that. I know that because I have very good intelligence sources, right at the very top. When the war is over, people will be surprised to find out who has been helping the *mujahideen*.'

'I suppose the Russians will only be prepared to withdraw, without conditions, when they are forced to by mounting casualties and mounting pressure from the rest of the world. When it is their only option; rather as the Americans were forced to get out of Vietnam.'

'Yes,' Masud said, 'I agree.'

I got up. It was after midnight and the others were sound asleep outside. The unanswered question that we left hanging in the still night air was: did the *mujahideen* have the military muscle to force the Russians to leave Afghanistan? It seemed to me, in the final analysis, to come down to that.

Masud slept on the roof again, and we breakfasted together in the morning. I had heard on the BBC World Service that Russia was making conciliatory noises to China by offering to withdraw some of its troops from their common border. This prompted Masud to return to the point he had raised the night before about a possible sell-out of the *mujahideen*.

'I think the Russians will make concessions on arms limitation, so as to get the Americans to forget about Afghanistan.'

I disagreed. 'I don't think American public opinion would allow that, even if an American administration wanted to do it.'

143

He was not convinced. 'It has happened before, many times.'

Since I felt I could raise anything with Masud and get an intelligent response, I said that, speaking as a television professional, we found it impossible to get enough film or video pictures of the war to give our viewers a proper service. Both the Americans and the Germans were training Afghan cameramen. Perhaps we should do the same.

'It's a very good idea. I will send you a very good man who, when he is trained, will stay with me all the time. He is a university science graduate and he's also an artist and a sculptor.'

'But will he take pictures when the bombs are falling?'

'Yes, he's very brave too.'

I told Masud the story of Newsreel Wong, a Chinese cameraman for Hearst Metrotone in the Thirties. He had covered the Sino-Japanese war, including the bombing of Shanghai. Newsreel, who later worked for ITN in Taiwan, told me how he had gone to the main station in Shanghai minutes after the Japanese attack. 'The whole place was in flames and people were rushing out of the station screaming and shouting. I had to fight my way in, filming like mad, and I had just about finished when I saw a baby lying on the platform screaming its head off. Its mother lay beside it dead, and I thought the roof which was on fire was going to crash down on top of us at any moment. I had only ten feet left, so I finished the roll on the baby, grabbed it in my arms and rushed out of the place as fast as I could. Well, I shipped my stuff off to New York, they made a still frame of the baby and it was published all over America. Roosevelt used it in one of his speeches, holding the picture up and saying, "Look what the Japanese are doing in China." That picture went round the world"'

Masud took the point. I said I would send him a copy of our documentary as well as a VHS player so that he could view it. He asked if I could also send him a series about war. I suggested Thames Television's 'World at War' and possibly the Central-PBS series about the Vietnam War.

'Yes, and anything about the history of mankind and educational films; we are desperately in need of that kind of thing. I also need a copier, because I plan to send out 5,000 copies of a weekly newsletter.'

I said I would find out and let him know. Khalili said to me later, 'He never told me he needed one or we would have sent it.'

That afternoon Jan Mohammed, who agreed with Napoleon that an army marched on its stomach, despatched a couple of boys to fish the Namakau River below the house. In due course they returned with a dozen beautiful trout which the master soon translated into another of his famous fish and chip dinners. Masud and Khalili arrived just as we were finishing. I apologised for starting without them: we never knew when Masud would appear. He waved the apology aside and he and Khalili made short work of the rest of the plateful.

We went inside and Masud spread out his map and explained his plans for attacking the Farkhar post in detail. Khalili translated while Noel filmed.

'The enemy is situated or is resided in five security mountain posts. The operation will be co-ordinated on first these two security posts and the base. Enemy is about three hundred people. They have one 75 millimetre, two Dashakas and three mortars, three or four mortars. They have got ammunition and food but it's difficult for them to supply the base.'

'So it could be quite a tough nut to crack?'

'If we have got experienced *mujahideen* and trained *mujahideen* it's easy to capture it. But as Commander said, they're new *mujahideen* under the process of being trained, then it'll be a little bit difficult because they've not seen yet any fighting. The forts are also strong enough: they've got underground bunkers also.

'Just with the help of God, the Commander says, we hope that we'll capture it in two or two and a half hours.'

Afterwards we sat and talked. I sensed that Masud was intellectually isolated and welcomed an opportunity for conversation, and I knew that he and Khalili often talked until two in the morning.

I asked him what was happening in the Panjsher and he said there was always some fighting: recently the *mujahideen* had knocked out several vehicles in a convoy and shot down a helicopter.

'What about the Salang, are there still many ambushes there?'

145

'Yes, there's a small ambush in the Salang almost every day. Three or four vehicles. The governor of the province once sent me a message asking, "How many trucks do you need each day?"' Masud gave one of his rare laughs.

'The ordinary Russian soldiers sell everything they have: tyres, ammunition, anything for a few thousand Afghanis. They sell to the shopkeepers in the Salang and then buy hashish. A Kalashnikov fetches about 30,000 Afghanis (£150). Sometimes if the *mujahideen* carry out an ambush, instead of counter-attacking with their long-range artillery, the Russians will arrive and accept payment instead, say 5,000 Afghanis (£25).'

'Is there as much drug-taking as there used to be among Russian soldiers?'

'Not just among the soldiers. The officers take drugs as well: hashish and heroin.'

'Is there any evidence that heroin, especially, is being shipped back to the Soviet Union?'

'I don't know, but they certainly buy drugs in very large quantities.'

I said I had been rather surprised to see fewer helicopters on this trip.

'Yes, they are using the Mi24 and Mi25 less, because we have been shooting a lot of them down. They use jets more, for bombing and for general attack purposes. But they still use Mi8s and Mi17s for transporting troops. And they still use Afghanistan to test their latest weapons, like the SU29.'

At one point in the evening, someone came in with a message and Masud got up, saying the first of the arms shipments had just arrived and he was going to inspect it. He reappeared half an hour later to announce excitedly, *'C'est la BM12 qui est arrivée.'* This was the BM12 rocket launcher.

Next day, while we were breakfasting, another small convoy of donkeys came trooping past the house. We wanted to film them so I shooed them back round the bend and held them there until Noel was ready to roll. The lead donkey was a handsome if conspicuous white animal, carrying two BM12 shells, one on each side.

We followed them to the village and filmed the unloading and storing of the ammunition in *sangars* – stone emplacements or fortifications used very effectively for sniping in their wars against the British. The BM12 shells, and the 75 millimetre recoilless rifle and Dashaka heavy machine-gun ammunition were stored inside the *sangars* and then covered over with stones. By the time the *mujahideen* had finished, the camouflage would have defied the most precise aerial reconnaissance. Masud now gave orders to assemble the BM12, explaining that none of his commanders knew how it worked and it was important to have a test firing.

We were waiting to film this when he suddenly announced, 'One piece is missing so they won't be able to fire it. Tomorrow.'

We walked back to the house for lunch to find a pile of saddlery strewn all over the carpet on the verandah and a large, bearded Frenchman sitting in the middle of it. Andy introduced him as a photographer called Pierre Issot-Sergent, who had come on his own, on horseback, to find Masud.

Pierre told me he had read my account of the Vietnam War in *Don't Worry About the Money Now* and particularly enjoyed my description of the acid-tongued Joe Fried, who used to make life miserable for the American briefers at the nightly press conference, nicknamed the Saigon Follies. This nearly won me over, but not quite, and I could not help feeling resentful that this stranger should suddenly arrive out of the blue, and sit himself down in our midst uninvited. He had not even informed Jamiat, with whom he had had a row in the past, so Khalili was not too pleased either. But he turned out to be an agreeable and intelligent companion and I soon felt ashamed of my churlishness.

We had arranged to interview Masud at four, but while he was washing in the stream, Khalili asked, 'Sandy, could we do half the interview now, and half tomorrow?'

I consulted Noel. 'Not really, the light will be different.'

I explained this to Khalili and added, 'But there's no problem. If he doesn't feel like it today, we'll do it tomorrow. It's important he should feel in good form.' A few minutes later Masud came walking up the hill and I saw that he did look tired; when I suggested we postpone the interview until the next day, he looked relieved.

'Commander says he's grateful. Tomorrow will be better.'

Next morning, I told Masud I heard a report on the BBC about the current Geneva talks on Afghanistan. The Russians had finally tabled their withdrawal plans, saying they needed four years to complete the operation.

Masud said, 'That's good for us.' I presumed he meant that such an extreme position was bound to produce a prompt rejection from the Pakistanis, who were then talking about a four-month withdrawal period. In fact this was exactly what happened and the talks were promptly adjourned.

Masud spent the rest of breakfast studying maps and immediately afterwards had another lesson with the mullah, not so much on the text of the Koran but on things like the prescribed ways of washing before prayers. He made these sessions lively and even humorous, quizzing some of the simpler *mujahideen* and poking gentle fun at them when they did not know the answers.

The ammunition and various groups of *mujahideen* were taking longer to arrive than expected and Masud was having to spend more time in one place than he liked: every day that passed increased the risk that our whereabouts would be discovered and that the Russians would take retaliatory action. But he seemed very relaxed about it all and came to have lunch with two young lawyers who had just graduated from Kabul University. I was curious to hear what life was like there under the Russian occupation.

'Most of the students are anti-Communist and are openly hostile to the very few party members in the class; maybe only two or three out of a class of eighty. Lecturers begin by asking how many students in the class are party members. Very often there are so few of them they are embarrassed to put up their hands and the lecturers say it is a disgrace that there are no party members in the class. The Russian lecturers get very few students in their classes. Everybody hates the Russians.'

One of the two explained that his father was a colonel in the Afghan army. Fascinated by this piece of information, I wanted to know what their relationship was, now that he had joined the *mujahideen*.

'He said if you want to support the government, come and work with me. If you want to work for the *mujahideen*, then go and do it.'

This divergence, if not the father's broadmindedness, seemed to me typical of any civil war, whether in Spain or Vietnam, or indeed in England in the seventeenth century: families split down the middle by conflicting loyalties.

The lawyers said that because of conscription, many girls were now at Kabul University. 'The majority of them have no time for the Communist students. They say to them, "You want to marry me, you a traitor, a supporter of the enemy, Moscow?"

'Some girls in Kabul make dates with Russians, and when they keep the date the men are often killed. On one occasion a Russian adviser and some of his friends went shopping in Kabul. Somehow a group of Afghans found out that they were planning to visit a certain shop. So they planted a bomb in the shop and set it off when the Russians were inside, killing them all.'

I said, 'It can't be much fun being a Russian in Kabul.'

That afternoon, Masud arrived as promised for the much-discussed interview and submitted himself to my questions for over an hour. He looked fresh and incisive, unlike the day before. Because of the translation difficulty, Khalili sat right beside the camera, with me next to him, both of us facing Masud. I asked the questions in English, Khalili translated into Farsi and Masud replied in the same language. After every three answers, we stopped and Khalili gave me a brief summary of the answers, just in case Masud had said something unexpected. The full translation would have to wait until we got back to London. In the event, it was a good interview, without being in any way sensational, and he had already made most of the points in general conversation. This was not surprising as we must have spent at least twelve hours talking privately before the interview.

He was very forceful on several points, especially when I asked him about Mr Gorbachev's announcement that the Soviet Union would withdraw seven or eight thousand men from Afghanistan by the end of the year.

'The withdrawal of six regiments of Russian troops from Afghanistan doesn't have any significance from a military point of view. First of all because the Russians have sufficient forces inside Afghanistan. Apart from that, and we've seen it many,

many times, whenever they have been faced with stiffer resistance they have brought in overnight, either by Antonov transports or helicopters, thousands of commandos from across the border to fight in Afghanistan.'

Masud claimed that the war was going badly for the Soviet Union.

'Russian casualties which mount up day by day are another problem they face. The many deaths that people in Russia hear about, in spite of very tight censorship, have caused protest movements against the war. The next problem is the loss of morale among the Russian forces fighting the war in Afghanistan, particularly the officers. At the moment, I can assure you Russian army morale is not what it was four years ago – it has gone down considerably. Apart from that we see that the Russian puppets in Afghanistan, the Parchamis and the Khalqis' – the two wings of the Afghan Communist Party – 'are constantly in conflict with each other and the Russians haven't been able to find a solution. Even among the Parchamis there's trouble between the various factions.'

As always, he came over well on camera.

Just as we finished the interview, a whole string of donkeys went past, loaded down with arms and ammunition. It would have made a good picture, but there was no time to re-position the camera and shoot the sequence. This is known as 'sod's law' and although it applies to life in general, it seems to be particularly applicable to the television business.

CHAPTER SIXTEEN

The clans were gathering in the little village of Nakshi Darra, in the valley of Namakau; among the latest arrivals was a man who for political reasons Masud had designated the commander of the Farkhar operation, Mullah Abdul Wadut, of Taluqan, in Takhar Province, accompanied by fifty *mujahideen*. He was a rather portly gentleman, well mounted on a dark bay stallion, who looked as if he would be more at home in a bazaar than on the battlefield. Indeed, Masud was the real commander but he was clever enough to give all the credit for the battle to Wadut.

The other, more interesting newcomer was Panna, with Gadda and Azim the third of Masud's senior commanders. I had met him briefly four years before but felt I knew him well through Andy, who had spent a lot of time in the Salang with Panna when he was Masud's commander there.

I studied him now as he came loping up the trail, a lean, hard-looking man in his early thirties, in Russian combat jacket and trousers, flat Chitrali cap and green scarf. He padded rather than walked, like a tiger, and there was in his offhand, laconic manner something feline and deadly.

'Here's your buddy,' I said to Andy.

'He's more than that, Sandy.'

They embraced one another with real warmth in the Afghan manner, three times. Panna speaks no English but Andy's Farsi is versatile if unorthodox, so there were a lot of jokes and inquiries about Andy's wife and small daughter. Then Andy brought out a little box with a handsome black Seiko in it, (exactly like Jan Mohammed's), its diving counter aglow even in the daylight. Panna, a man of few words, took it in silence, fastening it on his wrist with reverent fingers.

Panna had been the great ambush specialist in the Salang and Andy had filmed at least three attacks in his company. He clearly admired Panna as a fighting man and someone who led a charmed life.

'He's mad, you know, Sandy. Completely mad. Once, in the

Salang, he got in a bus with some other *muj*. They were stopped at a Russian roadblock, told to get out of the bus and arrested. They had no weapons, of course, so Panna grabbed one of the Russians' Kalashnikovs and started firing. He shot a couple of Russians and ran off up the road, dodging the bullets as they whizzed all round him.

'Another time, he was staying in a house in the Salang. Someone tipped off the Russians and they surrounded the house and called on him to surrender. So Panna gets up, kicks open the door and comes out shooting. He got away unhurt, but the other *muj* with him were killed.

'He hates the Russians because they killed his wife. I think the village was bombed, and she was in the house. Ever since then he's wanted to kill as many Russians as possible. When a convoy comes along, he just walks down on to the road and shoots it up. He's crazy. One day he'll get killed, that's for sure.'

Andy's boils were if anything worse; as soon as one burst, another formed underneath. Noel proved a dedicated practitioner of the hot bottle treatment. This consists of heating a small glass bottle, clamping the mouth over the boil and holding it there for several minutes in the hope that the ensuing vacuum will draw out the pus. The boil however proved extremely stubborn and Dr Jan Mohammed, called in to give a second opinion, predictably prescribed the hot onion remedy. Andy endured these ministrations in stoic silence, although they must have been agonisingly painful.

Masud came for dinner and brought with him a young doctor, recently graduated from Kabul University. Abdullah said that most of his former class-mates were now either in Pakistan as refugees, or were working for the government. 'I think I am the only one who has joined the *mujahideen*.'

Masud talked about a heavy attack by Russian and Afghan troops the previous autumn in the Darra, a big side valley of the Panjsher.

'Last November the Russians landed several hundred commandos and six hundred Afghan soldiers by helicopter. The *mujahideen* were present in large numbers and very soon wiped out most of the Afghan forces. The Russians also had many casualties. In fact the Russians would have had very heavy casualties but unfortunately one *mujahideen* attack was not carried out properly and it failed. Eventually the Russians withdrew. We had some losses but not too many.'

Western observers treat most Afghan accounts of the fighting with a very large pinch of salt. There is probably a variety of reasons for Afghan hyperbole: for one thing, most *mujahideen* are uneducated if not illiterate and have not been taught precision in numbers; there is also a natural desire to make the best possible case, so every skirmish becomes a battle and every battle a victory. However, in the past I had found Masud reliable and his figures, whenever one could check them, nearly always accurate. He admits mistakes and failures, which is by no means a typical Afghan trait. He often referred to his intelligence network and I never doubted it was first class.

'Some time ago I was sent a very important document by a very good source in Kabul. It was a Russian document, dated the end of 1984 and signed by twelve generals. It said that if the Russians wanted to win this war, they would have to send in a lot more troops. Either that or get out. The reason they gave was that they were fighting not so much a national uprising as a faith: Islam. The Afghan army was a liability since it was constantly weakened by desertions. The document also mentioned the widespread use of hashish among Soviet forces and said morale was low.'

I wondered if there was any chance of getting hold of the document; it would make a fascinating addition to the documentary.

'Unfortunately one of the conditions laid down by my source was that as soon as I received the original, I was to burn it. This was done. I'm not sure where the Farsi copy is.'

We had talked a number of times about Russian casualties and the subject came up again. I said the British had produced a figure of 8,000 Russian dead up to the early part of 1986. This was based on verifiable evidence, presumably names and addresses in Russian publications. The Americans estimated about 10,000 dead and 20,000 wounded.

'Eight thousand, no, that's much too low. Far too low.'

'Well, then, what do you think the figure is?'

'I don't know. We have no figures, but it is much higher than that.'

(I did not hear Masud say it, but Khalili quoted him later as having estimated that combined Soviet and DRA dead were twenty a day on average. Even if only a third were Russian, that would give a figure of 2,575 Russians killed in a year, and more than 18,000 in seven years, a not incredible figure. On the same basis DRA losses would be 5,150 dead a year, and more than 36,000 in seven years, also a credible figure in my view.)

'Tell me about the war in the Falklands. What kind of aircraft did the Argentines use against the British?'

'They had a small aircraft called the Pucara, which made some daring low-level attacks on British troops. But most of the damage was done by the French Mirages, equipped with Exocet missiles.'

'Exocet? What sort of missile is that?'

I looked at Pierre. 'Well, it's French, launched from an aircraft in this case, and homes in on its target. These were air to ship. They hit several British ships and caused heavy casualties.'

Either Andy or Noel said, 'The thing was the French supplied the Argentines with new Exocets during the war.'

Masud's eyes lit up mockingly, going from Pierre to the three of us and back again. 'Did that not upset the friendship between the French and the British?'

Pierre was highly critical of his own side. 'It was absolutely disgraceful that the French government should sell Exocets to the Argentines when they were clearly the aggressors in the Falklands War and fighting the British who are our allies in the Common Market and in the defence of Europe. I blame Mitterrand, *c'était vraiment dégoûtant!*'

Maybe Masud thought this was dangerous ground, because he went back to the subject of the Russians.

'They have many internal problems in Afghanistan, largely based on ethnic differences. Tajiks and Ukrainians take sides against ethnic Russians and there have been many reports of fighting breaking out between different units. Also, many of the officers are unpopular and treat their men badly, sometimes abusing them physically.'

Jan Mohammed interrupted to say that dinner was ready: another masterpiece, but instead of fish we had lamb and chips, with an excellent tomato and onion salad.

Monday 11 August, our thirty-fourth day in Afghanistan, dawned overcast again, which was good in the sense that it reduced Soviet air activity and the chances of Masud's build-up being detected. We had not heard a single plane go over since we arrived in Namakau, which was exceptional. We could only guess at the reasons: possibly the Russians were too busy elsewhere, trying to block the infiltration routes.

After breakfast Noel and I were debating what we should do when I spotted Masud, who was staying a little farther up, striding purposefully past our house, accompanied by Khalili, who made no sign in our direction, and followed by a big group of the recently arrived *mujahideen* from Taluqan.

'Come on, Noel,' I said. 'It looks as if something is happening.' We shouldered the rucksacks with camera and sound gear and walked after them. They had not gone more than about a quarter of a mile when Masud turned off the path and led the way to a flat, bare piece of ground.

He formed the *mujahideen* up in ranks and called out the first three with their rifles. A brisk word of command and they dropped to the ground, took aim at three white stones which had been placed on the slope a hundred yards away, and fired.

After the first shot, Masud stopped the man nearest to him and asked for his Kalashnikov. Standing with his legs well apart in the copybook position, he put the rifle to his shoulder, aimed and fired one shot at the target.

'Did you see that?' he exclaimed. 'Far too high.' He asked for the tool kit, which is kept in the butt of the Kalashnikov although in most of these rifles it was missing, and adjusted the foresight. He fired another round. Again much too high. Another adjustment. When he was satisfied the sights were zeroed and the rifle was more or less accurate, he gave it back.

The Taluqan commander stood watching impassively, as if it was all a mystery to him. It would have been very understandable if Masud had shown annoyance at the total lack of readiness the state of these rifles implied. No doubt they were captured weapons, perhaps recently acquired; but in any army with the slightest pretension to efficiency, a sergeant would have seen to the very elementary business of zeroing the sights: it was the sort of thing that a recruit in the British army was taught during his basic training. Yet here was the general doing a sergeant's work, quite happy to train some really raw recruits. Masud's passion for detail was undoubtedly part of his genius. One by one he put them through it until every *mujahid* had fired at least three rounds under his eye and had his rifle checked.

We then moved off fifty yards and he repeated the performance with the machine-gunners, most of whose weapons were also woefully inaccurate. Masud concluded the morning's training session by demonstrating how to construct a booby trap from a grenade and a tripwire, and delivering a brisk lecture on how to take a fortified post on a hill. His audience sat rapt as they underwent the full Masud treatment: a gripping lecture style, with constant questions to keep the audience on its toes and plenty of repetition to drive his points home.

We had had a good demonstration of Masud as the complete guerrilla commander: crack shot, weapons' instructor, staff-college lecturer and, of course, general commanding. A little later, his brothers Ahmed Zia and Ahmed Wali having just arrived from Pakistan, we saw him in the less familiar role of elder brother: the three of them walked away up the stony valley and, sitting on the ground in the open, had a long talk well away from any inquisitive ears, breaking off towards dusk for prayers and then returning to their discussion.

Next day, we celebrated the Glorious Twelfth with the long-awaited test firing of the BM12. This is a Chinese copy of a Russian weapon, one of a family of multiple rocket launchers, sometimes known as the Katyusha. This model had twelve tubes mounted in three rows of four, one on top of the other, and could fire twelve rockets in rapid succession.

A former Afghan army officer, who had recently defected to Masud and who seemed to be the only person who knew how the BM12 worked, took charge. The target, a white rock on the hillside about two miles away, was selected and we were ready for the demonstration. The actual firing is done by a Heath Robinson sort of remote control, an operator madly cranking a handle, like an old-fashioned telephone set, and pressing one of twelve buttons on the firing console. The effect, however, was anything but Heath Robinson.

The first rocket went off with a tremendous red flash and a loud *whoosh*, and then, after an awesome pause, another impressive flash as it hit the mountain, followed by the boom of the explosion. After the fourth rocket exploded on target, everybody voiced unqualified approval; even the inscrutable Panna seemed moderately impressed.

We had had a very Afghan problem on the way down and it was still waiting for us after we had finished filming: the tramp of so many *mujahideen* feet had shaken an already flimsy bridge to its foundations, leaving only one narrow tree trunk to span the raging torrent below. Afghanistan is not only full of fast-flowing rivers but also of precarious bridges which are usually narrow, shaky and without a handrail. Noel, who was carrying the camera, had circumvented this one very sensibly by sitting down astride the tree trunk and edging his way across, uncomfortably but safely. A kind *mujahid* had seen our plight and offered him a helping hand. Encumbered only by the tripod and the spare magazine, I thought it would be easier to inch my way across upright, but it had nearly proved to be the wrong decision. The return journey was no easier, but we accomplished it without dropping anything in the river.

On our return Ahmed Wali, Masud's youngest brother, who was studying in Britain on a British Council scholarship, dropped in for a chat. He could not make up his mind, he said, whether to study medicine or international relations. He had asked Masud's advice but was still waiting for his answer. I suggested he should complete his A-levels because it would give him another year to make up his mind.

He asked me how I found Masud. I said, 'Amazingly relaxed and confident. I don't remember seeing him quite so confident before.'

'I can't believe it either. And he makes so many jokes all the time. It's good to see him like that. But he has his problems too, you know. Getting all this equipment and all these people together in one place at one time is a big thing and has taken a long time. He's impatient to get on with the operation.'

Masud's sand table, which was really a large-scale relief model, was ready for the final briefing. It was an impressive piece of work, measuring about ten square yards, the mountains artistically sculpted from stones covered with earth and the five forts which made up the post realistically cut out of cardboard. Even the road through the camp was lined with small white pebbles. The whole thing had been supervised by the defecting officer who had served in Farkhar and knew every detail of the place.

He began by briefing Masud and the half-dozen commanders involved in the attack on the general layout of the post with details of each of the forts, the strongest of which was manned by the KHAD, the secret police; then he pointed out the minefields and the machine-gun positions on the hills above.

Masud then took over and outlined the plan of attack, walking about on the model and indicating the routes which the various groups would follow for the assault. His mastery of the details of the defenders' positions and armaments seemed to be complete. At the end, he threw open the discussion, inviting comments and criticism. Panna had quite a lot to say, as did Gadda who advocated the use of another assault group on one particular sector, which after discussion Masud accepted. Masud then summed up, which meant the operational plan was now understood and agreed by everyone.

As a piece of planning, it struck me as thoroughly professional, with a scale model, an exhaustive briefing and plenty of time for discussion. It certainly gave the lie to critics of the Afghan *mujahideen* who tend to dismiss them as undisciplined and disorganised. It showed what a guerrilla commander could do if he had the intelligence to learn from experience, as Masud had in seven years' often desperate fighting against a heavily armed and largely professional army: long gone were the days when the *mujahideen* were mainly up against raw Soviet conscripts. Increasingly, the Russians have been forced to deploy elite troops, the Spetsnaz, leaving the conscripts to carry out routine guard and convoy duties.

Masud's military talent was at least partly hereditary. His father had been a regular colonel in the Afghan army in the days of Zaher Shah. He had originally wanted to follow in his father's footsteps, but instead, after studying at the famous Istiqlal Lycée, where he learnt his French, he had gone on to do engineering at the Kabul Polytechnic, although he never completed the course. His guerrilla career started in 1975, when he took part in Gulbuddin Hekmatyar's ill-fated coup attempt against President Daoud. Masud was twenty-one and strongly opposed to Daoud's pro-Moscow policies; but he thought Gulbuddin's plan was incompetent and said so. Gulbuddin is said to have taunted him, 'Are you a coward, then?' This so enraged Masud that he took part against his better judgement. The coup duly turned out to be a fiasco and Masud fled to Pakistan where he began to interest himself seriously in guerrilla warfare, avidly reading everything he could lay his hands on, including, he once told me, the works of Mao, Che Guevara, Régis Debray, the French leftist, and an American general whose name he had forgotten.

Between 1975 and 1978 he travelled backwards and forwards between Pakistan and Kabul at least ten times, and he was in Kabul 37 days before Taraki seized power in the April 1978 coup. He immediately went back to Pakistan, returning shortly afterwards via Nuristan. 'All I had was 100,000 Afghanis (£500), although I borrowed some from friends in Nuristan. Six months after the Taraki coup I was back in the Panjsher with twenty men, two Kalashnikovs, two RPGs (rocket-propelled grenade launchers) one FN (NATO) rifle, nine rifles made in Darra (Pakistan), six .22 rifles and two or three Sten guns.

'A month after we arrived in the Panjsher we started attacking government forces and captured several hundred weapons. After two or three months I had between five and six hundred people. We captured Salang and Bulaghen, then, after forty days' fighting in the Salang, I was wounded in the thigh.

'It was a flesh wound but I couldn't walk and they had to carry me. After that, our whole effort collapsed because the government mounted a major attack on the Panjsher and we ran out of ammunition, so there was nothing we could do. I realised after that our training was not good enough so I started again with thirty *mujahideen*, including Gadda, Panna and Amon – there are only eight or ten of those original thirty left. This time we trained really hard and slowly we built up our strength and the rest of the story you know.'

On Friday 15 August, we rose early and left the sanctuary of our *banda* in Namakau at 4.30 a.m. It was a lovely walk down the river in the dawn, past the mud-walled farmhouses surrounded by a few poor fields of wheat and barley, with their modest flocks of goats and one or two undersized cows, the peasants still somehow pursuing their traditional way of life despite the threat of war, destruction and even death. I was struck once again by the tenacity of the Afghans, their truly stoic fortitude which had its roots in a civilisation older and more fatalistic than we in the West understand any more.

I felt happy, not only to be on the move again, but because we had 'in the can' the most detailed portrait yet of the most important guerrilla leader in Afghanistan who, luckily for us, was a television 'natural'. Masud never looked at the camera, indeed never seemed conscious of it at all, behaving in exactly the same way whether it was there or not.

Shooting a documentary is a long, painstaking business, in which the sequences have to be built up like a mosaic, piece by piece. We had had an unexpected bonus in being able to spend so long with Masud at a critical moment in his fortunes, when much of the planning and organisation he had devoted to the north was about to be put to the test. Both Masud and we, for different reasons, needed a success in the coming battle. It was vital for him because victory would set the seal on a year's work and consummate the legend of his military invincibility. We needed success because the battle was the natural climax to the film and it had to be a convincing climax.

Thanks to Jan Mohammed's excellent feeding, we were in good physical condition; even Andy's boils were on the mend and he was impatient to go into action. He had come a long way and waited a long time to shoot this battle sequence and he desperately wanted it to be his best: I told him I was sure it would be.

We climbed through fields of short-stemmed wheat and barley to the pass, which cannot have been more than 10,000 feet and which we found the easiest climb yet. Our lungs were now almost acclimatised and breathing was much easier. I got Noel to take a picture of me on the summit of the pass, grinning like an imbecile.

We stopped at the foot of the mountain for a brief rest and a drink from the stream and then Azim sent off the groups one by one in case of air attack. The country was bare, we were probably lower now than at any time since leaving Pakistan and the temperature was in the high eighties or low nineties. A few hundred yards on, we were stopped by local *mujahideen* who apparently did not think it wise for us to enter the village of Khost De since it was Friday and the start of the Id of Korban, a Muslim feast to celebrate the occasion when Abraham was preparing to sacrifice his only son Isaac and the angel of the Lord called out to him to stay his hand. In the Bible it says, 'And Abraham lifted up his eyes and looked and behold behind him a ram caught in a thicket by his horns: and Abraham went and took the ram and offered him up for a burnt offering in the stead of his son.'

We spent an uncomfortable hour trying to find some shade in a burning hot, stony *wadi* before finally being taken to the village where we found Khalili, Panna and the others ensconced under the trees beside the river, reclining on carpets and drinking tea in what might have been a scene from a Mogul miniature. Later we moved to another even more delectable 'garden' of young walnut and peach trees, their fruit, alas, not yet ripe, and were served with yoghurt, soup and *nan*. It was green and cool under the trees and also practical, there being an air-raid shelter dug into the hillside only five yards away.

Although the *mujahideen* did not celebrate the Id, we were told because of the war, we did see lots of little girls dressed in their Friday best running through the village. Apparently they go from house to house, paying their respects and receiving in return gifts of sweets. In the evening we saw through the trees a more serious procession. Scores of villagers trooped past in single file carrying armfuls of two-foot-long plastic tubes containing 75 mm Chinese recoilless rifle ammunition. Indeed, our whole stay in Khost De was an illuminating example of just how close most Afghan villagers were to the *mujahideen*. They not only fed and housed them, no doubt against payment, although here, unlike Nuristan, it would never be requested; they supplied the donkeys to transport the *mujahideen*'s guns and ammunition, as well as our cameras; and they provided intelligence about enemy movements. Once again, the conclusion was inescapable that the *mujahideen* and the peasantry were two sides of the same coin, inseparable one from the other.

Jan Mohammed appeared at eight and said Gadda wanted us

to split up our equipment, taking with us only what we needed to film the battle; the rest would be sent by donkey direct to Warsaj, to the south of Farkhar and on our return route. All the others now disappeared, presumably to sit at the feet of Masud, leaving us to our own devices. Our dinner did not arrive until some time between ten and eleven, by which time Noel, who was not feeling well, and I had both crept into our sleeping bags, leaving the indomitable Andy and Jan Mohammed to do justice to the rice. During the night, which was fine, tiny droplets of moisture, which I took to be dew, kept dropping on my face: in the morning I discovered the peach trees had sucked up so much water from the irrigation system that their trunks and branches were saturated; hence the 'dew' which continued to fall on us while we were eating our fried eggs. Even a jet going over very high failed to disturb the peace of the Id.

After breakfast, as we waited for word from Masud, I made a ceremonial presentation of my Sony radio to Jan Mohammed. He had never ceased to lobby for it through Andy, and he had certainly kept his side of the bargain, providing us with a steady diet of fish and chips. He seemed genuinely touched and Pierre took a celebratory photograph. At twelve, a boy brought us some cherries, small and black and quite tart, although they became less so as you ate them. Then came lunch and we had just finished when a messenger arrived and Jan Mohammed announced, 'We go now.'

We shouldered the camera equipment and after about an hour's walking came to a big bridge over a plunging river, the Warsaj. On the far side was a remarkable sight: in a bend of the river lay a wide expanse of soft green turf, the size of two football pitches, fringed with some splendid trees; and all round this expanse, sitting in groups of thirty or forty, were Masud's entire strike force for the Farkhar operation. Khalili laughed: 'Isn't this a beautiful place? It was the favourite camping spot of King Zaher Shah. He came to shoot *markhor* in the mountains and fish for trout in the river. They have the best trout in all Afghanistan here.'

CHAPTER SEVENTEEN

We dropped our rucksacks at the edge of the royal camping ground, beside a Dashaka on a tripod, and went for a stroll. Everywhere, groups of *mujahideen* sat on the grass, with their weapons beside them: recoilless rifles, RPGs, Dashakas and even eight SAM 7Bs, the Russian ground-to-air missile. Panna was busy checking a Dashaka's ammunition belt, in the case of an air strike. Masud had blocked the roads from Namakau, to stop information about his plans leaking out, but if the Russians had got wind of them Zaher Shah's old camping ground would have made an inviting target. It would have taken only a few minutes to cluster-bomb the assembled *mujahideen* and land special forces by helicopter to cut off their escape. Although the half-dozen Dashakas ready for action on their tripods indicated that Masud was not oblivious to the danger, there was no sense of impending nemesis: the atmosphere was more that of a picnic.

All afternoon and evening, a string of villagers, including old men and boys, walked across the bridge carrying ammunition: I counted 55 BM12 rounds as well as hundreds of recoilless rifle shells and RPG rockets. The RPG is an ingenious weapon and the curious bulbous head of the rocket with its sharp snout conceals its secret: the hollow or shaped charge, invented by an American, developed by the Germans and then the British, which concentrates all the power of the explosive on one spot the size of a twenty-pence piece, with such effect that it can drive its way through the armour plating of a tank.

At dusk, each group was given a final pep talk by Masud, ending with a rousing chorus of '*Allahu Akbar*'. As they marched off he inspected each man, the Dashaka and recoilless rifle teams, the mortars and the RPG men; no detail was too small or trivial to escape his eye. A fleet of old, battered Russian lorries was drawn up under the trees at one side of the ground and the *mujahideen* climbed aboard and went off waving and cheering in a cloud of dust and blue diesel fumes.

Khalili walked across to where we were sitting. 'Masud is

nervous because this is a vairy important moment for him; it's the first time he has attacked a big post outside the Panjsher; the first time a number of groups from different areas in the north have carried out a joint attack. It is also a training exercise and he wants to use it to build up the morale of the *mujahideen* in the whole of the north. So you see it is vairy important it goes well for him.'

We were sitting on the grass with a few small boys and a couple of old men, watching the last lot depart, when Masud came over to join us. He started talking to the boys, teasing one of them about the white cloth with garishly embroidered flowers he was holding.

'Do you want to give that to me as a present?'

After some hesitation, the little boy said, 'Yes,' and held it out to Masud.

'No, no, it was only a joke. Your mother might have something to say about that.'

But the little boy, who could not have been more than seven, insisted and Masud had to accept it.

'It's beautiful, thank you very much. Here, come and sit beside me, I want to talk to you.' The boy did as he was told without the slightest sign of shyness or embarrassment and, after asking him a lot of questions about himself, Masud persuaded him to recite several verses from the Koran and then something in Farsi. He did it beautifully, as far as I could tell, without a pause or hesitation, and when he had finished Masud applauded. I asked Khalili, 'Who was that poem by, Khushal Khan Khattak?' Khattak was a seventeenth-century Pushtun poet.

'No, much older. It was by Hafez, a Persian poet of the fourteenth century.'

We were almost the last to leave, walking past the bridge and then north along the river which foamed luminously below us in the moonlight. We had gone only a mile when we saw lights twinkling on the hillside and as our guide led the way over the stony ground, the lights grew bigger, resolving themselves into three or four hurricane lamps; something soft under our feet turned out to be a couple of *kilims* spread out to make a resting place and dinner table. Fat cushions were brought and pushed under our backs and eventually our peasant hosts brought food: rice and what was no doubt goat although the darkness made close inspection impossible, which was probably just as well.

An hour later, we boarded an ancient lorry which creaked and groaned its way over the bumpy road like a windjammer in a stormy sea. Noel and Andy climbed uncomplainingly into the back, but I was offered a seat in the cab next to a young Jordanian student.

'Where you come from, America?'

'No, we're British, from London.'

'Ah, London, London vairy, vairy good.'

'Is this your first trip to Afghanistan?'

'No, I come now three times. In my holidays. This my third time, to fight the *Jihad*. I am Muslim. I come to help my brothers fight the *Jihad*.'

The door flew open and the young Jordanian, who smelt as strongly as any of his Afghan brothers, leaned over me and slammed it shut.

'You have to close special way. Like this.'

We stopped a little farther on and the Jordanian and I got out for a few minutes. When we climbed in again, I failed to close the door in the way he had indicated, which led to another demonstration and another strong rush of BO. I was glad we did not stop again before reaching Farkhar at around midnight.

As we assembled in the dark on the outskirts of the village, I discovered to my shame that Noel and Andy had had a dreadfully uncomfortable journey, especially Noel.

'It was terrible, so terrible I had to laugh. The back was packed with *mujahideen*, all pushin' and shovin', and treadin' on our feet. I had this bloke next to me with a Kalashnikov and he kept jabbin' the butt in my face . . .'

'Noel, how awful.'

'Yeah. He kept hittin' me in the face, every time he turned round. I kept swearin' at him, but he didn't pay a blind bit of notice. It was so awful, I finally had to laugh. I just laughed.'

Andy had to go off with his group. We would not see him until after the battle.

'Good luck, Andy.'

'Thanks. Good luck to you and Noel, too.'

'Look after yourself, Andy. Good luck.'

Jan Mohammed, Noel and I walked into Farkhar, each house and garden enclosed behind high mud walls and shaded by tall trees, although it was so dark they were only a black canopy above our heads. The road, which was really only a track wide enough for pedestrians or horsemen, but not vehicles, ran beside a stream which meandered past the houses: European villages must have been very like this in the Middle Ages. We stopped at a house near the centre of the village and Jan Mohammed climbed the stairs to see if anyone was awake. He returned with a youth who led us to the guestroom, carpeted and cushioned but, as is the custom in Afghan villages, with no other furniture. A few minutes later, our host arrived to greet us and inspect us through his dark glasses. We apparently passed muster and were bidden good night.

Breakfast was disappointing: rather stale *nan*, tea from a thermos and very overcooked bits of meat, probably goat. Meat in Afghanistan is often boiled first and then fried, so it resembles nothing so much as an old boot sole in appearance and, I imagine, in taste too. Jan Mohammed, conscious that this was not the three-star service we had become accustomed to, tried to propitiate us with lump sugar and biscuits from the shop next door and then went off to find Masud. He was back in an hour.

'I speak to Masud. He ask me: "Sandy Gol, Noel, they all right? They have food and sleep good?" I tell him you have food and sleep good. He speak me, "You take good care Sandy Gol and Noel. I, Masud, come later and then we go."'

'Do you think the operation will take place today?'

'Yes, I think. Masud has close whole town. No one allow come in or go out. Too many spies who tell Roossians that Masud is here. Now you rest. Later we go.'

We did not get much rest in fact, because our presence attracted a string of visitors, wanting to see for themselves what these strange '*Angrezi*' were like. One was a biology teacher from the local school who brought us a bowl of yoghurt and his vocabulary notebook, in which he had jotted down a selection of English words, culled at random from his dictionary.

'Please you look here and tell me what this mean,' he said, passing me his notebook.

I read aloud. 'To-do, pell mell, peeking, and peckish.'

'Please, what mean this words?'

'They are quite unusual words and quite difficult to explain.' I was not sure if either my English or his was up to it. I started with the easiest one. 'Peckish means hungry. A to-do, is . . . a carry-on, you know, a fuss . . .'

The teacher looked blank. 'Please?'

'Pell mell. That's running or riding as fast as you can . . .' I had a brainwave . . . 'like *buzkashi*.' The look of incomprehension that had been on his face for the last few seconds cleared like mist on a Scottish moor when the sun comes out. He smiled broadly.

'Pill mill. Like *buzkashi*. Very good.'

One word defeated me. 'Bild,' I read. 'What does that mean?'

'Bild?' He passed his hand over the top of his head and giggled. 'When you have no hair.'

'Oh, I see, you mean bald.'

At least he was more stimulating than another of our visitors who came in, sat down in the corner and then lay down and fell fast asleep. He woke about an hour later, yawned and stretched, got up and walked out of the room without a word. I looked in some surprise at Jan Mohammed.

'Who was that man? Did he just come for a rest?'

Jan Mohammed looked pained. 'This man is *mujahid*. He fighting ver much. He ver tire.'

Jan Mohammed had not wasted his morning: the young man of the house now appeared carrying a plateful of fried fish for our lunch. They were small, brill or bream I guessed, but tasty, and Jan Mohammed said they came from the little stream, no more than a yard wide, which ran through the village.

I had hoped we would sample some of the trout from the Farkhar river which King Zaher Shah esteemed so highly. 'Next time,' Jan Mohammed promised. 'I fix for you trout next time.'

After lunch, we walked down to the river and waited for Masud. He appeared in about half an hour with his entourage, including Khalili, all on horseback. As he came over the bridge, Masud called out to me, '*Vous voulez un cheval? Je vous donne un pour vous deux*' indicating Noel and myself.

167

'*Oui, merci beaucoup*.' Masud gave an order and a *mujahid* jumped down and held his horse's head.

'Noel, do you want to ride?'

'No, I'm fine, you go ahead.'

So I mounted and we rode off along the river. After about fifteen minutes I realised that Noel was struggling under the heavy camera bag, while everyone else rode blithely ahead. I shouted to Khalili and Masud overheard and gave another order. A strapping *mujahid* shouldered the bag and at least Noel was able to walk unencumbered. The sun burned from a cloudless blue sky, we were much lower now, on the northern slope of the Hindu Kush, on the edge of the great plain that sweeps down to the Amu Darya and the Russian border.

In half an hour or so we came to a small village where our progress was halted by enthusiastic locals all anxious to shake Masud's hand. He dismounted and went off to the mosque to pray while we were shown to an airy upper room where a feast of ripe, juicy melon and home-made sweets was spread on the carpet. Tea had just arrived when a young *mujahid* put his head into the room and said breathlessly, 'Hurry up, they're leaving.'

By the time we reached the road, they had left; indeed Masud and most of his party were already half a mile out of the village.

'Why didn't they tell us they were going, instead of leaving us sitting up there?' I knew I was being querulous, but I was angry at the lack of planning. Here we were with the battle only a few hours away, left to our own devices, with one horse between two of us and no one to carry the camera.

'Bloody mad,' said Noel. The man who had been carrying the camera had disappeared and I was just in time to stop my horse following suit.

'Hey, wait a minute, I want to ride.'

The owner, a local man I presumed, grinned obligingly and helped me to mount. Noel picked up the camera bag again but after a few hundred yards it was clear he could not carry it much farther. I appealed to Jan Mohammed, who, thank God, was still with us.

'Noel can't carry the camera all the way up the mountain. What the hell are we going to do?'

'Here, you put camera here. Give me, I show you.' He grabbed the rucksack with the camera and lenses and hooked one of the shoulder straps over the pommel of my saddle.

'No,' I shouted in exasperation. 'If that strap breaks, the camera will be smashed and we might as well all go home.'

I struggled to hook both straps over the pommel, eventually succeeding after much tugging and cursing and despite the doubtful help of the horseman. I had to ride with my left foot virtually out of the stirrup because of the rucksack, but it was a small price to pay. The track soon became steep and the horse's owner wanted me to dismount, pleading that the heat and the load were too much for it. I responded by kicking the animal on and shouting at its owner loudly in English, 'The horse is perfectly all right. Let's go.' Then in Farsi, *'Birra, birra.'*

Near the top of the hill, it became so steep that I had to dismount, but the camera stayed on the horse's back, swinging about precariously. I walked up another hundred yards or so and came on Masud, with Khalili beside him. Masud was busy on the radio, a British-made, Racal battlefield communications set.

When he had finished his call, Masud strode off up the hill and I waited for Noel who arrived a few minutes later, looking hot and blown. We climbed up a long, grassy slope, passing groups of local *mujahideen* whose cheerfulness probably reflected their distance from the battle zone, and halted under the brow of the hill. Noel began to get the camera ready for shooting. Ahmed Zia, Masud's brother appeared with the tripod, which he had nobly carried all the way up for us. I thanked him and he said, 'Masud has gone farther up the hill. You should come now.'

'We're just getting the camera ready. It will only take a couple of minutes and we'll follow you up.'

Noel was under pressure, his fingers hurrying to program the complicated time code device which, although sound and picture are shot separately, enables you to synchronise the two later, or 'synch' them up, as the jargon has it.

'If only they'd bloody well tell us what's going on, it would make life a lot easier.'

'I know. It's always the same. No planning as far as we're concerned and then a mad rush at the last minute.'

We found Masud a quarter of a mile away, near the top of the mountain, sitting with his back against a Dashaka machine gun, earphones on and calling up his commanders in turn: Gadda, Panna, Azim, Amon. They were all in position and ready for the order to begin the attack. Masud looked at his battered Japanese watch: twenty minutes to go. There had been one bad moment when they had been moving into position the night before. One of Azim's men had set off a mine, fortunately not wounding himself, but there was a tense moment as they all waited to see if the guards would raise the alarm. But nothing happened; the defenders presumably thought a dog or a fox had set off the tripwire.

At 5.15 Masud moved another fifty yards to the crest of the mountain and for the first time we had a good view of the post below. It nestled among the hills, looking peaceful and harmless in the evening sun and very like the model. Masud made a last check call to each of his commanders and then at 5.30 he gave the order for the start of the attack.

'Put your trust in God and start firing.'

The barrage started slowly but with impressive weight. '*Thump ... Thump ...*' Then came the crash of the BM12 which was sited well back, and the slam of the 75 millimetre recoilless rifles. Smoke began to drift across the front of the sand-brown forts, pinpricked by red flashes as the *mujahideen* fire found the target. The defenders took several minutes to recover from their initial shock and then their Dashakas began to return the fire in a long rattle, like an angry woodpecker.

Masud sat tensely on the bare earth, headset clamped over his hat, talking non-stop to his commanders in the heat of the battle below. His radio operator squatted next to him, the set's long aerial waving above his head like the antenna of some strange insect. Masud became excited when after six minutes Azim captured the first machine-gun post on a little hill above the main forts. Within fifteen minutes he had taken two more.

As the light faded, Masud was impatient to clinch the battle, shouting over the radio to Panna, who seemed to be held up and out of contact. Finally the radio operator announced he had Panna on the net.

'Commander Panna, Two Five, Two Five, can you hear me? This is Headquarters.'

'Yes, I can, go ahead.'

'Where are you? Where are you?'

'I've reached the minefields.'

'Listen, don't worry about the mines. Don't worry about the mines. You can go by the road. Two forts have been captured. Use the road. Hurry.'

Two more forts fell shortly afterwards; only the fifth and last, defended by the KHAD secret police, was still holding out. Knowing that to surrender might be to sign their own death warrants, the detested KHAD tended to fight to the bitter end.

Masud's commanders were trying desperately to take the last fort. But one machine-gun post, which gave it covering fire, had for some reason not been captured and was still in action.

The light had almost gone, the sunset was a lingering glow in the darkening sky. Noel was shooting wide open, on fast stock. It was a scene of great drama and beauty. Masud, with the little circle of his brothers and close friends round him, was silhouetted against the sky with an almost full moon shining palely silver above his head. When it was almost dark, Masud got up and walked down the hill, Noel following him with the camera until he ran out of film.

While Masud went on down the hill, we had to walk back to the top to recover the rucksacks, the exposed magazines and the tripod; by this time we were almost alone on the mountain, the sound of gunfire still crackling angrily below us. A familiar figure loomed out of the dark.

'Sandy, Noel. This way.' It was Jan Mohammed, who had discreetly remained at a lower level during the battle and then come looking for us. He quickly took charge.

'Masud go down long time ago. Why you so slow?'

I started to explain that making a film was a slow, laborious business and then realised he was not listening. Jan Mohammed had seized the tripod and started off at speed down the hill.

CHAPTER EIGHTEEN

We spent the night in a house which was so full of *mujahideen* that we had to sleep in the garden, where we were mercilessly bitten by mosquitoes. Pierre arrived late and gave us a vivid description of Azim in action.

'Azim, 'e is incredible, 'e fought like a lion. You know 'ow quiet 'e is normally. Well, when the battle started, 'e was like *un homme possédé*, 'e was always at the front, leading 'is men forwards.

'We took a lot of prisoner, a 'undred maybe, and a lot of arms. I went into one post where the DRA officer was just about to sit down and 'ave a glass of vodka and something to eat. Yes, the bottle was lying on the floor, broken, *hélas*. Otherwise I would 'ave 'ad a drink. I needed it.' Pierre gave a big laugh. ''e 'ad been killed by a rocket. It was a direct 'it. 'e must 'ave been killed immediately.'

During the night, they brought in two wounded and in the morning, the *mujahideen* put them on stretchers and carried them, grimacing with pain, to a waiting lorry. They had been given first aid by the Panjsheri doctor, a jolly old man with long white hair who carried his surgery on the back of his horse. No doubt he had done his best but his supply of medicines was fairly limited.

In the back of the lorry were two dead *mujahideen*, their faces and bodies covered by *pattus*, with only their feet, still clad in black Russian army boots, sticking out. Another lightly wounded *mujahid* appeared and was helped on board. Two dead and three wounded were amazingly light casualties by any standards, but not untypical for the *mujahideen*.

We bumped our way down the road, the dead and wounded being jolted about unceremoniously in the back. Noel clung to the side of the lorry and I balanced precariously on the roof of the cab, expecting to be thrown off at any moment as we lurched through the enormous potholes.

After half an hour or so, we stopped by a group of *mujahideen*, including Panna, who told us to climb down. I wondered at first if he did not like the idea of us riding in the lorry with the dead, but I soon realised I was being over-sensitive; it was merely that we had reached our destination. A local farmer wearing a striped brown seersucker jacket, rather like one I used to have from Brooks Brothers in New York, beckoned to us to follow and led us across the fields towards his house by the river. Our destination turned out to be not the house, but a raised earthen dais, like an outdoor concert platform, between two magnificent sycamores (*chenar*). The dais had been covered with a carpet and we were bidden to make ourselves comfortable: even in the midst of war and all the privations that went with it, the niceties of Afghan hospitality were still scrupulously and even graciously observed.

While we waited for the tea and *nan* to arrive, I asked Jan Mohammed, 'Where on earth would a man in Farkhar get a jacket like that?'

Jan Mohammed looked surprised at such a silly question. 'In bazaar, in Kabul. Many, many like this in Kabul bazaar.'

'Really? Can you still get jackets like that?'

'Plenty, plenty.' Jan Mohammed indicated his own jacket, a pseudo-English tweed with a blue overcheck. 'This one I buy in Kabul bazaar.'

'It's very smart. How much did it cost?'

'How much this one? This one cost 50 Afghanis (£2.50).'

'Can I see where it was made? It must have a label.'

Jan Mohammed took his jacket off. 'Ah, here it is. What does it say? Wait a minute. Ro ... man ... Roman Export. It must be Romanian. Good Lord, fancy an English-style tweed jacket from Romania.'

Jan Mohammed looked as if it were the most natural thing in the world. Before the war, and even still, apparently, second-hand clothes from Europe do a roaring trade in Afghanistan. I wondered if I would come across some of my own cast-offs.

A stream of locals arrived to view the *farangi* (foreigners) and Jan Mohammed regaled them with what sounded like a vivid account of the previous night's battle. As they listened avidly to his recital, scores of dragonflies darted about, staging an aerobatic ballet above the maize field that separated our dais from the river. Their flight and shape, apart from the abrupt changes of direction, bore a remarkable similarity to the Mi24 helicopter gunships which had made me so nervous on my previous trips; and I wondered why there was still no aerial reaction from the Russians after last night's attack. It was altogether too peaceful and that in itself was ominous.

The thought of an air strike, the flatness of the valley and the intense green of the rice fields made me think of Vietnam. It was not so much the visual similarity as a matter of suggestion: the villages hidden among their thick screens of trees had the same secretive air; down by the river, a boy showed me an air-raid shelter dug into the river bank; and the people who came to meet us and gave us *nan* and tea were as devoted as any Vietnamese villagers to the cause of the guerrillas. Perhaps more so: there were plenty of villages in Vietnam where neither the Vietcong's terror tactics nor the predatory ways of the South Vietnamese army, always ready to steal a chicken, or worse, were welcome.

Here in Afghanistan, I had never seen the *mujahideen* ordering villagers about or helping themselves to their possessions: I think the strict tribal code and the Afghan sense of honour prevented that. Leaving aside Nuristan, which is a special case, I estimated that ninety-nine, if not one hundred per cent of the villagers we saw were behind the *mujahideen*. But then that was hardly surprising, since they *were* the *mujahideen*, their own flesh and blood, their fathers, uncles, brothers, sisters and wives. Khalili said there had been 'mistakes', made by 'bad *mujahideen* commanders', in the past, but that these had been stamped out by people like Masud and were practically unknown now.

During my first visit to the Panjsher in 1982, we had deliberately avoided several villages on the way in because our Jamiat escort said they were Hisbe and therefore hostile. And sometimes that hostility might lead them to help the government, as happened to Ashem. In the same way there might be villages in the north which were pro-government, or neutral, but in a month of travelling there, moving from village to village and from house to house, depending entirely on the hospitality and friendliness of the local population, we never came across a single one. Quite the reverse: popular support for the *mujahideen* seemed to be total. Everywhere Masud went, he was treated as a hero. Of course, the north is basically

Tajik-speaking, so in a sense he was on his home ground, although a long way from the Panjsher Valley. But his appeal, it seemed to me, was more than ethnic. He was one of those archetypal Afghan warrior-leaders, like Ahmed Shah Durrani and Abdur Rahman, who so often in Afghan history appear at a time of crisis to save the nation. True, Masud was not yet a national leader and might never be, but there was certainly no one else in Afghanistan with anything like his by now almost legendary prestige.

After a delicious lunch of mutton and rice, accompanied by an onion and tomato salad, a message arrived summoning us to Masud. It turned out he was only about a mile away, resting under some trees farther up the hill, surrounded by local bigwigs. I walked up and asked him in French, 'Did you capture the last fort?'

'No, we didn't. But I'll give you a full briefing later.'

Soon afterwards everyone got up and we discovered that the dead, now numbering three, were to be buried on the hill above the village. Masud led the way, stopping at the mosque where a large crowd of villagers was gathering. I buttonholed Khalili.

'Where are they going to take the bodies? Inside the mosque?'

Khalili asked some villagers who were queuing up to climb through an opening in the high wall surrounding the mosque. 'First, they will take the bodies into the mosque and then after they have said prayers they will take them out and bury them.'

Noel asked, 'Where are they going to bury them? We want to get there in advance.'

'Let me ask . . . Yes, in the cemetery.'

'Where's the cemetery?'

'A moment . . . It is some distance. Here, this boy will show you. Please go with him.'

We followed the boy up the dry river bed for about a hundred yards and then, just as we turned left to climb the hill, we heard a shout behind us. It was Pierre.

Pierre was wounded in Vietnam and walks with some difficulty. He seemed to be moving very slowly and we kept chivvying the boy to hurry up. But, not understanding, he kept turning round and waiting for Pierre. Finally we saw the cemetery in front of us, perched on the top of a steep little hill. By now Noel and I, weighed down with the camera equipment, were becoming increasingly short-tempered.

'It's all very well for Pierre. He only has to carry a couple of small cameras and needs no time to set up.'

Noel, on the other hand, would need several minutes to have the camera and sound gear ready for shooting and to set the time code. The boy was still dawdling up the hill with the tripod.

'Hey, get a move on, they're coming.'

Approaching by another, more direct route was the cortège with the three stretchers, the bodies covered with white sheets.

'Shit, and he brings us the long way round. Here, fetch us the bloody tripod.' Noel was angry. The cortège was advancing at a rapid pace, and was soon at the foot of the hill. He punched in the time code, so infuriating to have to do under pressure, but so essential for editing, swung the camera on his shoulder and was just in time to get a shot of the first body.

A man like a dervish, naked to the waist and with his face and hair matted with pale brown dust, advanced on the first grave and leaped down into the vault, waving his hands excitedly and shouting orders. This, clearly, was the chief gravedigger. The three graves were dug extremely deep in the sandy soil and lowering the bodies into them took a lot of effort, discussion and above all noise. The air was filled with loud voices, dust and emotion. Masud and his *mujahideen* stood on the edge of the first grave, watching with sorrowful intensity as ten feet below they laid to rest one of his oldest and dearest comrades in arms, Sofi Miraj.

Sofi had fought at Masud's side in many engagements in the Panjsher over the years and this time Masud had told him to stay well back, even giving him a sniper's rifle. But Sofi had pleaded to be allowed to take part in the assault and a fierce argument ensued, ending only when Masud had slapped him across the face. Later his remorse at having struck an old friend was so strong that Masud relented and let Sofi have his way. He gave him permission to take part in the assault and Sofi had been killed.

The chief gravedigger was now supervising the walling up of the tomb with large stone slabs. Once they were in place, the tomb was sealed with large handfuls of mud passed down by a human chain of helpers. That done, he seized a long-handled spade and began to fling the earth down on top of the grave, the dust rising in clouds which were whipped away by the stiff breeze. After a few seconds, Masud stepped forward, took another spade and started to shovel the earth on to Sofi's mortal remains in a final tribute to his friend. He looked deeply distressed.

Noel, heroically I thought, went downwind of the grave and shot the final scene through an inferno of dust. In the middle of all this Andy arrived, unscathed but not entirely happy.

'Andy, very good to see you, how did you get on?'

'I think I've got some good stuff, but we got pinned down and they couldn't take the last fort. Masud finally called off the attack at about half past two this morning. He didn't want to risk any more casualties. I got lots of good bangs, though, and I got a direct hit on the KHAD fort, too.'

'Fantastic.'

'I was lucky. The camera was running when the shell exploded right on target. There was a big flash and a lot of smoke. It should be a good picture.'

'That's marvellous, Andy.' I was considerably reassured because I knew from experience how difficult battles, especially guerrilla battles, were to film.

'I filmed until the light ran out, but there was so much fire coming from the KHAD fort that we couldn't move. So I just lay down and went to sleep until about eleven. When we left at about two or two thirty, Azim was still attacking. What a man.'

'You must be bloody tired.'

'We had to walk all the way back and I haven't had anything to eat since yesterday, but I'm OK.'

The burials over, the mourners sat down and listened attentively to the mullah's sermon. It went on for a long time and was followed by a local commander who paid his own tribute, Homeric in length, to the dead. Finally, the mullah intoned a prayer and, with the sun beginning to set behind the mountains, everyone started to leave.

We walked back to the spot where we had met Masud and found him stretched out under a tree, having a nap. One of the *mujahideen* tiptoed up and gently covered him with a *pattu*.

177

We had made ourselves comfortable and were just settling down for the night when Jan Mohammed announced we were moving. I always found these sudden changes of plan infuriating.

'I thought we were staying here for the night?'

'We go house. Very near.'

'*Nim sat?*' I asked facetiously.

'No *nim sat*. Five minute. House is better than here.' Jan Mohammed looked round disparagingly.

But it was not. We had to wait a very long time for dinner and when it came it was hardly worth eating: cold rice and a small bowl of salad. Noel was exhausted and after eating a few mouthfuls unrolled his sleeping bag in the corner and went to sleep. The room was small and stuffy and I asked Jan Mohammed if Andy and I could sleep on the roof instead. It was a selfish demand and put our hosts to considerable trouble, but after a good deal of talk a young man brought a *kilim* from the house next door and with difficulty hoisted it on to the roof. When I made my suggestion I had not realised that the only way up to the roof was by using a tree as a ladder. Mattresses and pillows followed by the same route and Jan Mohammed, Andy and I finally bedded down under the stars, the soughing of the trees our lullaby.

Masud arrived with Khalili after breakfast to give us the promised briefing. He was friendly, as always, and business-like.

'We had a number of problems which prevented the operation being a complete success. First of all, Panna was delayed by a minefield which we didn't know existed. We had no intelligence about those mines. One 75-millimetre recoilless rifle was not working. But the biggest problem was the machine-gun post above the KHAD fort. The group that should have attacked it had no covering fire: the Dashaka that should have provided it had no firing-pin. Finally, we ran out of ammunition so I called off the attack at three o'clock yesterday morning. But to sum up, the operation was highly positive and successful.'

Masud then went into detail. 'This was a difficult operation in many ways.

'First, different groups from different areas had to combine, and second, weapons had to come from many sources. The two things together make for a difficult operation. But, despite the lack of training of some of the groups, it went better than I expected; and politically it was a success with the local people.

'Two-thirds of the enemy garrison were eliminated: between eighty-five and a hundred were killed or wounded; another fifty defected to Hisbe-i-Islami; and fifty-three were taken prisoner. One crack unit was destroyed and the commander and second-in-command killed or captured.

'We captured a lot of stores: the garrison was supplied for the next six months; also, most of the weapons were captured or destroyed and the buildings burnt. They will have to send a big convoy to resupply the base; it will have to go through Taluqan and the *mujahideen* will attack it.'

'Why do you think there have been no air strikes?'

'Because no Russians were involved. Panna is going to attack again tonight and try to capture the last fort. For me and my commanders it was a very important experience. For the *mujahideen* too. We have all learnt a lot.'

'How does this compare with other operations you've been involved in?'

'I've been in bigger operations when we've been attacked, but it's the second biggest offensive operation I've ever taken part in, after Pushghour. I think it'll be a turning point for the *mujahideen*, because it was a combined operation involving nine groups from five different provinces.'

He went through the order of battle.

'One mobile group each from the Panjsher, Khost, Farkhar and Kishem. Two local groups from Taluqan, one local group from Ishkamish; and two central groups.'

The central groups were the best troops, recruited from all over the north, including the Panjsher, and could be deployed anywhere. In other words, they were not troops who could only fight on home ground and they were a key part of Masud's plan to nationalise the war.

'How many commanders? We had one from Badakhshan, one from Kunduz and three senior commanders from the Panjsher.'

The briefing was over and he now made a little speech of the utmost courtesy, thanking us all for coming so far to see him.

'It is a very long way, over our mountains, especially if you are not used to so much walking.' He permitted himself a grin. 'I hope your film will tell the world the truth about what is happening in Afghanistan.'

I asked if he had any message he would like me to give to President Zia.

'Tell him: "If you want to see us beat our common enemy, send us the weapons. If not, give them to General Akhtar and let him sell them in Darra (on the North-West Frontier) or in the bazaars of Pakistan."'

I did not say so, but I thought that while the first part of the message was unexceptionable, the second part might have to be diplomatically toned down.

'Now, your movements. I'm going to send you in the pick-up first to where you can see the prisoners and then it'll take you on to Warsaj.' We walked down to the centre of the village where someone stopped him with a request. Masud sat down on a stone, took out a ballpoint and paper and started to write a letter. It was so characteristic of him that I took a picture. But he was looking down, frowning, so I said, 'Ahmed Shah.' He looked up obligingly, grinned and gave me my last picture of him.

Azim and Khalili walked with us down to the truck, a battered Russian equivalent of a Ford pick-up, embraced us and waved us goodbye.

We spent an hour filming the prisoners: I counted them and Masud's figure of fifty-three was correct. They included about a dozen boys aged between nine and eighteen who said they had been press-ganged into the army from surrounding villages. When we asked if they would like to join the *mujahideen*, perhaps not unexpectedly they all put their hands up. There was a weasely-looking, crew-cut little man with hardly a tooth in his head who I was told was the *uluswali*, the assistant administrator of the district.

'What will happen to him?' I asked Wali, Masud's youngest brother.

'He's an old Communist. Maybe they will try him.'

'And the others, the officers?' There were half a dozen.

'Some of them were already in touch with us from inside the *garnesion*. So they will probably join the *mujahideen*.'

I looked at the prisoners. Most were fairly young. Who knew what devious and tortured thoughts were going through their minds, although no doubt survival was uppermost? I gave a last glance at the wizened little Communist. He looked confident, almost cocky, but perhaps he was putting on a brave face. It is a commonplace that of all wars, civil wars are the cruellest.

CHAPTER NINETEEN

When we had finished filming the prisoners, and were ready to leave, we discovered that the pick-up had disappeared.

Wali said he would walk back to our starting point, find the missing vehicle and rejoin us. I thought this was a piece of characteristically Afghan logic but merely said I hoped he would catch up with us soon, since he would be a valuable travelling companion: I knew we would soon be parting company, alas, with Jan Mohammed. So we tramped south towards the King's old camping ground, watching the moon rise over the mountains, softening the harsh landscape with its silvery magic.

We stopped for some food and slept until two, when Jan Mohammed roused us to watch our equipment being loaded on four donkeys. As we departed across the royal meadow, I listened for ghostly laughter from more gracious days, but there was no sound except the rush of the river and the clink of our little convoy. Suddenly, like a swimmer from the depths, a troubling thought surfaced in my mind.

'What the hell are we doing here? We should be filming the attack on the fort. It's only just occurred to me. God, what a fool I am. Masud told us yesterday morning he was going to make another attack last night.'

'I never heard him talking about it,' Noel said.

'It wasn't very clear, just a passing remark; like an aside.' Andy's voice was soothing.

'It's entirely my fault. He said it, I remember him saying it, for God's sake, but somehow I didn't react. We allowed ourselves to be rushed away. To have come so far and then to leave before the climax, it's enough to drive you mad.'

Andy tried again to calm me down. 'Maybe he thought the attack would fail and he didn't want us there to see it. Or he may have been worried about the chances of an air strike, and us getting killed. I wouldn't worry, Sandy, we've got some good stuff.'

I strode on in silence, trying to recall every word of the

conversation. How was it that when he let drop something so vital, I hadn't picked it up? That none of us had picked it up? Why on earth hadn't Masud, usually so alert to the benefits of publicity, not suggested himself that we film the final assault? Even if he was worried about our safety during the attack, he could have let us film the aftermath, once the last fort had fallen: the prisoners, the captured arms, himself taking possessions of the fort. What a picture that would have been! The missed opportunities crowded into my mind, torturing me with what might have been. Now only time and fatigue – and there was no shortage of that – would dull the sense of failure.

We walked on as the moon set, the pre-dawn darkness cloaking the mountains and blacking out the road. First light was at four and dawn came at about five, wonderfully fresh and promising. We walked until seven through a landscape as bare as a volcanic crater, the green silt-laden river keeping us company on our left. Small fields bordered the road and below a village we came on some men threshing wheat with a team of oxen. The oxen were yoked to a wooden pole and driven round and round, treading the grain from the stalk; it was a scene that could hardly have changed since the days of Alexander the Great.

I halted to take a picture and the farmers immediately stopped work and came over to shake hands. One man wanted us to go to his house in the village, but we declined, knowing it would take at least an hour. Well, then, surely we'd sit down and have some tea and bread?

Jan Mohammed and I sat down, gratefully and in my case stiffly, and let ourselves be waited on as if we were kings: but then in Afghanistan the traveller is a kind of king. It was only *nan* and tea, but it was served as if it were caviar and champagne.

We said goodbye to our friends and half an hour later reached a *chaikhana* where Andy and Noel were already installed and savouring their first pot of tea. Noticing that there were chickens running about in the yard, Jan Mohammed ordered fried eggs, *nan* and lots of tea with sugar for those who wanted it. Sugar was sometimes unobtainable but not often; the Russians had to keep the economy of Kabul going for their own purposes and were unable to prevent the *mujahideen* turning it to their own advantage. Thus, despite the destruction of agriculture in many parts of the country, the basic necessities were generally available, although at highly inflated prices.

Half an hour later, back on the road again, Jan Mohammed and I walked together, past farms where they were busy harvesting.

'This place very like the Panjsher Valley at Astana.' He pointed at a narrow gorge through which the river poured in a green flood. Above the gorge, the valley broadened and scores of cattle and donkeys grazed the wide water meadows. We passed a lorry parked under some trees and our hopes rose.

'Any chance of getting them to give us a lift to Khanaka?' Khanaka was the main town in Warsaj district. My legs were beginning to feel very weary. Jan Mohammed spoke to some men waiting by the side of the road.

'They say they like take us but they have no petrol.'

'Ah, well, it was worth a try.'

'But this mens who have lorry, they say Panjsheri family have big farm, not too far from here.'

Heartened by this information, we marched on in the heat of the day, finally coming to a collection of houses hidden among trees, owned by a Panjsheri patriarch who had lived there with his sons and grandsons and their families for twenty years. The Panjsheri connection, and the magic name of Ahmed Shah Masud, ensured that their hospitality was doubly generous. Carpets were spread under the trees at the edge of the river where it was delightfully cool and a big lunch served *al fresco*. After we had eaten our fill and were reclining on cushions drinking our tea, Jan Mohammed said the patriarch was offering to provide us with horses and some of his numerous descendants to escort us back to Chitral. We had been planning to hire horses in Khanaka, but we were still some distance away and it seemed a tempting idea.

'What are the horses like? Are they any good?' I asked. I knew I was no expert, and I suspected neither were Andy nor Noel.

'Good, good,' said Jan Mohammed with great conviction, as if there were no such thing as a bad Afghan horse. 'You look horses. You like, you take. You no like, you no take.'

Filled with food and weary from the long march, I lay back lethargically and watched the patriarch's sons lead the horses into a nearby field.

'Isn't that grey a bit old?'

'Which one? The white horse? Is good horse. All good horse.'

I realised we were not going to get a dispassionate verdict from Jan Mohammed. We were still several miles from Khanaka and quite naturally he saw this as a heaven-sent opportunity to complete the journey on horseback.

'What do you think, Andy?'

'I'm not an expert, Sandy. I'm sure they're OK.'

'OK, we need five horses. Yes? Five horses. How many horsemen will there be?'

An animated discussion followed.

'This four men,' Jan Mohammed said finally. I looked at them. They seemed sturdy and reliable.

'All right. Five horses, four men, how much?'

'Forty thousand Afghanis. One horse.'

I did some mental arithmetic. 'That's two hundred thousand Afghanis for five horses. One thousand pounds. All in, everything included?'

'Everything.'

I wanted to be sure there were no arguments later. 'Jan Mohammed, they will take us to Chitral, five horses, for two hundred thousand Afghanis. No extras. Is that right? Please make sure.'

Jan Mohammed repeated the arrangement in Farsi and heads were nodded. 'Is good. Is OK. We go now. They make horses ready and come later.'

We crossed a torrent by a wooden bridge and came on a group of men sitting in a field by the side of the road. They looked as if they had been having a discussion, their faces serious. Thirty yards away, the women sat in another group, their red dresses and *chadors* making a bright splash of colour against the stony earth. Some of the younger women were unveiled and strikingly good-looking. Jan Mohammed stopped to talk to the men.

'Who are they, refugees?'

'Yes, they come from Taluqan. They say they leave their

villages because too much bombardment.'

'By the Russians?'

'Russians, of course. They say Russians bomb their villages, their houses, kill many people. Then Russian soldiers come into the villages, they kill the old people and burn the houses. They cannot stay there any more. They must leave their villages.'

'Why are they waiting here?'

'They want to go to Pakistan, but Masud has close the road. The *mujahideen* stop them and tell them they cannot go. So they wait here.'

I remembered Masud saying he and the other commanders in the north had given the order that no more refugees were to leave the area. Here was the proof that his writ really did run throughout the north.

We had been walking for a good half hour, with no sign of either the horses or Khanaka, when uncharacteristically Jan Mohammed exploded. 'Half hour. They say half hour to Khanaka. Why these people say half hour when it two hour, maybe three hour? Why they say this when they no know? They crazy people, these people.' I had never seen him so angry. He must have been as fed up with walking as I was.

The horses eventually caught up with us and we mounted; Noel and I found ourselves on the two slowest animals, mine being highly uncomfortable as well because of the bulging, straw-stuffed pack saddle which had no stirrups. Having a horse under him soon returned Jan Mohammed to his usual good humour and he trotted off smartly, waving his whip in approved Afghan fashion. I was the last to arrive in Khanaka, my muscles so exhausted by the discomfort of straddling the stirrupless pack saddle that when I dismounted I could hardly stand. The narrow street was crowded with people and the sight of a *farangi* tottering bow-legged up it provided the locals with much innocent amusement. Haji Saleh, Masud's man in Warsaj, immediately took us off to his house, a ramshackle but beautifully situated remnant of King Zaher Shah's summer residence. It stood in an apple orchard above the confluence of the two rivers which join to form the Farkhar, so the King would have had his fishing on the doorstep.

Haji, a prosperous lapis dealer with two wives and numerous

children, was a refugee from Dasht-i-Raiwat in the Panjsher. He proved a most generous host, providing us with an excellent dinner and comfortable and clean bedding on the floor. After dinner, he summoned two of his sons, one nine and the other ten, to entertain us by wrestling Afghan-style, which they did with great energy and some painful-looking falls. As soon as we decently could Noel and I pleaded exhaustion and retired to bed: I calculated it had been a nineteen-hour day.

Next morning we breakfasted at a leisurely hour, having decided that Thursday 21 August, our forty-fourth day in Afghanistan, would be a rest day for us, while the horsemen made their final preparations. Haji produced a sort of semolina porridge, made from the root of a purple flower which grows in the mountains of Badakhshan and Takhar, and sounds disgusting but tasted rather good. Afterwards, I enjoyed a lazy hour reading Robyn Davidson's book, *Tracks*, a fascinating account of her journey across Australia with two camels. Australia's first camels were imported complete with their Afghan drivers and the author had studied the mysteries of camel behaviour under one of them. While I was engrossed in Miss Davidson's remarkable journey, so much harder than our own, Haji's sons sat down beside me and peered at the cover of the book, which depicted the author and her camels crossing the desert.

'This Afghanistan?'

'No, this Australia.'

From their faces it was clear they had never heard of Australia. I drew a very rough map of the world for their benefit, starting with India, Pakistan and Afghanistan, and then moving on to Russia, China, Japan and Australia with tiny little Britain away up in the top left-hand corner. Because of the war these boys had received no proper schooling which was a pity because they were both intelligent. When Haji made them sing *mujahideen* songs for us, they did so with *élan*, reciting verse after verse without a pause. One of the songs had a refrain which went . . .

'*Ay askari, Masud-i . . .*' 'I am a soldier of Masud . . .' with the emphasis on the 'i's.

After the geography lesson, I strolled into the town, soon getting lost in the maze of narrow side streets which zigzagged between high walls. These were beautifully built of round stones from the river, each row slanted in alternating diagonal patterns. I eventually found the bazaar which consisted of a few small shops like rabbit hutches and in one of them I discovered Jan Mohammed. The walls were stacked with bales of garishly coloured cloth from India, Japan, Russia and North Korea as well as Afghanistan. There was also some beige cloth from England, which the shopkeeper said he sold for men's shirts and baggy trousers.

This shop also sold Russian army boots and Russian brown soap – both probably taken from convoys ambushed in the Salang – and Afghan raisins, sweets, matches and dozens of other articles. With Jan Mohammed's help, I stocked up for the homeward journey with sugar, including sugar crystals, raisins, sweets and tea.

After lunch, which was served by Haji's sons, Jan Mohammed told us that the horsemen wanted to go to another village. 'This men say other village have ver good bazaar. No good here, no food for the horses.'

This was a typical horseman ploy. They always wanted to move to another village where there was a better bazaar, or to another area where the grazing was superior, and always at the most inconvenient time. Andy and Noel wanted to spend all afternoon sorting and packing our sixty-odd rolls of film before the journey, so I put my foot down. 'No, we can't move anywhere this afternoon. They're to stay here and be ready to move off first thing tomorrow morning.'

That evening, a boy came into the house where I was reading and summoned me by dumb show. I rose and followed him across the orchard and over the wall which bounded Haji's property. Coming towards us across the broad expanse of King Zaher Shah's former lawn was a small group among whom I identified Haji and Jan Mohammed.

'Come, Sandy Gol, look here,' Jan Mohammed shouted. A man carrying a basket thrust it under my nose.

'My God, look at all these fish! How wonderful, Haji, how very kind of you to go to all this trouble.' I had pestered Haji, as I had pestered Jan Mohammed before him, with my passion for fish. Haji had hired a man from the village on the other side of the river and he had been fishing all afternoon with a net to catch our supper. Although he had already filled the basket, at

Haji's bidding he demonstrated his technique for me by wading into the freezing cold river in his bare feet, and casting his net with a dexterous discus-like swing, grinning broadly that such an everyday act should excite such curiosity. We took the fish back to the house, and Haji's unseen wives cooked them beautifully. I had observed a couple of trout in the basket and they were delicious: the others, which might have been a kind of bream, were bony and rather tastless; I didn't think the King would have approved.

We left Haji's desirable residence at half past six next morning, and started up the valley, heading south. It was a beautiful ride, sometimes high above the river, sometimes dropping down to splash through the shallows and then climbing again past fields of wheat where the locals were busy harvesting. The only thing that marred my enjoyment was the difficulty of riding *à l'Afghane*, on top of a pile of saddlebags and sacks of barley – fodder for the horses – which had an infuriating habit of slipping to one side. This meant that as you rode along you had to keep yanking the whole lot straight to maintain your and your horse's equilibrium, sometimes while negotiating a narrow path with a hundred-foot drop to the river below.

We passed through several pretty, shady villages to which I thought it would be wonderful to escape for a honeymoon or to finish a book. At the entrance to one village, where the river made a big green pool below a cascade, I counted five large trout indolently floating on the upcurrent, waiting for a tempting titbit. I suggested that we stop to try to catch them, or have a local boy catch them, but I was brusquely overruled.

It was in one of these villages that the sad moment came to take our leave of Jan Mohammed. He had obviously been told by Masud to make sure we were well on the road to Pakistan before he left us and he carried out his instructions to the letter.

'Sandy Gol, I say goodbye.'

'Look after that radio,' I joked.

'I thank you ver, ver much.' He put his hand on his heart in that touchingly courteous Afghan gesture. 'Goodbye, Andy, you bastard man.' They would have embraced, but for the fact that Andy was on horseback. 'Goodbye, Noel.'

'Jan Mohammed, take a last picture, would you?' I handed

him my camera, trying to stop my horse turning its backside to the lens.

There was also a final deal to be done, with the help of Jan Mohammed.

'Horsemen say they want money to buy food for horses.'

'I thought they had already done that?'

'They want take money now. Five thousand Afghanis each horse.'

'I see. They want an advance, in other words.'

'Please?'

'They want five thousand now, and the rest when we arrive in Chitral?'

'Ah, I understand. Advance, yes.' Jan Mohammed laughed. 'Advance ver good.' The horsemen looked on unsmilingly as I counted out the notes which they then divided among themselves.

Impatient with all this delay, the horses started to barge their way out of the village and I had to turn in the saddle to wave goodbye to Jan Mohammed, catching a last glimpse of the burly figure with the half happy, half sad clown's face as he stood surrounded by villagers in the little square. I had suggested to him that he come with us to Pakistan, but he had just smiled. 'I go back. Masud need me do ver ver much work.'

The valley now became more open and full of birds: I noted grey and pied wagtails, golden orioles, hoopoes, a pied chat, the male very handsome in his black and white plumage, redstarts and for the first time, I think, a pair of white-tailed stonechats, equally handsome with dark heads and cream and russet chests. There were also warblers and countless shrikes, sometimes called the butcher bird because of its nasty habit of impaling its prey on thorns and eating it at leisure. They have cruel beaks and a dark stripe through the eye which gives them the look of a masked highwayman waiting for a victim.

In the afternoon, at the top of the watershed, we passed a narrow, intensely green lake about a mile long: it looked so deep and mysterious that I expected an arm to emerge from its waters brandishing if not Excalibur at least a Kalashnikov. We stopped in a small mountain village for tea at about five and decided to spend the night in the mosque. From it we could gaze at a mighty mountain, the top pyramid of rock covered in snow, and contemplate without enthusiasm the pass, our tenth, we would have to cross tomorrow. As soon as the sun set, the temperature dropped sharply and I was glad when it was time to get into my sleeping bag. There was still no sign of the wandering Wali and I began to wonder if we would ever see him again.

CHAPTER TWENTY

The horsemen were still loading when we left the mosque at six o'clock on empty stomachs and marched up the valley towards the distant peaks. Not far from the village the river tumbled through a narrow gorge, spanned by the best-built bridge I had seen in Afghanistan, a solid wooden arch at the top of hundred-foot cliffs. I had been cold all night and it was not much above freezing now: I could not remember my hands being so cold since the winter of 1945–46 when I did my national service in the RAF at Melksham in Wiltshire. But that had been in the middle of winter. Here, it was supposed to be high summer, August the twenty-third, to be precise. It was eight o'clock before the sun came over the mountains and my hands began to thaw out in its first warming rays.

We were climbing a long grassy shoulder when I heard a shout from behind and turned to see my horseman spurring after us, apparently stricken by a rare fit of remorse: most horsemen are quite happy to let you walk while they ride the horse that you are paying for. After helping me to mount he tried to make amends for our lack of breakfast by offering me an apple and later, when we had caught up with Noel and Andy, he undid his *pattu* and shared out his supply of hard, home-made biscuits, called *kulcha*.

The grassy uplands gave way to a great saucer of mountains in the middle of which lay two glass-green lakes and beyond them a steep rock escarpment. We had caught up with a party of *mujahideen*, one of whom spoke a little English.

'Is that the *kotal*, the pass, there?' I asked hopefully, pointing at the escarpment. It was steep but not very high.

'Yes, yes, *kotal*, *kotal*.'

'Really? *Kotal*? *Hubas* (Good).' Then to Noel, 'I can't really believe it, can you?'

'It would be great if it was the pass.'

Noel started up the rocks and I followed in the wake of some friendly but slow horsemen, one of whom gave me an encouraging sweet, and some even slower donkeys. At the top, I found Noel casting about for the right path.

'It's not over there, that goes back down the way we came. So it must be up here.' We looked up at the forbidding face of the mountain in front of us and the last faint hopes of a relatively easy ascent vanished. Very slowly and reluctantly, we started to plod upwards to the real, but still invisible pass. The words 'lofty' and 'inaccessible' flashed on and off in my mind, like lights in a disco. The going was shaly and slippery and the path wound backwards and forwards in a maddening manner. Having been misled by the map the night before into thinking this was a gradual, rounded summit, Noel and I found ourselves panting up one of the steepest passes yet: it was called Zard which, phonetically at least, conveyed something of the harshness of the place. As if to mock us, two magnificent lammergeier vultures now appeared and soared with tantalising ease just above the summit, no doubt calculating our eligibility as carrion.

At two o'clock we stood on the top of the pass; my heart was pounding and my lungs heaving but the first few seconds of triumph were, as always, sweet. After a brief rest, photographing one another against a mighty, snow-capped panorama, we walked across a gently sloping plateau from which the snow had only recently melted and where clusters of tiny blue flowers made little cushions of delight on the bare earth. Snow buntings flitted tamely among the rocks and ravens swooped and croaked overhead as we went hurrying down, trying to make up for the slow ascent, eventually coming on Andy sitting with his back against a rock, puffing his pipe.

'I think there's a *banda* a bit farther on where we might get some tea,' he said encouragingly.

It proved to be a long hike down before we sighted a black Kuchi tent belonging to an almost toothless ancient; he greeted us with great friendliness, offered us tea and *nan* and explained that he had been in these parts for four months.

'He and his family came up from Jalalabad in the spring. He says that the Kuchis are always getting bombed by the Russians as they move from one place to another. They've lost a lot of camels from the bombing.'

The old man said something and Andy laughed. 'He thought we were Russians from Tajikistan, and he was a bit worried at first. When I told him who we were he was much happier.'

The tea and *nan* arrived, brought by two of his pretty little daughters: or were they granddaughters?

'I think we ought to give him something, Sandy. He says that a lot of *muj* stop at his tent and ask for tea and *nan* and he doesn't look very rich to me.'

I took 200 Afghanis out of my pocket and held them out to the old man. He immediately backed away, saying he did not need any money, but when I thrust them into his pocket he took them, although with every sign of reluctance. I was glad that Afghan pride had its limits because life on that mountainside, even in summer, must have been very hard. For centuries, the Kuchi nomads have travelled with their camels and herds and their black tents from one end of Afghanistan to the other, wintering in the warm valleys round Jalalabad and across the border in Pakistan and in summer trekking north to the high pastures. The Kuchis have always been moneylenders as well as herdsmen, transacting their business in the villages they passed through; they would lend in the spring and collect in the autumn and many of them were said to be rich. But since the war Russian bombing and ground attacks have wreaked such incalculable damage on the Kuchis, as on the vast majority of Afghans, that the entire nomadic pattern of their lives has been disrupted if not destroyed.

As we approached Chamar and the *qarargah* where we had left our saddles and spare kit, we passed a long line of *mujahideen* heading for Farkhar. They had heard about the battle: word travels quickly in rural Afghanistan despite the lack of telephones or other modern means of communication, and they wanted to know all the details. I did my best in my extremely limited Farsi.

'*Jang hubas, bisjar hubas.* (The battle was good, very good.) Ahmed Shah Masud, Panna, Azim, Gadda, *hubas, hubas, Daulat bus* (the government post is finished),' accompanied by a sweeping movement of the hand.

This news was greeted with enthusiastic cries and a lot of questions which I had difficulty understanding let alone answering. When they realised they would get no more information out of us they shook hands warmly and strode off like men anxious to reach the scene of the battle before it was completely over.

A little farther on we passed a friendly farmer who took a handful of peas and beans out of his pocket and thrust them into our hands to sustain us on the march. But we were now nearing the end of the day's journey: the top of the Panjsher Valley opened out welcomingly in front of us, green and peaceful in the evening sunshine; and the mountain where we had interviewed Issa, the Dashaka gunner, so long ago it seemed, was actually below us on our right. A steep descent took us into Chamar village, where we had to dawdle behind a flock of goats, finally reaching the *qarargah* on its bluff above the river at seven, just as the light was fading. We climbed wearily to the upstairs room and found Andy reclining in his usual place at the far end, pipe in mouth.

'Hallo, Sandy. Hallo, Noel. I've ordered some tea.'

It came soon afterwards and tasted like nectar. The horsemen arrived at half past nine, just as we were going to bed. We had been on the road for thirteen hours at a stretch.

After a day like that, the first moments in the sleeping bag are, for me, akin to bliss: tired muscles stretch and relax, dissolve almost, and then sleep comes swiftly, like a hawk over the hill. But just as my eyes were closing, I heard muttered curses and frenzied movement and Andy rose from the floor and rushed out of the room, clutching his sleeping bag in one hand and holding his trousers up with the other.

'What the hell's wrong, Andy?'

'Bugs. I'm getting bitten to hell.'

Fleas and other bloodsuckers are part of *qarargah* life and, temporarily abandoning sleep, I sat up and having found my insect spray gave my sleeping bag a generous dose. It worked. I had an untroubled night whereas Noel and Andy were badly bitten. When Noel inspected the inside of his sleeping bag next morning, he discovered a large number of small black invaders which Andy soon identified.

'Crabs. They're real bastards. I think they're the ones which must have got me too.'

Around mid-morning, more deadly intruders shattered the peace of the upper valley: a couple of Russian jets dropped bombs somewhere in the region of Zard Pass.

'They might have been looking for us. Or Wali,' Andy said. Rashid, the commander at Chamar, said he had heard that

Wali had arrived at Najmuddin's house and he expected him to appear at any moment. Apart from the pleasure of Wali's company, we were anxious to borrow 100,000 Afghanis, without which we would have difficulty completing the homeward journey – the money I had lost on the way in had never turned up and Masud had been short of money himself, so I had not been able to borrow any from him. The jets went over a second time while I was sunning myself after a cold bath in the river; but this time I did not hear any bombs.

Just before lunch, Andy and I strolled out to see how the horsemen were faring and came on a gruesome sight. Andy's horse, a grey, was lying on the ground, roped by the legs, with two of the horsemen and the boy sitting on it while the third horseman, blood on his hands, seemed to be in the middle of some operation. At first I thought the horse had cut its face and that he was stitching it up. However, on looking closer, we discovered that he was cutting a slit in the side of the horse's nose. One nostril had already been sliced open and we were just in time to see the second part of the operation. Feeling almost sick at the sight of the poor beast smothered in blood, writhing on the ground, Andy and I left them to it.

'Do you think they were bleeding it?' I asked.

'Dunno. It might have a bad stomach or something like that.'

A couple of hours later, as we got ready to depart, the horse still looked badly shaken. 'I don't think it's strong enough to carry me to Bala Chamar (Upper Chamar), so I'll walk,' Andy said. But, amazingly, after a few days the horse seemed to have recovered and managed to complete the journey. We never did discover what the drastic cure was supposed to achieve. But I had often noticed that donkeys had similar slits in their nostrils, so I imagine it was a standard Afghan remedy.

With still no sign of Wali, I got Andy to explain our predicament to Rashid and in return for an IOU he obligingly handed over 100,000 Afghanis, mainly in nice big 500-Afghani notes. Feeling much happier now that we were solvent again and, after nearly seven weeks in the interior, about to start the final stage of our journey, I enjoyed the ride up the familiar valley to Bala Chamar and the *chaikhana*. In particular, there was one happy ornithological moment when I came on a hoopoe sitting in the grass, offering me a splendid view of his long, delicately curved beak and striped crest. When I got to within a few yards of him, he rose into the air in a leisurely fashion, as if not at all afraid, showing off his handsome black and white wing bars and cinnamon tail.

Noel, however, who had walked up with Andy, had had a much less agreeable time. They had passed a boy and a girl with a large, fierce dog.

'I dunno if they thought Andy and I were Russians, but they deliberately set the dog on me.'

'Good God. Are you sure, Noel?'

'Positive. They were shouting at the dog as I passed them – Andy was on ahead – and I happened to look round. Just as well I did. The dog, a bloody great fierce brute, was just about to spring at me. Luckily I was carrying my stick, and I gave it a hell of a belt on the side of the head. It yelped like anything and ran off. But the kids tried to set it on me again. The second time, though, I just had to show it the stick and it buggered off.'

This time, we fared much better in the *chaikhana*. The one-eyed owner installed us in a snug *sangar* with a canvas roof, ejecting all other customers, brought us rice and tea and generally made a fuss of us. I had to get up in the middle of the night to answer a call of nature and found the valley flooded with the silver light of a full moon. It was astonishingly beautiful and very cold, and next morning there was frost on the grass and ice in the streamlets.

Chamar is not a very difficult pass from the north: in fact, as a rule, all the passes are easier from the north, since the tilt of the land is slightly from north to south. To my delight and I must confess slight surprise, I fairly romped up the mountain; at least that was the word I used in my diary. But I suppose it would be more accurate to say I laboured to the top with slightly less difficulty than usual. Andy and Noel had gone on ahead, the horsemen were well behind, so I enjoyed the magnificent views in solitude, taking a couple of pictures of Mir Samir, standing like some great white sentinel guarding the entrance to the Panjsher, and then hurried after the others.

At the foot of the pass, where the shepherd's dog had tried to bite me, both shepherds and dog had departed and so there was no tea. When Andy heard that the horsemen were still a long way behind, he strode off impatiently to the next *chaikhana*, about four hours' walk away, leaving Noel and me to sun ourselves on the grass. When the horses arrived, the horsemen immediately set about rearranging the loads which had slipped on the way down, Noel's saddle being almost round his horse's neck. The horse carrying the film promptly tried to lie down and roll with its load on, leading to much shouting and waving of arms. It then kicked or bit my horse and sent it bolting across the grass shaking off its load, which included my small rucksack with the sound gear, piece by piece as it cantered crazily round and round with the horsemen in hot pursuit. While they were reloading the wretched animal, I noticed that there were only two horsemen and the boy.

'Where's the other horseman?' I asked Noel.

'Isn't that him, lying asleep beside the rock?'

I questioned Tazomir, the headman, by raising my eyebrows and nodding in the direction of the sleeping figure.

Tazomir replied by pointing to his forehead and shaking his head.

'Oh, I see. He's got a headache.'

'They're all a bloody headache, if you ask me,' Noel said.

We were now down to three horsemen, one of whom was sick, and the boy, who was not strong enough to pull the girths tight on Noel's horse. As a result, the saddle kept slipping, which can be dangerous. The fourth horseman, we had just discovered, had decided to wait for Wali, but had omitted to tell us.

Near the *chaikhana* we came on a group of refugees from the north who, despite their privations, were extremely friendly and quite happy to have their photographs taken. I took a picture of one tiny girl, asleep on the back of a donkey, and another in her father's arms. An old man offered me a handful of wheat grains and *tut*, which I munched gratefully and found unexpectedly delicious. How typical of Afghanistan, I thought, that the first thing a refugee does is to offer you something to eat. Their leader was a dignified old man in a blue turban. I tried by sign language to explain that we wanted to film the group next day.

'Ax, ax (photograph),' I said, waving my arm to take in the fifty or sixty refugees.

He smiled and nodded. '*Baksheesh?*'

'Yes, yes. *Baksheesh.* Tomorrow.'

They were on the road early, passing our *chaikhana* while we were still saddling up, led by four or five determined-looking ladies with veils. Then came the children walking or riding on donkeys, or on their parents' backs. The mother of one child, which was wriggling and screaming, dealt it a blow that would have felled a grown man, threw it over her shoulder like a sack of rice and marched past.

Our plan was to film them on Kantiwar, the next pass, so we caught them up and passed them later in the morning. As we were overtaking one family of a young husband and wife and several young children, their heavily loaded horse, a nice-looking grey, slipped on the rocks and fell heavily. Other refugees came running to help, but it lay sprawled almost upside down and they had to unload it before it could get to its feet.

We reached the last *chaikhana* before the pass in the afternoon. Clouds were swirling round the summit of Kantiwar and a few large spots of rain, and later, according to Noel, some flakes of snow as well began to fall. The *chaikhana* consisted of a small stone *banda*, with a fireplace for cooking and a draughty tent with a very dirty *kilim* on the ground. We were standing outside, waiting for the kettle to boil, when a small party of *mujahideen* came round the side of the mountain below us. One of them, on horseback, looked familiar.

'Good God, it's Wali.'

He rode up, grinning broadly. '*Salaam aleikum.*'

'Good Lord, we thought you'd decided to stay behind. What kept you?'

'I have something very important to tell you.' The *watandar* brought the tea and we went into the tent.

'The last fort was captured very quickly, Masud was very happy. Panna was in command, with three groups. They attacked at five in the morning and it was all over by six. First they captured the machine-gun post on the hill above the fort. After that the fort fell very quickly. Many of the defenders gave themselves up. They took a lot of prisoners and hundreds of weapons and lots of food and supplies.' Wali's face shone with excitement.

'The commander of this fort and his deputy escaped across the river but they were captured. Their clothes were dripping with water and they were very unhappy. Masud questioned them. He kept asking them why they had run away. But they did not know what to answer. They just looked all the time on the ground. Lots of people came to shake Masud's hand. He was so happy, not because they had captured the post but because all the people came to see him.'

Then came a depressing piece of news.

'When I got back after I left you, Masud suggested to me to take a car and bring you back to film the operation.'

'Was there a car?' I used the Afghan English idiom, although I knew he meant a jeep or pick-up truck.

'Yes, a very good car.'

'Would you have had time to come and fetch us?'

'Yes, because the attack wasn't until the next morning at five.'

'Why didn't you come for us, then?'

'Masud Khalili told me not to. He said you had closed your cameras.'

'The cameras are never closed. All you do is take them out,' Noel said.

'Masud Khalili told me not to go. That's why I didn't come. And my brother said several times, what a pity you could not have been there to film the capture. Because after they captured it, the *mujahideen* poured petrol over everything and burned it.' There was a moment of anguished silence as we thought of the pictures we could have taken of the burning fort.

'Was there any bombing?'

'One helicopter came and flew over the fort. Panna took a Kalashnikov and fired some tracer bullets at the hillside to make the helicopter think that was where the *mujahideen* were. It dropped one bomb, maybe two, and then flew away.' Wali laughed happily at the resourcefulness of Panna.

It was an odd story and I knew we would never get to the bottom of it. Perhaps it was better to follow the Afghan example and conclude that it was the will of God.

Wali and his companions left before dawn, but much as we

would have liked to have gone with them I was determined to wait for the refugees. It was a key sequence and I knew we had to have it. While we were waiting a large group of *mujahideen* from Kunduz stopped at the *chaikhana*. They were heading for Pakistan to collect weapons; not Kalashnikovs, they told Andy disparagingly, but rocket launchers and heavy weapons.

'They say the Russians have made a lot of attacks in Kunduz and there's been some very heavy fighting. The Russians also burnt all the wheat just as it was ready for harvesting.' One man held out his hand to show how high it had been. Another *mujahid* came up to me, pointing to his rather bald head and then to his stomach. At first I thought he wanted a pill to make the hair grow but then it turned out he had a headache. Apparently a bomb had exploded very close to him and although he had not, apparently, been wounded, the blast had given him a permanent headache.

When by mid-morning there was still no sign of the refugees, we sent Tazomir back to hurry them up.

'Tell them Masud personally wants us to film them on the top of Kantiwar.'

But even that white lie did not help. He soon returned saying that the horse we had seen fall the day before was so badly injured that it could not move and the whole party was going to wait until it was better. I was impressed by their community spirit but irritated that luck or the will of Allah seemed to be against us.

'Bloody hell, are we never going to get this sequence? And we've wasted half a day as well.'

We told Tazomir to load up as fast as possible. We still had to climb Kantiwar.

Whether frustration lent us wings or acclimatisation was finally working, I do not know, but Kantiwar turned out to be an almost enjoyably easy climb; although it started badly for me when I tripped over some rocks at the foot of the pass and cut my hand and lip, banging my chin so hard on the ground I thought at first I had broken a tooth.

Coming down the far side we passed a convoy of eighty-five donkeys and horses, carrying three tons of stores and medical supplies. With them, climbing slowly with pained expressions which I instantly recognised, were a dozen French doctors and nurses – one or two of the latter very pretty – and one Dutchman, from *Médecins sans Frontières*, one of three French voluntary organisations which have provided virtually the only medical service for the *mujahideen* inside Afghanistan since the war started. I stopped to speak to one of the doctors. 'We stay for one year in Badakhshan, where we 'ave two 'ospitals. Some of us 'ave been there before, so we know what it is like, for others it is the first time.'

CHAPTER TWENTY-ONE

We were travelling faster than on the way in and stopping less often, and just above Kantiwar, where the valley makes a great V and a distant peak fits with perfect symmetry exactly in the middle, we met up again with the *mujahideen* from Kunduz. The place reminded me of Scotland: a steep, rocky hillside covered with gnarled Scots firs, or the Asian equivalent, and a stream at the bottom. As we sat in the shade while the *mujahideen* fed us with tea and *nan*, I sketched the valley and jotted down some thoughts about the nature of the war.

'It is a war on three levels.

'Firstly, it is a religious war, a *Jihad* between believers and non-believers.

'Secondly, it is a civil war, of Afghan against Afghan, the anti-Communist majority against the Communist minority.

'And, thirdly and most importantly, it is a war of national liberation against a foreign invader: the Russians. Take away the Russians, 115,000 of them, with another 50,000 along the border, available for cross-border operations, and the Communist government's forces would soon be overwhelmed and the government itself collapse.

'That is really why the Russians find it so difficult to pull out. That is presumably why they talk in terms of their withdrawal taking four years – the Soviet negotiating position in August, 1986. Four years, provided the Communist government in Kabul can by then stand on its own feet. But if not, not. No withdrawal. Unless casualties and world condemnation finally make them bite the bullet and accept the unpalatable truth: Communism has no appeal to the vast majority of Afghans and they have been unable to impose it by brute force, hard as they've tried.'

Kantiwar without the *jirgah* was only a little less crowded, being full of *mujahideen* travelling north to Badakhshan with arms and ammunition. Andy's friend, Haji, invited us to stay and immediately he saw Andy's saddle asked if he could have it. No sooner said than done. 'It's yours,' Andy told him. 'And the bridle as well.'

'That was very generous of you, Andy.'

'Well, you see, I once stayed with Haji for a month and the next time I came to Afghanistan I brought him a few presents. Unfortunately the horse carrying the presents fell over a precipice on Mum (Pass) and they were all lost. So I'm pleased I can finally give him something.'

We had thought of avoiding Mum by making a slightly longer detour by the river, which also had the merit of being very pretty, according to Andy. But Haji and his brother pooh-poohed the idea, saying it would add another day to the journey and that much the best route was by another pass called Sim.

'They say it's easy, you can ride all the way up and it's grassy at the top.'

So we set off in optimistic mood next morning, but soon began to realise that once again we had fallen victim to Afghan hyperbole. We hauled ourselves up rocky gorges, across snow-fields, over a series of screes, more snow and several false crests until, finally, six hours after leaving Haji's house, we stood on the top of Sim. There was no sign of the grassy summit that Haji had talked about so plausibly.

'He's probably never been up here,' Andy said.

Going down, Noel and I stopped to film an arms convoy on its way to the Panjsher. We heard later that hundreds more horses were on the road: one man said fifteen hundred horses had just left Chitral.

In Parun, we spent the night in the mosque where, the others told me, my loud snoring nearly drowned out the sound of the old men at their prayers. Afterwards, a blind man came creeping round the wall of the mosque and was surprised to come across the recumbent figure of Noel, who got up and led him gently to the exit.

On the way to Papruk, our fourteenth pass, I saw my old friend, Güldenstädt's redstart, magnificent in his black and red livery and snow-white cap, and a new friend, a red-heded finch who looked almost as handsome and self-confident. To complete my good fortune, as we approached the pass I spotted a couple of crested tits in a wind-bent cedar, the only ones I had seen in Afghanistan.

Andy made us climb Papruk by the *direttissima*, a steepish rocky chimney, which at first looked horrendously difficult but proved to be quite manageable and much quicker. Papruk village on its hilltop, which we reached next day, was as unfriendly as ever, but the *chaikhana* at the foot was crowded with *mujahideen*. Fifty horses and donkeys were tethered among the trees, and ammunition for the BM12s, recoilless rifles and RPGs was scattered everywhere. Nuristan has become Afghanistan's Ho Chi Minh Trail, or perhaps one should call it the Ahmed Shah Masud Trail.

One of the horses, the grey that carried the film, was now very lame and beginning to hold us up. It had to be unloaded before we crossed Papruk and one of the horsemen was fully occupied looking after it. A Nuristani at the *chaikhana* wanted to buy it and I encouraged the horseman to make the sale.

'Either that, or he stays here with the horse until they come back. But we can't afford to be held up by a lame horse that doesn't carry anything.'

A furious argument ensued, with Tazomir urging him to sell and the horseman shouting that he would not.

'Why the hell doesn't he want to sell?'

'Apparently it's not his horse. It belongs to somebody else and he says he's responsible. He says he can't sell it and he has to get to Pakistan.'

'All right then, but Tazomir had better tell him to get a move on and not hold us up.'

After that conversation, the lame horse always left early and arrived late, but to be fair it never held us up again.

As we neared the border, we came across several arms convoys, each of a hundred or a hundred and fifty horses; I estimated that we passed five or six hundred horses altogether. I also counted three new BM12 rocket launchers, but there may have been many more I did not see. On one occasion, we had to wait by the side of the track until two or three hundred Badakhshanis, all carrying new weapons, marched past us in single file. We often saw spy satellites criss-crossing the night sky, Russian as well as American presumably, so I imagine that the Russians knew all about the arms convoys. But it remained a mystery that throughout the summer of 1986, and especially in late August and September, when the traffic was at its peak, the Russians did not once bomb the trail.

The climb to the *chaikhana* at the foot of the fifteenth and final pass turned out to be a long, exhausting stumble in the dark. Nuristani bloody-mindedness and a growing penchant for bureaucracy delayed us. First, Tazomir had to go back into Peshawarak village to get a *laissez-passer* from the local commander. Then we had to negotiate a checkpoint, where, as so often in the Third World, red tape turned out to be a pretext for extorting a little money. Our way was barred by a gentleman in a Ruritanian uniform with a very real Kalashnikov, backed up by a number of young Nuristani bloods. Tazomir talked to him and then explained the situation to Andy.

'He says he wants to see all the film.'

'Tell him that's ridiculous. It's impossible.'

'We've already told him that, but he insists.'

'Can we give him something?'

'Tazomir's working on that. He says he thinks five hundred (£2.50) will do. Have you got five hundred, Sandy?'

'That's no problem. Is that enough?'

'Tazomir says that's fine. But not here. I think we'd better be fairly discreet.'

We walked on a few yards and I counted out five hundred Afghanis.

'There you are, Andy. I hope that does the trick. I'd hate to lose the film at this stage.'

'I'm sure it will be OK.'

After an anxious moment or two we saw Tazomir emerge from the *banda* and shake hands with the Ruritanian general. The feel of five hundred Afghanis had been enough to dispel his desire to inspect the inside of our film cans.

I cursed Nuristani bureaucracy many times that evening as I slipped and stumbled in pursuit of Noel's torch up what seemed to be an endless mountain. At one point we saw lights in the darkness and thought we had reached the *chaikhana*. To my near despair, it was merely a group of *mujahideen* who had bedded down for the night by the side of the path. One of their horses had laid down on the path itself and we had to walk round it. Eventually, truly exhausted, Noel and I staggered into the *chaikhana* and found Andy, like the wise old soldier he was, ensconced in the kitchen with a group of fierce-looking but hospitable Nuristanis, all as big as bears and almost black with sun and dirt. A huge cauldron of water from which one ruffian constantly replenished a string of small blue teapots simmered on the open fire.

'Sit down and have some tea,' Andy said. 'This is the best place, beside the fire, and these blokes are very friendly.'

We did as instructed, experiencing once again the almost magical effect of hot sweet tea on a totally exhausted body. Within ten minutes, the memory of the last three hours had been almost washed away by numerous pots of Nuristani *chai*.

The head ruffian told us we could sleep 'in the mosque', which turned out to be a bare piece of rocky ground, open to the elements but presumably out of bounds to donkeys and horses. We unrolled our sleeping bags in one corner and thanks to Andy's entrepreneurial skills were brought a last cup of tea in bed by the *watandar* when he came to pray. It was a short, cold night on the frozen ground, but no one minded as we all knew that, unless things went very wrong, it would be our last in Afghanistan.

Dawn, with the tops of the mountains glowing a virginal pink, was cold and austerely beautiful. After drinking a cup of tea with a rather subdued *watandar* we started the final ascent at half past six, leaving the horsemen to follow. It was an advantage to have camped so high the night before, but I still found the climb exhausting, my snail-slow rhythm constantly interrupted by two men on horseback who kept overtaking us and then stopping on the path, forcing us to climb round them. At these altitudes every extra effort is doubly exhausting.

We reached the summit of Peshawarak Pass soon after eight, to be rewarded by a magnificent view of Tirich Mir and away to the right what looked like an even higher peak, perhaps K2. Knowing we had climbed the last pass and were standing on the border induced a wonderful sense of achievement and we sat down happily to wait for the horses and the camera. As a lammergeier planed above us I rehearsed the plan of campaign.

'Noel and I will stay up here at the top of the pass and wait for the next lot of refugees. If they don't come today, we'll have to wait until tomorrow.'

'That's right. We'll just have to sit it out. We must get that sequence,' Noel said.

'Andy, as discussed with Noel, you'll be a few hundred yards below us and film the refugees going down. The best shot will probably be on one of those Z bends.'

'I'll try and get close-ups of them going past me,' Andy said. After half an hour or so, he disappeared down the steep track below us and Noel and I made ourselves as comfortable as possible out of the wind. It was a brilliant day, the sky a pale, gentian blue and completely cloudless for the first time, as far as I could recall, of the whole journey. Tirich Mir dominated the distant skyline, the sun glinting off the icefields near the summit.

Looking down from our eyrie, we could see a convoy of horses with arms toiling up the pass from Pakistan; and at the same time a group of refugees appeared from the other side. As luck would have it, they reached the top of the pass at the same time, the horses getting in one another's way and kicking up clouds of dust. To complicate things further, a party of *mujahideen* came and sat themselves down on the rocks beside Noel, staring infuriatingly into the camera and making him swear.

'Why don't these bloody *muj* bugger off? Go on, buzz off, shoo, go away!'

'*Birra, birra,*' I shouted, waving my hands in the direction of Pakistan, but they either just grinned or looked uncomprehending.

Noel filmed with furious concentration until all the refugees had disappeared.

'Well, I began to think we'd never get that sequence. But there are some very nice shots, especially the kids: the one being carried down the hill on its father's back and the other little kid on the horse looking straight into camera. Now I just want to do a couple of GVs (general views) to finish off.' He clambered up among the rocks to where there was an uninterrupted view in both directions: back into Afghanistan and ahead of us, to Pakistan.

It was noon by the time we had finished and started down the mountain, a lammergeier giving us a last majestic fly-past, the white on his wings like creamy snow, his wing tips black and upcurling. He planed away over a rocky ridge with superb control, making even the ravens, which were doing dives and half rolls, look insignificant. I cast a last glance backwards at Afghanistan: a hundred peaks, dazzling white in the midday sun, marched like an undefeated army to the horizon.

CHAPTER TWENTY-TWO

Because of the need for security, we had been strongly advised not to film in the refugee camps near Peshawar before we went into Afghanistan. And yet an essential part of the film was to be found there: evidence of Russian atrocities which could only be obtained through interviews with the survivors. So while Andy departed for London, Noel and I set to work.

Everyone who understood the situation in Afghanistan knew that there had been countless atrocities committed by Russian soldiers in the course of the long and bitter war. But it had always been difficult for many reasons, including time and distance as well as language, to get the facts quickly enough to interest the world's media. For example, if there was a massacre in a village in the north of Afghanistan, say in Kunduz or Badakhshan, it might take six or eight weeks for the survivors to reach Pakistan. There they would be swallowed up in the refugee camps, and although the story would be picked up by the relief agencies and the handful of Afghan news services, it would probably get no further. There are no full-time Western journalists in Peshawar, and the Reuter and Associated Press correspondents in Islamabad, a hundred miles away, although presumably aware of the reports circulating in Peshawar, rarely if ever follow up atrocity stories.

A good public-relations firm like Markpress, which represented the Biafran cause in the Nigerian civil war in the late Sixties, would have made it its business to find the most articulate of these survivors, the ones with the most horrific experiences to recount, and arranged for them to tell their story to the world. In a handful of instances, a few individuals or bodies interested in human rights, like Michael Barry and the International Humanitarian Enquiry Commission on Displaced Persons in Afghanistan, have crossed the border and made detailed on-the-spot investigations. Michael Barry first did this with notable effect in 1982 when he brought the Logar Massacre to the world's attention.

But on the whole, the grim business of Russian atrocities has gone largely unreported. The Afghans themselves have lacked the publicity skills to put the story in front of the world's media and the world's media have shown themselves singularly uninterested in digging out the story for themselves.

I saw this aspect of the war as a vital part of the documentary and had explained to some of my Afghan contacts that I wanted to do a series of interviews with eyewitnesses when I came back. As I might have guessed, nothing had been arranged and Noel and I had to start from scratch. We went first to the Jamiat headquarters in Peshawar, and after a good deal of discussion there decided we would drive to a refugee camp halfway between Peshawar and Islamabad where, it was said, we would find some survivors of a recent massacre in Kunduz.

Squashed in a small Japanese car (the only cars available for hire at the Pearl Continental Hotel in Peshawar) Noel and I, a young Jamiat official who spoke a little English and a large Afghan called Kakar who knew some of the survivors arrived after an uncomfortable journey. There turned out to be not one but half a dozen camps, and we spent an hour finding the right place. Various men with a story to tell were assembled and Noel set up the camera for the first interview.

'Everything OK, Noel?'

'Hold on a tick, Sandy. Can everyone keep quiet, please . . . Yeah, there it is again. There's a pump or something in the background, all the time. Once you're aware of it, it's very distracting.'

We all listened, and although it would have gone unnoticed in ordinary circumstances, under interview conditions it was immediately and irritatingly audible: the persistent, rapid beat of a small petrol or diesel engine.

'Do you hear it, now. That . . . hear it?'

The Afghans smiled indulgently. 'Oh, that's the water pump.'

'Can we turn it off?'

'Very difficult. It very very long way away.'

'We'll have to go somewhere else, then. Can't do the interview with that noise. It'll be there, on the soundtrack, all the time.' Noel's clipped tones reflected his exasperation.

'OK, let's go somewhere else.'

Too polite to say so, but clearly convinced we were quite

mad, the Afghans debated long and loud and finally led us off into the middle of some maize fields. There, apart from the occasional interruption, we managed, as the afternoon drew to a close, to record the stories of several men from the Chardarra area in Kunduz Province, near the Soviet border. I only discovered later that the Chardarra incident had occurred in 1985. But it was typical: the *mujahideen* had been in action against Soviet troops – very often this takes the form of an ambush – and in reprisal the Russians had sent a big punitive force to sweep through the area.

The first survivor was a man of about fifty, wearing a dirty white turban. He was a prosperous small farmer, a minor village headman. He spoke fluently, almost too fluently perhaps, because he had told the story so many times before. I cross-checked it later and was told it was confirmed by many other eyewitnesses, although his figure of seven hundred and seventy dead seemed improbably precise and too high. A British diplomat, on the basis of other reports from survivors of the Chardarra massacre, put the figure at about four hundred. But the main facts, he said, were not in dispute, including the death of the Soviet general.

'My name is Ghulam Nabi. I'm from Imam Sahib, in Kunduz. When a hundred and seventy Russian tanks entered Chardarra we, the *mujahideen*, wanted to resist. They scattered through the village and the battle started. When they lost thirty-six tanks, they started fighting the civilians and they destroyed at least three to four hundred houses. The *mujahideen* surrounded the Russians, but forty to fifty aeroplanes came towards us from Kunduz and the Russians succeeded in rescuing their soldiers. But one Russian general was killed by the *mujahideen*. The *mujahideen* had to withdraw as they couldn't fight the air battle. The Russians were angry because their general had been killed and in revenge they destroyed the village by tanks and gunfire . . .

'Seven hundred and seventy people were killed. They stole many carpets and radio cassette players as well as cash. Little boys were hung up and killed, women's breasts were cut off. You may think I'm exaggerating but believe me I'm not. That's what I saw with my own eyes. It took us three days to bury the dead. Twenty to thirty people were buried in one mass grave. We had no time to dig a grave for each. Later we decided to load some of the dead on carts and asked the old men from the next village to take them and show them to government officials, to the governor or someone, and we sent at least ten carts to them so they could see what they are doing to us. They were the bodies of men, women and children. The governor saw them and said, "It's out of my power to say anything. We have no power over the Russians. We can't tell them not to kill civilians. You killed their general and they killed seven hundred of your people."

'We took the dead back to the village, it was cold and the ground was hard to dig.'

The second interviewee, also from the Chardarra area, was a youngish man, a simple peasant farmer who despite being nervous of the camera told his story with quiet conviction. He did not give his name and, as in all these interviews, I had only a very general idea of what was being said until everything had been transcribed and translated when we got back to London.

'They killed children because, for example, if there was shooting somewhere in the village, the Russians would come and ask who did it and the children would say they didn't know. The Russians would start killing them with their bayonets or with their Kalashnikovs. Even if it was not proved to them that someone had fired from this house, they would still kill them. Not just the people but the animals too and they would steal their things and their food. For about three days they came; they fought every day and the *mujahideen* fought them but the *mujahideen* were killed. Most of their bodies were in the river for days.'

An old man in a blue turban with a fine aquiline face said he came from Khanabad, one of the principal towns in Kunduz and only about thirty miles from Farkhar. We had heard accounts of the bombing of Khanabad when we were in the north and Masud had told us that the Russians had deliberately destroyed the crops there. He was a recent arrival, his story dating from the first half of 1986.

'Eighteen hundred Russians were killed, you understand. They closed the school and took the boys away. They closed the factories and took the workers away. They said we don't need schools or work now, it's time to fight. That's what we need. Then they started killing civilians, women and children, and the rest were taken away by the patriotic [government] soldiers. They wanted us to tell them where the *mujahideen* were. And nobody would tell them. The Russians attacked us for seventeen days and nights in Khanabad from the air and on the ground. They used Mi3s* on the ground. For seventeen days they attacked us. I was there all the time. What can I say? They killed everyone. They didn't leave anything. They hit houses, mosques and took farmers and shepherds away as hostages from Khanabad to Kunduz. I was there for seventeen days and then I came here.'

The figure of eighteen hundred dead Russians is undoubtedly wildly exaggerated: many Afghans, especially simple peasants, have an unfortunate habit of inflating figures and for many years this virtually destroyed the *mujahideen*'s credibility with the media. I say unfortunate because although the figures may be exaggerated, the description of events is in nine cases out of ten, I believe, correct.

Two days later, we went to a Jamiat orphanage in Peshawar and interviewed half a dozen boys aged between seven and fourteen, all of whose fathers had been killed by the Russians. In most cases their mothers had survived and were living in refugee camps where the boys went at weekends to visit them. I have already quoted, at the beginning of this book, the terrible story of the little boy with a scar on his forehead, whose house was forcibly entered by Russian soldiers and whose father and elder brother were shot in front of his eyes. Apart from his, perhaps the most moving story was told us by a nice-looking boy of twelve, with close-cropped hair. The Afghan in charge of the orphanage said he might be too upset to tell his story, but that he was willing to try.

---

* No such weapon exists, but this was the word he used.

'My father, my brother and a friend were at the front. One day they decided to come and see if we were all right at home. They left their weapons with the *mujahideen*, but when they arrived, they found that the Russian forces were already there. They thought they couldn't fight them bare-handed, so they decided to go back to the front ... They were on their way back when two Russians stopped them and asked if they were '*dost*' [friend] or '*dushman*' [enemy]. In their hearts they were '*dushman*', but they pretended they were '*dost*' and put their hands up. They thought it was just these two soldiers, so they fought with them. They shot my father with three bullets in his chest, his shoulder and the back of his neck.' He pointed to each in turn. 'He fell down and was martyred [killed]. My brother and his friend the commander got very angry and fought with them.

'My brother jumped up and grabbed one of their weapons. At this point, more Russians came and they cut off my brother's fingers with their bayonet.' The boy began to sob. 'They cut them with the bayonet. So, of course, he was helpless. After all his fingers were cut off, they beat him. They shot him in one ear and the bullet came out of the other. He was martyred too. There were more bullets here and in his legs. Then they turned on the other one, the commander, what do they call it, what do they call it? ... a Kalashnikov. They put it against his head and one side of his head was blown off. And he was martyred too. My uncle heard that the Russian forces were in the village and he was wondering why my father was late getting back. He came to the village: lots of people were dead. He was looking for my father. He fainted as soon as he saw my father. The forces had gone away. More relatives gathered and they took the bodies to the big house for a few minutes and the same night the *mujahideen* buried them.'

A ten-year-old boy with cross eyes, which made him look especially vulnerable, had a less dramatic but equally heart-rending story to tell. He spoke compulsively, no doubt because of what he had been through. He described how the Russians had surrounded his village in the Panjsher Valley.

'The tanks went towards the hillside. The soldiers got out and spread everywhere. My father was already with the *mujahideen*. Whoever came out of their homes, they shot. We thought it was better to stay at home. We decided to escape at night. We went towards the desert and headed in the direction of the *mujahideen*. My father was already there with the commander. They fought, came down off the hillside and they were firing from the hillside. The Russian infantry were still there. Later they came towards the village. The rest were stopping the *mujahideen* coming to the village. Two tanks were moving next to one another. They were firing. They were coming towards the houses. They were firing and firing. The *mujahideen* wanted to counter-attack. My father told us a big battle was going to take place and we had better leave the area. We set off for Bulaghen. As we were leaving the fighting started. At night the infantry came towards the village and started searching people. Some of them were destroying the fields. Most of the crops were burnt . . .

'My father managed to escape from the Nahabad side and came towards us. When we heard that the Russians had left, he suggested that we went home. My uncle was also with us, and my father was with three or four of his armed friends. My father suggested that he and his friends should walk ahead. We were behind them and we had all our belongings, food and whatever we had on our pack animals. We were behind with my uncle. We were halfway there when we saw a cloud of dust and when we went close we saw they were all lying dead, killed by mines. When we looked at them, one of my father's friends was still alive, but he had a big wound on his neck and he kept saying "Allah, Allah . . ." My father was wounded behind the ear and he was lying on the ground. Just one of them was alive. Three of them were dead. My father . . . was dead. One person stepped on the mine, the others were killed by shrapnel. My father and one other friend were killed like that. When we got close to their bodies, we left everything behind. We said to hell with the things. We were all crying. My uncle was with us. As we went towards the village some of the people who had run away were coming back. We told them what had happened

216

and they came with us, with several beds. We collected the dead and went back to the village and we buried them at home.'

I had tried, through our interpreter, Shwayb, to explain to the boys that they should stick exactly to what they had seen and on the whole they did this faithfully. I was also very conscious that we were asking them to relive intensely harrowing experiences, but I felt it was justified if we could bring before the British public and ultimately, I hoped, the world, something of the catastrophe that had befallen the Afghan people; a people whose only crime was to want to decide their own future in their own way.

The fourth boy, who was about twelve, told his story with no outward show of emotion and it was only after it had been translated that I appreciated the full horror of it.

'My name is Mohammed Zaher and I come from Parwan. The Russian tanks and lorries were blown up by the *mujahideen* mines. Many of the Russians were killed. In revenge they attacked a village called Baba Khel, but the *mujahideen* fought them off and the Russians were defeated.

'They came to our village and entered our courtyard. My brother was going for a swim. They threw stones at him and told him to call my father . . . When my father came they beat him up. They pulled and pushed him and they were swearing at him and then they killed him.

'My brother screamed and ran away. Four or five of them went after him and dragged him back from the other courtyard. And then they martyred him too. They shot him right here, and blew his brains out of his head. They shot my father in the ear and blew his ear in. They did it with a Kalashnikov. When my sister saw what they had done to my father and brother, she started to scream too. They shot her with three bullets and wounded her: one bullet here, one bullet in the arm, and one in the knee, right here.

'Then they went away and we, with our other brother, emigrated from Afghanistan to Pakistan. Now I go to school, I study in the fifth grade.'

I felt we had probably recorded more interviews than we

would be able to use, but now Shwayb reported that he had found several boys who had been wounded in the fighting and were in hospital.

'Do you want to go and see them?'

'Yes, of course. How many are there?'

'Two in one hospital, the Khyber Surgical, and another boy we can bring to the Jamiat office.'

We went first to the Khyber Surgical Hospital, which is staffed and run by Pakistanis. One of the two Afghan boys had just been discharged but the other lay on a bed in a dark room, his leg horribly burned.

'Too dark in here. Can we take him outside?' Noel asked.

'Yes, of course, where would you like to go? On the balcony?'

'Yes, or better still what about down there, on the grass?'

We looked down on a small patch of grass surrounded by a few dusty flower beds.

'Yes, that'll do fine.'

The boy hopped happily down the stairs on to the grass and his little face beamed as he sat and faced the camera.

'The story is a large force came, every day three aeroplanes. One would come from one side, one from another and one from another side. We didn't care, we used to play and enjoy ourselves. Lots of boys would play and go towards the fields. It was then that they dropped bombs. I started to run away and I thought, well, boy, you won't survive. And I stopped running.

The next bomb dropped and I was burnt. I had a terrible pain in my leg. A really bad pain. About ten boys were injured . . . My father took me on his back and carried me all the way to Jalalabad. We stopped on the way just so that I could have a pee. Immediately afterwards he picked me up again and he ran fast all the way. I passed blood in my urine. When we came here, my father gave a pint of blood. It was for me.'

Unlike the boys in the orphanage, and despite his wound, he seemed a happy person. By contrast, the boy who was waiting for us at the Jamiat office seemed deeply disturbed. He had lost a leg in an air raid on his home in Herat Province, near the

Iranian border, and wore a clumsy artificial limb which he had been given in Iran.

'Two helicopters were bombing Roken at twelve o'clock. About one o'clock they came to our village, Naobahar, and until two o'clock they were bombing – two hours, three hours they were bombing . . .

'My brother was sitting on the wall. One bomb dropped next to him. He jumped down from the wall. A rocket hit below his legs. He jumped down and ran towards the other house and closed the door and locked it. The rocket exploded, hit my leg and I fell down and two pieces of shrapnel hit my mother, one here and one here, in these two places, and it hit my aunt here, the shrapnel.

'My brother had gone to bring ammunition to fight the Russians. They were still bombing when he arrived with a tractor. The tractor took us to the road. When we reached the Roken road my mother was martyred . . .

'For one day and night they didn't do anything to me, they didn't operate. From here to here the bone was broken. The doctor cut off my leg from here.' He pointed to his thigh, well above the knee. 'The next day and night my father came – it was about evening prayers when he reached me. I opened my eyes then I closed them again. I was unconscious . . . I was four months in this hospital. My father asked the doctor to discharge me . . .

'"Isn't it better that we go away than all of us be killed here? I think it's better if I take my children to Iran." The doctor said, "Of course it's better if you go to Iran."'

Early one morning, Noel and I went to the airport in Peshawar and boarded a Pakistani army helicopter which flew us over some of the nearest refugee camps: there are nearly three hundred in Pakistan altogether. The pilot was excellent and immediately understood what Noel wanted: slow tracking shots of the endless rows of refugee dwellings, tents in the newer camps and mud-brick houses in the older ones. Indeed, the older camps look like any other village in this part of the world.

We also needed some pictures on the ground: this turned out at first to be nearly impossible since every time Noel set up the camera, we were mobbed by hundreds of shouting, pushing boys who all wanted to have their photograph taken. I managed to divert some of them by pretending to take pictures of them with my small camera, but as soon as Noel moved to a new spot, they raced after him uncontrollably. Several older men came up and scolded the boys but they paid no attention. Luckily, that evening I bumped into a friend, Wakil Akbarzai, a member of Pir Gailani's National Islamic Front, one of the three 'moderate' *mujahideen* parties, who took us to a camp just outside Peshawar where he seemed to have complete control. A number of new refugee families had just arrived; they had practically no possessions except their clothes and some sort of blanket or covering for a makeshift tent. To my surprise one woman, with two small children, did not object to my photographing her.

'Do you think she'll give us an interview?' I asked Akbarzai. It is almost impossible for a stranger to talk to an Afghan woman, let alone photograph or interview one.

'Let me ask her ... Yes, she'll do it. Tell me the questions and I'll translate.'

'Can she tell me where she comes from and why she left her home?'

Akbarzai, squatting on the ground beside us despite his considerable bulk, questioned the woman. She was about thirty or thirty-five, with a strong, peasant face that was not unattractive. She wore one or two pieces of silver jewellery, no doubt the only things she had been able to save. Her two small children clung to her skirts as she told us she came from the north, from Kunduz, like so many of the more recent refugees.

'There were aeroplanes, there were tanks. They burned our food, they burned our crops. They took away the men [including her husband], most of them were killed. We had to come, we had no choice – what do we want from this land?

'Now we're thirsty and hungry and wanderers. Two children are with a relative because my brother-in-law wouldn't keep them. He gives me money for only these two and in return I bake him bread and work for him.'

An older woman with one child sat a few yards away and with Akbarzai's help we persuaded her to talk to us as well. Again, to my surprise she did so unveiled. It turned out that the tearful child in her arms was her granddaughter.

'They were bombing our house. Quiet. Quiet.' The child began to cry so she pulled her shawl over its head and rocked it in her arms. 'My daughter-in-law was killed by the bombing, our house was destroyed. The other [her son] went mad. I brought him here to the doctor. Now it's about five days since he disappeared. Yes, he disappeared here. He went mad because of the bombs. My house was destroyed by bombs.'

CHAPTER TWENTY-THREE

There are hundreds and hundreds of stories like these: thousands, possibly hundreds of thousands. Five million refugees represent at the very minimum 500,000 families on the basis of ten people to a family. Virtually every Afghan family that has left its home and fled the country has been driven out by the sort of experiences I have just quoted. In some cases, they may not have been victims themselves of Russian atrocities, merely neighbours or relatives of victims. But in every case I know of, families have uprooted themselves, with all the hardship that implies, because they no longer were able, or felt able, to live safely in their homes.

As a final example of what is really happening in Afghanistan under Soviet occupation, I want to quote perhaps the most telling single incident of all, recounted by Michael Barry in his report to the International Humanitarian Enquiry Commission on Displaced Persons in Afghanistan, dated November 1985. Barry and a Swedish doctor, Johan Lagerfelt, travelled for more than 400 miles through the south-eastern provinces of Afghanistan in September and October of 1985. They recorded many accounts of atrocities committed by Russian soldiers, including the following incident at Bed-Moshk (Musk Willow) village near Ghazni. Barry and Lagerfelt say the Soviet soldiers responsible were under the overall command of a General Osmanov.

Preliminary bombing in the morning of October 3 killed a large amount of livestock. Then heliborne Soviet commando troops were deposited in the village. Four young men covering the flight into the mountains of fellow villagers were killed (the four sons of peasant Shahzad-Gol: Abdollah-Jan, 30, armed; Mohammed Amin, 20, armed; Mohammad Sharif, 16, armed; and Mohammad Shafiq, 14, unarmed). Narrators of the following included Shahzad-Gol, father of the four slain partisans, and Mohammad Anwar, uncle to Mohammad Nabi whose own father, Mohammad Asef, although present, could not bring himself to utter a single word; five other villagers, also witnesses to the events, were present and contributed to the testimony:

'The four boys were able to kill one Russian. Then Abdollah-Jan said: "We are going to die. Let us sing them a song of *Jihad*, the Holy War!"' [Narrator and other witnesses interrupt narration to weep.] 'When they were slain, the Russians pulled off their boots and wristwatches. Now Mohammad Sharif was a most handsome young man. We believe that the body of a holy martyr is a splendid and fragrant one. But they poured over his face a product which blackened it all at once. Thus they caused his father and mother to despair.

'Then the Russians found two children in hiding behind rocks: Esmail, 10, and Mohammad Nabi, 14, "*Dost? Dushman?*" [Friend? Enemy?] They asked this in Persian. "Friend," said the little Esmail, but Mohammad Nabi, the older boy, said "Enemy," as a challenge to them. The Russians tied them up and dragged them off to their camp with them, cuffing and buffeting Mohammad Nabi all the while. They passed through the village of Petawak, the village you just visited, where they stole the water-pump; it was the only water-pump in the village, it belonged to Haji Sattar. They loaded it on the shoulders of Mohammad Nabi and forced him to walk like that.

'At their camp, little Esmail showed himself docile. He denied having any sympathy for the *mujahideen*. But Mohammad Nabi behaved proudly, he refused to drink their water and to eat their bread. So they broke all his teeth, they kicked in his face, and they opened one of his shoulders with the blade of a bayonet. It was little Esmail who told us all about what happened in the camp the next day, and we all saw Mohammad Nabi the next morning, hardly to be recognized, with his eyelids all puffed up and blood all over his face. Suddenly the Russians said "*Pul?*" [Money?] And both children, to save themselves, said their parents had some. The Russians had a Tajik translator.

'The next morning, the Russians brought the children back to the village. We ourselves had returned to the village over the night. Mohammad Nabi called for water, but when an old man offered him water in a basin, the Russians knocked it out of his hands with their gun butts. The Russians asked for little Esmail's house. The boy's parents gave them 200 Afghanis (US$ 2.50). That was enough for them, they let the boy go.

'Then they were taken to Mohammad Nabi's house. His mother and sisters were there, they gathered together all their money, more than 200 Afghanis; the Russians took it, then they said it wasn't enough, that Mohammad Nabi was one of the bandits, the *ashrar*. Neighbours contributed money too, but the Russians first took it then said it still wasn't enough. And to make fun of Mohammad Nabi because, on the previous day, he had refused to drink their water and eat their bread, they stuffed Russian bread in his broken mouth. And he was so thirsty!

'And then they tied him to that tree over there; you can't go near it to see it tonight, it's much too close to the watch-post where they are now. He had his hands tied over his head, like this' [witness shows], 'and there was a rope tight around his neck fastening him to the tree. And that's the way he was when they shot him.

'Afterwards, they came back to take our wristwatches, our cash, and the jewellery of our women.' [Narrators weep.]

Testimony taken down on the spot, at dusk of October 6, 1985. We note that Mohammad Nabi's body was unfastened from the tree in the course of the day of October 5, for burial. The tree of execution referred to above was, it turned out, indeed too dangerous for close inspection, since only a line of poplars protected us from the view of a government watch-post less than two kilometres away, as we could make out in the last light of the day. To take down the testimony, we hid in one of the houses of Bed-Moshk until late at night, then escaped to a safer hiding-place in pitch darkness.

Villagers thanked the Commission for having come so far and taken these pains to record their story.

Is it not time the world awoke to the reality of what has been happening in Afghanistan since December 1979? Let me quote once again what Felix Ermacora had to say in the conclusion to his report for the United Nations.

> Continuation of the military solution, will, in the opinion of the Special Rapporteur, lead inevitably to a situation approaching genocide, which the traditions and culture of this noble people cannot permit.

It is indeed arguable that Felix Ermacora is being over-cautious when he says that continuation of the war will lead to a situation 'approaching genocide'. I believe that that situation has been reached and passed: that the Russians have been pursuing a policy of genocide – the extermination of a race – in Afghanistan since Christmas Eve, 1979; in other words for seven and a half years as I write. And yet the world has turned its face away from the tragedy, one of the most terrible in the history of a twentieth century already redolent with blood. Or should one not say, rather, the world's media have turned their faces away and largely ignored the Afghan war? After all, how does the world know what is going on except through its television screens, its radio and its newspapers?

Many people have asked me why it is that we hear so little of Afghanistan, despite the fact that terrible things are known to be happening there, especially when it is the Soviet Union that is involved, a country, what is more, that lays claim to operate the best and fairest political system in the world: Marxism-Leninism.

Is it because, as Mao Tse-tung said, 'All power comes from the barrel of a gun'? It was Stalin, of course, who asked derisively, 'How many divisions has the Pope?' the same Stalin, let us not forget, who exterminated 20 million kulaks in his determination to implement the New Economic Policy. So what are a few hundred thousand, or even a million or two Afghans, sacrificed on the altar of a brave new Socialist world?

My own view is that my profession, the media, have failed the world in not telling it exactly what is happening in Afghanistan, as we undoubtedly did in Vietnam. The reporting of Vietnam, in which I played a modest part myself, was intensive, extensive, and exhaustive. The reporting of Afghanistan has been spasmodic, superficial and almost sub-liminal. And yet in both cases a superpower has been involved;

each vies for our acclaim and support; each competes for the leadership of the world. Christ said, 'By their fruits ye shall know them,' and when Mrs Thatcher went to Moscow in 1987 she said much the same thing: Russia's assurances that it wants to live in peace with its neighbours will be judged by its behaviour in Afghanistan.

Meanwhile the killing goes on. The Afghans, being an ancient and proud people, will never beg for the world's sympathy. Since they still live in the age of chivalry, as opposed to the age of chicanery, they will fight their *Jihad*, their Holy War, until they have no more blood to spill. Let us leave the last word with Ahmed Shah Masud.

'If the Pakistan border is closed and help doesn't reach the interior, it won't make the slightest difference to our determination. We will carry on fighting until we achieve victory – or death.'

I sincerely hope it is the former rather than the latter, for it will be a victory for liberty, justice and a small nation's independence. Let us also hope it is the Will of Allah.